# CLIMBING THE
# MISSISSIPPI RIVER
# BRIDGE BY BRIDGE

## VOLUME ONE

*From Louisiana to Minnesota*

To Mary Lee and Rick,
     Best wishes and happy
'Climbing'!
                    Mary C. Costello

Written and Illustrated by
Mary Charlotte Aubry Costello

*This book is dedicated to my six children—*
*Pat, Barb, Judith, Tom, Roger, and John—*
*for their enthusiasm and steadfast*
*support throughout this wonderful experience.*

**CLIMBING THE MISSISSIPPI RIVER BRIDGE BY BRIDGE**
Volume I– All the bridges from New Orleans
to the Minnesota border

Copyright © 1995 by Mary Charlotte Aubry Costello
All rights are reserved including the right of reproduction
in whole or in part in any form.

Publisher • Mary C. Costello
Designer • Marlo Buzzell
Printer • Von Hoffman Graphics
Illustrator • Mary C. Costello

**Library of Congress Catalog Card Number 94-96856**
ISBN 0-9644518-0-8 Softcover
ISBN 0-9644518-1-6 Hardcover

First Edition: March 1995
Second Edition: November 2002

MANUFACTURED IN THE UNITED STATES OF AMERICA

<u>COVER</u>

This is a scene of the Rock Island Arsenal Bridge with the Davenport skyline in the background, illustrating this span's three modes of transportation—pedestrian, train and vehicular travel. These three are possible on only one other bridge on the whole Mississippi—the Eads in St. Louis, which carries only light rail traffic. The Arsenal Bridge was selected for the cover because it is in the approximate location of the first railroad bridge that crossed the "Great River" in 1856.

# Contents

**Appendix**

The study of bridges is both romantic and technical. For more information on technical terms, please consult the glossary in the back of the book.

**Reader please note:**
New Bridges and Bridge Changes
since 1995
on page 198

* Twin Bridges
+ Originally called "Greater New Orleans Bridge"

# Introduction

*M*any Mississippi River bridges are masterpieces of design that compare favorably with the greatest bridges in the world. Among the more than 200 bridges on the extended winding waterway are greatly varied and ingeniously engineered structures. But even more than their beauty and engineering, the Mississippi River bridges should be recognized for their great service and historical contribution to the United States. The railroad bridges unified our nation in its beginning, and highway bridges continue to do so today. If you question this, just imagine the Mississippi River with no bridges to span it.

Bounded by ten states, the Mississippi River, extending almost as far north as Canada and as far south as the Gulf of Mexico, divides the United States into two parts. The name "Mississippi," given the waterway by the Ojibway Indians, means "Great River"—the highest tribute the Ojibway knew to give this powerful body of water that crossed their land.

From the Revolutionary War until the Louisiana Purchase, the Mississippi River served as the western boundary of the United States. But farmers east of the Mississippi were not able to float their produce to market down the river through French-owned New Orleans. What were they to do? Temptation might be to secede. Therefore, President Jefferson in 1803 bought the land from the Mississippi River to the Rocky Mountains, including New Orleans, (the Louisiana Purchase) to save the Union from splitting apart.

By 1820, with the advent of the steamboat, the Mississippi became a very important north/south highway. However, in going east and west across the Mighty River during the movement West, settlers generally found the river treacherous or impossible to ford; therefore, until 1855, they used boats or the winter ice to cross to the other side. In that year, the first bridge was erected in Minneapolis, Minnesota. Perhaps more important, though, is the fact that in April of the following year(1856), the first railroad bridge was completed near the middle of the Mississippi, linking Rock Island, Illinois, and Davenport, Iowa. This first railroad bridge created much anger and fear on the part of riverboat owners, who objected to it as an impediment to navigation. Boat people were very concerned about future bridge construction and competition from the railroads. The United States Government, on the other hand, was delighted because the railroad would unite the western two-thirds of the country to the East and again save the nation from breaking apart. There was good reason to fear that the West Coast settlers would solve their transportation problems by separating from the East and

becoming an independent country. The railroads and the requisite Mississippi River railroad bridges saved the day.

The fear of railroad competition on the part of riverboat owners back in 1856 was more than well founded, for by 1878 fourteen railroad and one elevated highway bridge had been constructed across the "Mighty Mississippi." (Warren 1878, 68) The once busy Mississippi River traffic declined as the railroads expanded not only east and west but north and south, until barge traffic on the Mississippi became almost extinct.

Railroads continued to grow and build Mississippi River bridges until the end of the nineteenth century. The two Huey P. Long Bridges (one in New Orleans, 1935, and one in Baton Rouge, 1940) were the last Mississippi River railroad bridges built, except for reconstructions. The heyday of the railroads began after the Great Depression in the 1930s and extended through the 1940s. In the 1950s, large trucking and revived barge traffic cut into the railroad freight business, and travelers found that jetliners were a faster means of transportation than trains.

Just as the horse and buggy were replaced by the automobile, which dominated the roads after World War I, the old wooden "wagon" bridges were supplanted by steel and concrete "highway" bridges. Today, wider, stronger and more aesthetically pleasing bridges are constructed to accommodate the ever-increasing vehicular traffic which includes thousands of trucks carrying interstate commerce.

With the sagging farm economy beginning in December 1979, triggered by the U.S. grain embargo on the Soviet Union as a response to the invasion of Afghanistan, the Midwest farmers were no longer economically able to buy farm machinery, and many lost their farms. In the 1980s, this situation closed many farm implement plants, one of the major industries in the heartland along the Mississippi. In the 1990s, cities bordering the Mississippi River tried to restore the river to its former economic position of importance with riverboat gambling and river excursions.

Although the methods of moving goods and people in our country have changed with the times—from steamboats to trains, from trains to trucks, and back to barges and excursion boats—the unheralded bridges of the Mississippi have been the connecting links. The Mississippi River bridges have been the constant, unsung heroes that bind our land into one. "Shipping built the harbour cities, automobiles the suburbs, and [but] only bridges and tunnels can hold them together." (Billings 1961, 108)

# Preface

*I*t all began about twenty-two years ago with a teaching unit on the "Local Mississippi River Bridges". As an elementary school art teacher in Davenport, Iowa, I learned from other teachers' investigations about the Quad-City bridges and taught my students about them. They drew the bridges and created a model-bridge they, personally, would like to see built. Each student was his/her own designer/engineer/builder. An enormous display in the school hallway of every kind of bridge in all stages of professionalism culminated the unit. The fifth graders as a whole loved the project, and I developed a "love affair" with the Mississippi and its bridges.

With my interest in bridges aroused—actually growing year by year—and with time made available to me by early retirement, I decided to write the bridge book that I often challenged my students to write. Since there is no book written about all the bridges on the Great Mississippi—the only exception being one written in the late nineteenth century of the bridges between St. Paul and St. Louis (Warren 1878), long since outdated, I felt there was need for such a researched publication. To enhance the written record, illustrations of each span seemed a requisite and, with my art background, I was eager to take up that challenge.

Therefore, I left teaching and traveled the entire length of the Mississippi River alone, visiting and sketching each bridge from Lake Itasca, Minnesota, to New Orleans, Louisiana. Originally my intent was to write this book for children. However, as I discovered a tremendous interest in my project from people all along the river, and as I became more fascinated with bridge stories and structures myself, the concept of my book changed and expanded to include adults.

My personal experiences are an integral part of the Mississippi story, making the book a blend of history, facts, personal observations and experiences. My intent is to make people more aware of the beauty, unique features, style and history of "their" bridge. Although some bridges may be deteriorating and in need of replacement, their place in the area history is recognized and appreciated.

As I prepared for my bridge tour, I knew it would be exciting, but never did I think it would be as exhilarating and enjoyable as it became.

My plan was to take sketchpad, camera, binoculars and traveling clothes in my little red Datsun, first to the north, and then to the south. I had contacted people all along the way concerning possible lodging. One friend had a summer cabin in Crosslake, Minnesota, another a "loft" at O'Brian Lake in northern Minnesota. I had two daughters in Minneapolis and so it went. When "in the field," sometimes distance or darkness meant a local motel.

Although I traveled from north to south on the Mississippi, I have reversed the order in my book, putting the larger and more impressive bridges at the beginning.

My state maps were vital aids in finding bridges, but often it was necessary to question strangers. Whenever I arrived on the spot, I photographed the bridge, then sketched it. Finally I took notes on the colors, sounds, surroundings, and incidents that happened while I sketched.

After three weeks of driving and sketching up north, I went south. By September of 1986, I had finished the major part of my traveling, though I have gone north four more times for missed bridges.

Surrounded by three stuffed sketchbooks of drawings, photos, notes, and articles, I sat down to the computer. Sometimes I spent the normal eight-hour day before that "wonder" machine; other times I started very early in the morning or ended very late at night. The telephone was an important part of my spare-bedroom "office" equipment.

From countless interviews with engineers, bridge designers, construction workers, railroad workers, bridge tenders, historians, librarians, tourist center staff and citizens living along the river, I learned statistics that couldn't be found anywhere in print. The bridge histories have come from newspaper articles written, for the most part, when the bridges were constructed. The individual state Departments of Transportation (DOT), railroad companies, the Coast Guard, Corps of Engineers, city libraries, and historical societies were helpful sources.

After the writing was completed, then began the work of redrawing the sketches from my originals and from on-site photos. This task was every bit as enjoyable as the writing had been until I compared my more recent drawings with my first ones. I redid about 35 bridge sketches.

In the years of writing and illustrating my bridge book, I have learned so much, traveled so far, and made so many new friends that I would gladly do it over again. <u>Climbing the Mississippi River Bridge By Bridge</u> has been a labor of love.

# Acknowledgements

*I* wish to thank the many individuals who contributed to this endeavor. In particular, my thanks to Margaret Bolich, Phyllis Ammeter and Sister Maria Trinitas Rand, CHM, for their unending encouragement and generosity of time, thought and expertise in editing my script, and to Sister Clarice Eberdt, CHM, for her masterly critique of my sketches. I am grateful to my proof readers: Margaret Kester, Dennis Sievers, Don Denhardt, Caroline Copeland and Rebecca Schellenger. A special thanks to my husband, Ken, now deceased, for shifting for himself while I traveled and for switching domestic roles with me so that I could continue to work on the book. My undying gratitude to my six children, who have all been a marvelous support throughout, but especially to Judith and Patrick for their valuable time and assistance at any hour of the day or night. I am also very grateful to those who were so hospitable as I traveled the river—my daughter, Barb, and her husband, Greg Burke, Mark and Drew Burke, Charlotte Fogel, LaVerne Sifert and Ethel Willow. For their kindness and generosity I want to acknowledge my indebtedness to those wonderful people in the Corps of Engineers at the Rock Island Arsenal, to Roger Wiebusch with the U.S. Coast Guard in St. Louis, as well as to bridge designers, especially William B. Conway (Modjeski and Masters in New Orleans), and Harold Sandberg (Alfred Benesch and Company in Chicago), for checking accuracy from an engineer's point of view. And last but not least, I express my deep gratitude to the obliging archivists in historical offices, to various railroad personnel and to engineers from the many Departments of Transportation along the Mississippi from Louisiana through Iowa.

*Special thanks to*
*Mark Bawden*
*for his generous support*

# PART ONE

# Higher Than Ships

The Mississippi River between Cairo, Illinois, and New Orleans, Louisiana—the Lower Mississippi—is a giant, reaching depths of 200 feet. The river grows and matures with each tributary's input on its way to the Gulf of Mexico. It nearly doubles in size as it makes its way southward from Cairo.

This southern Mississippi River once was the bay of the sea. However, in the last 50,000 years, the fast-moving, earth-pushing upper river has gradually filled the inland sea and forced the gulf 1,000 miles further south. The Lower Mississippi is far different from the rest of the great waterway. It has no locks and dams, no small towns lining its corridor, but boasts of exceedingly high bridges, a few large cities and high levees along its shores. Until 1927, flood protection in the South was not sufficient, and the river still found "room to roam." The 1927 flood lasted up to three months and caused 214 deaths. Consequently, an important change was made—the levee was elevated to 25 feet along the 1,608-mile-long earthen dike. (The levee is the same height as the Great Wall of China today, but greater in length if one considers the connecting alluvial valley. This makes the Mississippi River flood wall a total of 2,202 miles long).* Taller than rooftops, the levee has kept the "Daddy of All Streams," for the most part, within its bounds.

Historically, the Lower Mississippi River was the site of the river's first steamboat, the "New Orleans," which puffed its way from Pittsburgh, down the Ohio to the city on the Mississippi whose name it bore. At that early time (1811), there were no bridges across the

Mississippi. In 1827, Abraham Lincoln, at the age of 19, took a flatboat with a friend from Spencer County, Indiana, to New Orleans. After crossing to the east bank by boat, they probably walked the long way home. For certain, they crossed no bridges, because there were no bridges to cross. In the 1840's great numbers of ornate side wheelers and sternwheelers were outdoing one another in beauty, size and luxury, floating side by side or, perhaps, even racing! But they had no problem avoiding bridges because there were no bridges across the Mississippi. In the 1860's iron-clad ships fought naval battles in Vicksburg and New Orleans, but had no bridge battles because no bridges existed in the region. After the Civil War, flatboats still delivered groceries to riverboat settlements because no bridges crossed the Mississippi below St. Louis. Until 1892, ships with tall masts had no problem as they made their way to and from southern wharves because...you're right...you guessed it...there were no bridges across the Mississippi in the South.

Today, there are seventeen bridges across the Lower Mississippi. Countless towboats pushing as many as 36 barges are common sights. Also common in Louisiana waters today are ocean-going vessels from all countries, often with small tugboats towing them as they travel the Great River's waterway to inland ports. In the Lower Mississippi, the river runs deep and the bridges rise high..."higher than ships."

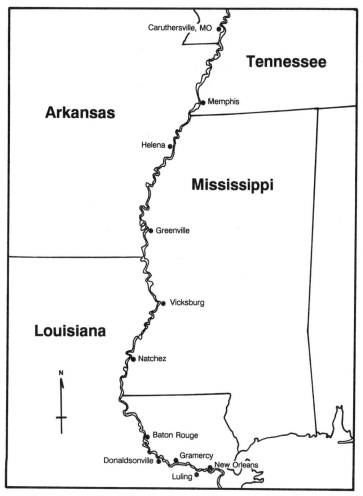

Caruthersville, MO

Tennessee

Arkansas

Memphis

Helena

Mississippi

Greenville

Vicksburg

Louisiana

Natchez

N

Baton Rouge

Donaldsonville          Gramercy
                     New Orleans
        Luling

---

*The Great Wall of China today is 2150 miles long (main wall), though at one time it was much longer. (1989 World Book Encyclopedia, Volume 8, 373.

# Crescent City Connection Bridges, US-90 Alternate
## (The Greater New Orleans Bridge)[1]

$\mathcal{S}$amuel Clemens, better known as Mark Twain, earned his river pilot's license just 100 years before the first Greater New Orleans Bridge was completed on the lower curve of "Crescent City." To read Twain's impression of this gigantic cantilever bridge, if that were possible, no doubt would be a delight. He once described the Mississippi Valley as "...reposeful as dreamland, nothing worldly about it...nothing to hang a fret or worry upon." (Wisconsin tourist folder, cover) Things have changed from those quiet times. In fact, because of the heavy traffic load on the 1959 bridge, a second bridge was constructed and completed for use in 1988. It took eight years and the coordinating efforts of ten design consultants to build the second span. Both bridges are giants and are located in a now very "worldly" New Orleans.

The Greater New Orleans Bridges, now called Crescent City Connection Bridges, are just 95 miles from the Mississippi River's mouth—so close to the Gulf that saltwater backed into the shrunken river during the 1988 drought, threatening New Orleans' drinking water.

The Crescent City Connection Bridges hold many honors. They are first in position in the lineup of bridges starting at the lower Mississippi. The matching structures have the longest spans and the highest vertical clearance of any bridge on the entire Father of Waters. In the United States they rank second, and in the world, fifth longest among cantilever bridges. Truly, no other bridge on the Mississippi can compare with these "twins."

The new span is identical to the original in truss design, pier placement, height and clearances. However, the second bridge is wider and has two innovative features. Using the latest criteria for "load-factor design," Crescent City Connection Bridge #2 is lighter by 3,000 tons. The other unique feature refers to the use of bolted redundant side plates at critical places on the bridge instead of welded connections. This latter change saved $9 million.

Looking at the sketches of these mammoth truss spans that gently arch over the Mississippi, I recall the helpful people I met when attempting to find my way to the bridges—the customers in the donut shop who volunteered suggestions, even to drawing the route for the best view—the man in the tan pickup who led the way to the West Bank road—the "Bridge Policeman" who gave me a ride in his tiny patrol car for my first view of the gleaming silver bridge profiles and who later returned to take me to my car near the 1984 World's Fair remains. New Orleans hospitality cannot be surpassed. Twain might describe this hospitality as "...cheering to the spirit."

By the time I put my last stroke on the sketch of the Greater New Orleans Bridges, the sinking sun bathed the building across the river in brilliant red-orange. The warehouse, sitting among olive green trees and under a white-splashed China-blue sky, made a spectacular color play. For the moment everything was peaceful. The only discernible movements were a jogger and two white riverboats, the "Cotton Blossom" and the "Creole Queen." The giant twin bridges enhance this ethereal southern scene and, like rungs on a ladder, are the first steps as we climb the length of the Mighty Mississippi—2,552 miles![2]

---

**Use:**
Access route to New Orleans from the West Bank suburbs, Highway US 90 Alternate

**Location:**
Between New Orleans and Algiers

**Style:**
3-span single cantilever truss

**Length:**
Channel span - 1400 feet clear
1575 feet total
Total length - 13,428 feet

**Width:**
Old Bridge - 4 lanes
New Bridge - 6 lanes with
2 lanes for public transit

**Clearance:**
170 feet MLW

**Date completed:**
Old Bridge - September 1959
New Bridge - 30 September 1988
opened for traffic

**Designer:**
Old Bridge - Masters & Henderlite
New Bridge - Modjeski & Masters

**Bridge:**
Old #2830801701, New #2830802440
in Orleans Parish

**Owner:**
Louisiana Department of
Transportation and Development

**Unique feat:**
Second longest cantilever bridge in the U.S. and fourth in the world (Collier's Encyclopedia 1992, Volume 4, 545)

Crescent City Connection Bridges                    Mary C. Costello

*T*en miles upstream from the Greater New Orleans Twin Bridges is the Huey P. Long—the oldest Mississippi River bridge in the state of Louisiana. Constructed in 1935, the Huey P. Long is named after the former governor, who persuaded the state legislature to authorize the financing and construction of the bridge.

Work on the Huey P. Long began in 1933 but only after engineers solved the problem of how to construct the pier foundations. What was uncommon was that bedrock in the New Orleans area is thousands of feet beneath the soft alluvial sediment of the Mississippi. This situation meant a solid-rock base was out of the question. Therefore, a sand-island technique was used. A large island was created by driving steel sheet piling, higher than the water level, into the riverbed and filling it with sand. In the center of this sand-island was placed a caisson made of double-steel walls filled with concrete and having a cutting edge of steel plate. Excavation was done inside the caisson's open cells with a clamshell bucket. When enough earth was removed and depth attained, the caisson sank under it own weight. Then concrete was poured into the bottom, the wells were flooded and the caisson sealed with precast concrete. On this foundation rests one pier.

It is interesting that most of this steel high-level railroad bridge, possibly the longest length in the world (4 1/3 miles long), is in the approaches over low, swampy terrain. This swampiness is probably due to the flatness of the New Orleans landscape, which is so often inundated with flood water. (Even the New-Orleans dead are buried in tombs above ground, since water is found only two or three feet below the earth's surface.)

I parked my car by the earthen levee which protects "Crescent City" from the ravages of the Mighty Mississippi. The parking spot I chose was next to one of the bridge's towering piers. I estimate my Datsun would fit 40 times into the bottom of just one of the two columns forming each pier, to say nothing of how many stacks of Datsuns it would take to get to the top.

Having just arrived in New Orleans the day before, I was totally unfamiliar with the Huey P. Long Bridge as I stood below it in awe. I didn't realize until I saw a train crossing that this was a railroad as well as a highway bridge. Both were on the same level but the trains (I saw four of them) went through the superstructure while the vehicles traveled on roadways outside the trusses. From below I could hear more than see the autos as they passed on the high span.

Besides the car sounds, there was sandblasting on the bridge. Workmen were painting it silver. In silent contrast, a tug named "Jack" pushed 25 barges upstream; then the ship "Ereaga" glided under the 50-year-old bridge without a sound. Another jeweled facet of the river is that it can magnify or deaden sound. Contradictions like this make the river and the bridges that grace it fascinating.

---

**Use:**
Major railroad crossing by Southern Pacific and Union Pacific Railroad plus US 90 vehicular traffic

**Location:**
New Orleans to Bridge City, Louisiana

**Style:**
8-span cantilevered steel truss

**Length:**
Channel span - 750 feet clear
790 feet total
Total length - highway - 8,076 feet
railroad - 22,996 feet
with approaches

**Width:**
4 vehicle lanes, 2 train tracks

**Clearance:**
153 feet MLW

**Date completed:**
December 1935

**Designer:**
Modjeski, Masters and Case, Inc., Consulting Engineers

**Bridge:**
#0060100001 in Jefferson Parish

**Owner:**
New Orleans Public Belt Railroad Commission

**Unique feat:**
Longest continuous structure of any kind in the world with its combined approaches (Plowden 1974, 257)

Huey P. Long Bridge, New Orleans

Mary C. Costello

# Hale Boggs Bridge, Luling, Louisiana, I-310

*M*y immediate response to first viewing the Luling Bridge? "Oh-h-h-h-h-h-h!" I was rounding a curve on Highway 18 when the bridge suddenly appeared through the trees. Perhaps it was its enormous size, but more than likely, its simple unique beauty prompted my vocal reaction. My not having been forewarned made the moment much more pleasurable.

Luling's cable-stayed design looked majestic with its two A-shaped towers from which glittering wire stays radiated like spokes from a hub. I was impressed with the clean simple lines and rich brown color of the towers, and the long horizontal box-girder sides. The Luling Bridge is fabricated of weathering steel and is constructed to withstand hurricane forces from the Gulf of Mexico—a "first" for this kind of span. All cables are encased in polyethylene tubes. Rectangular cross-girders go under the roadway anchoring the cables. The deck surface itself is epoxy asphalt concrete (2 1/4 inches thick).

Traveling across the Hale Boggs Bridge, named after a U.S. Congressman from Louisiana, was a joy. Because of the bridge's enormous height, only sky and the tower ahead were visible. The four-lane roadway was roomy, and a concrete railing topped with additional pipe provided a wonderful sense of security as I crossed. However, when I was exiting the bridge on the Destrahan side, my muscles tensed. The speed limit changed drastically to 25 mph on the three-spiral ramp to the ground. In shock, I dropped to 15 mph and felt dizzy by the time I reached the bottom. Future exit ramps would not have these carnival-like curves, I was told.

Back on the flat Luling side again, I parked and climbed the levee to sketch. It was here that I noted the only color besides the brown steel—an orange band between the two towers at railing height, which piqued my curiosity. I learned later that a researcher was given permission to test his paint for weather conditions to which the bridge is subjected.

During construction of the bridge a terrible accident took place. On 20 October 1976, the Norwegian tanker "Frosta" hit a ferryboat carrying workers and college students. The ferry overturned, killing 78 of the 91 passengers and 4 crew members. I found it hard to understand, since the ferryride takes only 3 1/2 minutes and there was no fog or other obstruction to the tanker pilot's view. Investigation showed that the accident was the result of drinking on the part of the captain of the ferryboat, "George Prince."

The 1976 tragedy emphasized the need for a bridge. The resulting 1983 span not only provided for a secure crossing but was an aesthetically attractive addition to the landscape as well. A design of the future made to withstand Nature's worst elements and, at the same time, appeal visually, the Hale Boggs Bridge is a real "thing of beauty."

---

**Use:**
Local traffic now; future I-310

**Location:**
Between Luling & Destrahan, St. Charles Parish, Louisiana

**Style:**
Cable-stayed box-girder bridge

**Length:**
Channel span - 1200 feet clear
1222 feet total
Total length - 10,700 feet

**Width:**
4 lanes with 10-foot outside shoulder, 4-foot inside shoulder and 2-foot median

**Clearance:**
154 foot MLW

**Date completed:**
6 October 1983

**Designer:**
Joint venture—Frankland & Lienhard/Modjeski & Masters

**Bridge:**
#4503700001 in St. Charles Parish

**Owner:**
Louisiana Department of Transportation and Development

**Unique Feat:**
First high level, long span, cable-stayed bridge in the U.S. Received the 1984 Outstanding Civil Engineering Achievement Award

Luling - Destrahan Bridge, Louisiana          — Mary C. Costello

9

# Gramercy/Wallace Highway Bridge, Louisiana

*W*hen questioned, many local residents were unaware that a bridge was being built between Gramercy and Wallace, Louisiana. Even after the bridge had been under construction for three years, they were uninformed! At this point in time the bridge had its four main piers, and one-quarter of the steel work completed.

This was the state of the Gramercy Bridge when I arrived. Actually, I was pleased to be on the site of a bridge under construction. It was even more exciting to have the bridge engineer, Jim Turk, invite me into his mobile office to discuss the bridge. Here he gave me copies of the bridge plans and valuable information about cantilever-bridge history and terminology.

When we finished the interview, Jim put on his hard hat and went back to overseeing the bridge work while I put my pen and sketchbook to work. I was between pier 3 and 4 with an excellent view from below of the steel "anchor arm"—the section of the superstructure between the shore and pier. Green netting hung below the bottom chord of the bridge. As I thought about the reason for the netting, Mr. Turk passed close enough for me to ask. He said it was not to catch tools, as I had thought, but to catch men. In fact, bridge foremen do not want tools to land in it. When asked if any men had fallen into the net, Jim hesitated a long time before answering. Then he replied, "Yes, one man fell into it." That was the extent of the information, however. He then suggested we move to a safer spot.

It was a busy place, though manual labor was going on with workers so far apart and at such heights that work appeared to be standing still. A temporary metal bracing from the ground to the underside of the bridge, known as falsework, helped support the end of the anchor-trusses above my head. The men working high above looked like ants on the giant beams. Behind the trees was a crane moving large bridge sections which had arrived by train. In the river a stiffleg derrick on a barge hoisted parts for the "cantilever arm" being built out over the water. Every worker certainly had to know his job and have no fear of heights.

Piers are an interesting part of any bridge. At the bottom of the square concrete, Gramercy pier is a built-in bumper composed of horizontal wooden beams evenly spaced and protruding from a heavier concrete base. This is to protect the pier from boat damage and eliminate the need of a separate wooden bumper. The proposed bridge plans called for the normal timber fender, so there appears to have been a design change.

In speaking with the design engineer, I discovered that the steel for the bridge was fabricated in Japan and Korea, shipped to the Port of New Orleans and then to Gramercy via the Mississippi River. There the various steel parts were welded or bolted together into the Gramercy Bridge superstructure.

At publication time the main span is complete, the East Bank is 93% finished and the West Bank only 24% ready. There are no plans "to connect" as yet. Money is a big consideration since it will cost 9 million dollars more to make the bridge usable.

When the bridge is complete, I am sure that the proud Gramercy/Wallace residents, at first so unaware of their bridge, will be boasting about its features.

---

**Use:**
Local and highway traffic when finished

**Location:**
Between Gramercy & Wallace, St. James & St. John the Baptist Parishes, Louisiana

**Style:**
Cantilever steel truss

**Length:**
Channel span - 1426 feet clear
1461 feet total
Total Length - 3010 feet abutment to abutment
(the rest of bridge incomplete)

**Width:**
4 lanes plus 2-foot median, and 4-foot inside and 8-foot outside shoulders

**Clearance:**
164 feet MLW

**Date Completed:**
No date has been set

**Designer:**
E. Lionel Pavlo Engineering Company Consulting Engineers, New York

**Bridge:**
#4340100001 in St. James Parish

**Owner:**
Louisiana Department of Transportation and Development

Gramercy Bridge, Louisiana

Mary C. Costello

11

# The "Sunshine Bridge," Donaldsonville, Louisiana, SR 70

*B*ridges can be named after many things—people, places, events, shapes—but this bridge was named after a song! Governor James H. Davis, co-writer of the popular tune of the '40's titled "You Are My Sunshine," liked the song so much that he named the high truss bridge after it. At least this title gave the bridge a reason for being, since it was much maligned as "the bridge that went nowhere." There were no large towns or major roads in the area when the bridge was built. Actually, the span started 167.5 miles above the mouth of the river on the west side and ended in sugar cane fields on the east. The bridge with its sunny name, however, brings an identity to the area. Whatever may have been said of it in the past, I found the Sunshine Bridge to be busy with travelers and people from Donaldsonville and Union, towns built after the bridge.

The silver-grey span was very impressive, even on a hazy gray day, with its four kingposts above the deck and stately tapered piers below. It is hard to imagine the height of these supports until one compares them to a familiar object. For those people living on the Mississippi—the piers would be twice the height of the "Mississippi Queen" (the largest overnight paddlewheel steamboat in America), or three times the height of the "Delta Queen" (the larger boat's sister ship). For people not acquainted with the famous Mississippi paddlewheels, one might compare the piers with eight one-story houses, each 20 feet high, piled on top of one another. The three beautiful concrete piers built in the water are surrounded by high wooden fenders, which protect them from passing ships and barges.

Watching traffic pass under the high-structured Sunshine Bridge, I realized that the Mississippi is truly a link between world merchants. Two ships sailed by—the "Sentinel II" from Monrovia and an all-black painted "Powanwiec Warzanski" from Czechoslovakia. A third ship's name and homeland I didn't record because the heat and humidity were starting to make me extremely uncomfortable and the dark sky indicated I should hurry on.

Originally, in 1964, a toll was charged on the Sunshine Bridge, but in April 1977, after the Bridge and Ferry Authority gave the bridge to the State of Louisiana, the toll was removed. That was one day when the Sunshine Bridge made people happy even if "the skies were grey."

**Use:**
Louisiana Highway 70

**Location:**
Between Donaldsonville and Union, Louisiana

**Style:**
5-span cantilever steel truss

**Length:**
Channel span - 750 feet clear
            825 feet total
Total length -  8,236 feet

**Width:**
4 lanes

**Clearance:**
167 feet MLW

**Date completed:**
August 1964

**Designer:**
Palmer & Baker, Consulting Engineers

**Bridge:**
#4260200721 in St. James Parish

**Owner:**
Louisiana Department of Transportation and Development

Sunshine Bridge, Donaldsonville, Louisiana          Mary C. Costello

13

# Horace Wilkinson Bridge, Baton Rouge, Louisiana, I-10

"*W*hat are you doing? I can confiscate your camera and take out the film!" That was the way I was greeted on the levee in Port Allen, Louisiana. It was a time when transportation was the target for terrorists around the world. Security had been greatly increased with recent headlines about hijackings and partisan activities. I realized that the man feared I was a saboteuse.

I was just beginning my sketch as the Horace Wilkinson Bridge started to shed the early morning fog. No one was around. I was glad to see the sun pierce the low cloud on the other side of the river when a little white Security Police car drove up to me. The driver was really gruff and upset at my not having obtained permission from one of the guard houses at either end of the embankment to photograph and draw the bridge. After warning me to "ask from now on" and not take pictures of the ships, he left.

I resumed my work. To the right of the double kingposted truss bridge was a wharf warehouse with wooden pallets stacked, waiting for use. Its metal roof glistened in the eerie light of sun through the clouds. Eventually I recognized an aerial tower and gray shapes of an industrial area across the river in Baton Rouge.

Although the fog lifted so I could see the bridge clearly, from my position I would not have guessed that the I-10 Bridge was 6 lanes wide. The structure's great height above me and the length of the main span stretched out so that the bridge appeared narrower.

Modjeski and Masters informed me that in building the piers for the bridge, workers called "sandhogs," working inside a caisson under pressure, hand dug the matter from under the piers, causing it to settle to its lowest elevation. Although the work was very dangerous, the pay was good.

Just as its "big sisters," the Crescent City Connection Bridges (formerly the Greater New Orleans), this Baton Rouge Bridge is not centered over the river. It is designed as usual with the main span over the deepest part of the Mississippi, but that span happens to be nearer Port Allen. The I-10 Bridge is symmetrical but is askew of the river.

Later in the day the West Baton Rouge Parish Library provided me with an aerial photo of the bridge interchanges at Port Allen. They are the most complex mass of "concrete spaghetti" in Louisiana.

Men were working on train tracks behind me, fire-ants* were working at my ankles, and I was working to make the guard-imposed deadline. I don't know about the men on the tracks, but the rest of us, the ants and I, made it. I left after an hour and a-half but my ankles itched for three weeks!

---

* Fire-ants are a variety of ants found in the South, Louisiana in particular. The welt made by the bite remains itchy for two to three weeks. The bites can even be deadly.

**Use:**
I-10 highway traffic in Louisiana

**Location:**
Between Baton Rouge and Port Allen

**Style:**
3-span cantilever steel truss

**Length:**
Channel span - 1120 feet clear
1235 feet total
Total length - 14,150 feet

**Width:**
6 lanes

**Clearance:**
165 feet MLW

**Date completed:**
November 1967

**Designer:**
Modjeski & Masters

**Bridge:**
#4500900001 in Baton Rouge Parish

**Owner:**
Louisiana Department of Transportation and Development

**Unique Feat:**
Last bridge on the Mississippi River under which ships can travel; also seventh longest cantilever bridge in the world (Colliers Encyclopedia 1992, Volume 4, 545)

Baton Rouge Port Allen, I-10 Bridge

Mary C. Costello

15

# Huey P. Long Highway/Railroad Bridge, Baton Rouge, US 190

*T*his is the end of the line—for ships, I mean. Ocean-going vessels require deep water; south of this spot in Baton Rouge, the Mississippi River channel is 40 feet deep or more, but just north of the US 190 Bridge the channel is, at most, only 12 feet.[3]

This second bridge, bearing the name of the Louisiana Governor, was built five years later than the one in New Orleans, and is in a site 128 miles north of that city. At first glance three things were unusual about the Baton Rouge Huey P. Long Bridge: the mustard color of the structure; the long, straight, high trestle; and the angled approach from the ground. I understood all of these peculiarities when I drove across. The unusual color was no doubt a primer paint, since the bridge was undergoing major rehabilitation. The center of the bridge, under the superstructure, was for trains only and was the reason for the high straight trestle (its descent would be long and gradual). The ramp that descended to the ground was a part of the vehicular highway. My drive up the narrow, two-lane ramp and across the bridge to the other side of the Mississippi was a scary one, with one lane of traffic just skimming by the other.

With great trepidation I made the return trip across the "Old Baton Rouge Bridge." Arriving safely, I went under the bridge where the cement trucks, construction equipment and most of the workmen's cars were located. Conveniently, it was lunch-time. As the workers ate in the shade of a black metal shed, the foreman volunteered some information. They were widening the bridge four feet on each side...starting on the far lanes. Therefore, all traffic was routed to the opposite side of the high superstructure. The foreman stated that during the bridge reconstruction the railroads had agreed to have trains travel only at night. During the day, "cherry pickers" on the ground lifted heavy bridge materials to and from the elevated work-site. Since the bridge is owned and operated by the Louisiana Department of Transportation and Development, the Kansas City Southern and Union Pacific Railroads are "paying tenants" and are very cooperative.

As I ate my lunch in a small gas station/snack bar near the Baton Rouge US 190 Bridge, I talked to the nephew of the superintendent who built the bridge. As many as 1,000 men worked on the structure above the swirling current of the Mississippi. My informant said that the bitterly cold winter of 1938 made the work extremely difficult. The foundation for the piers had to be sunk 180 feet below water. While concrete was being poured for one of these piers, a man disappeared. Thinking that he had fallen into the concrete, co-workers searched the best they could but he was never found. For years, on the anniversary of that fatal day, a woman could be seen laying a wreath at the pier.

---

**Use:**
Highway US 190 & two railroads: the Kansas City Southern and the Union Pacific

**Location:**
Approximately 3 miles north of Port Allen to Baton Rouge

**Style:**
Cantilever Steel Truss Highway/Railroad Bridge

**Length:**
Channel span - 748 feet clear
850 feet total
Bridge length - 3300 feet

**Width:**
4 traffic lanes with a single train track between them

**Clearance:**
112.8 feet MLW

**Date completed:**
August 1940

**Designer:**
Bridge Design Section of the Louisiana Highway Commission, Norman Lant, chief engineer

**Bridge:**
#0071000001 in Baton Rouge Parish

**Owner:**
Louisiana Department of Transportation and Development

Huey P. Long Bridge, Baton Rouge                                    Mary C. Costello

17

*I*t was Sunday and no one was working at the Natchez Bridge scene. For that I was sorry. The river front would have been a very active place any weekday because a span was being built parallel to the 1940 bridge. A parked dump truck looked like a toy below me on the Vidalia side of the river where I stood. The ground was spread with concrete mattresses, which the Corps of Engineers has waiting to spread where needed on the riverbank and sometimes on the river bottom, to prevent erosion. A "Drive Slow" sign near the river's edge showed that a safety committee had been at work.

The second through-truss span between Natchez, Mississippi, and Vidalia, Louisiana, was about half finished at the time of my visit. It took two years to build the concrete piers, which were in place that Sunday afternoon. Another two were needed to construct the steel superstructure and roadway. The completed new bridge is 16 feet wider than the 1940 span and has parapets of concrete instead of steel. Essentially, it is a twin to the original five-kingpost bridge and carries eastbound traffic while the older bridge carries vehicles going west.

When speaking before the American Society of Civil Engineers in Davenport, Iowa, 6 April 1944, Ned Ashton, the design engineer for the first bridge, said the whole bridge structure is 375 feet high from the bottom of the pier to the top of the superstructure. (One hundred feet of that 375 are in swift flowing water, with another 70 feet embedded in the river bottom.) Ashton had the audience imagine the bridge standing on Main Street. "It would tower about 30 stories high," he stated. The tallest building in Davenport (the Davenport Bank Building) is only 250 feet tall, two-thirds the height of the total southern structure.

This is an ideal spot for a bridge because Natchez has a high natural bluff on which the duo bridges rest. The Louisiana riverbank, however, is flat and low, requiring a long approach to ease to ground level. Ferries carried people across the Mighty Mississippi from Vidalia to Natchez for 150 years before the first bridge was built in 1940.

Natchez is the oldest settlement on the Mississippi River. Beginning as a French military post in 1716, before New Orleans was founded, it was occupied in succession by Indians, British and Spanish before the United States took over in 1798. This river town was capital of and first incorporated town in the Mississippi Territory in 1803.

Standing on the high grassy levee overlooking the Mississippi River, I could imagine friendly Natchez Indians (1542) on the bluffs across the river watching Hernando DeSoto's expedition approach by boat, greeting and taking them to their Grand Village. Without difficulty I could transpose those same friendly Indians into the 1980's bridge-construction setting, viewing derricks, cranes, barges and revolving cement mixers at work. How unbelieving they would be to watch the steel beams cantilever, seemingly unsupported, across their Great River and to see the suspended span float into place on barges. How impressed the early Indian would be witnessing the completed five-span bridge. Would "Great Sun" meet with the bridge engineer to work out a way for the Indians and Whites to co-exist?

When I finished my sketch, I hurried down the grassy dike to my car parked on Concordia Street. There I took my water jug from the newspaper insulation and enjoyed a refreshing drink.

**Use:**
US 84, 98 and 65 highway traffic

**Location:**
Natchez, Mississippi to Vidalia, Louisiana

**Style:**
5-span cantilever through-truss

**Length:**
Double channel spans each -
849 feet clear
875 feet total
Total length - Old   8,135 feet
New   8,448 feet

**Width:**
Old bridge -  2 lanes
New bridge - 2 lanes, plus 6 & 10-foot
shoulders

**Clearance:**
127 foot MLW

**Date completed:**
Old bridge - October 1940
New bridge - July 1988

**Designer:**
Howard, Needles, Tammen and Bergendoff
(both bridges)

**Toll:**
1940 to 1952, 35 cents (car & driver)

**Bridge:**
#026010000l Louisiana
#2100084001000001 Mississippi

**Owners:**
Mississippi and Louisiana Departments of
Transportation and Development

*Natchez - Vidalia Bridges*                     *Mary C. Costello*

19

# Vicksburg I-20 Bridge, Mississippi

According to local folklore, an eleven-year-old boy is credited with saving the economy of the city of Vicksburg after the Mississippi River changed its course in 1876. When the river bypassed the bustling river town, it was difficult to transport the cotton, timber and agricultural products to market. Everything suffered, and Vicksburg's economy declined. Had nothing been done, possibly there would be no Vicksburg or Vicksburg Bridges today. The youth's suggestion was to connect by a canal the Yazoo River, north of town, with the Father of Waters. This is what the Corps of Engineers did in 1904 after two years of study, thereby channeling water to the Mississippi River past Vicksburg via the Yazoo Diversion Canal (located where the dried-up-river channel had been). Vicksburg was given renewed life.

When determining in the 1960's which style bridge would facilitate highway traffic, since the old Vicksburg span was inadequate by that date, Lionel Pavlo design engineers considered five different types of bridges and concluded that the cantilever through-truss style was best for the location. It was also decided that to accommodate navigation, the new bridge had to be built either close to the already-existing bridge or 1 1/2 miles downstream. After many studies and much discussion the position 330 feet from the railway/highway bridge was chosen.

Today, Interstate 20 (the main East/West thoroughfare) crosses the Mississippi River south of Vicksburg a short distance from where the canal flows into the river. Completed in 1973, the "ultra-modern" Vicksburg Bridge looks similar to the "old truss bridge" in overall contour and pier line-up except for one pier on the east shore. The similarities end there. The I-20 Bridge is twice as wide as the earlier bridge, constructed of a simpler truss plan (Warren truss design), and of solid I-beams throughout instead of holed or trussed ones. The last span on the east, to accommodate the wishes of the Louisiana Levee Board, crosses without a support in the levee. The massive new through-truss Vicksburg Bridge appears low, wide and unencumbered. In fact, while crossing the bridge one feels the spaciousness. The I-20 bridge has been painted a rich blue-green color, in strong contrast to the older bridge's somber black.

My memory of the Vicksburg I-20 Bridge involves more than the bridge itself. Memorable are its surroundings: the one-story brick Visitors' Center overlooking both bridges, with its Doric-columned veranda, providing cool shelter and gracious hostesses offering a refreshing beverage to all tourists—the steep hills in the downtown area which held caves for women and children's safety during the Civil War "Battle of Vicksburg"—the attractive civic buildings so well-kept and effectively spotlighted at night—and lastly, the kindly townspeople giving assistance and information on the river bridges. I know why a young man who supposedly came for an overnight visit is still living in Vicksburg after fifteen years. Vicksburg is one town I would surely enjoy calling "home."

**Use:**
Highway traffic I-20

**Location:**
Between Vicksburg, Mississippi and Delta, Louisiana

**Style:**
Cantilever steel through-truss

**Length:**
Channel span - 846 feet clear
                870 feet total
Total length -  12,974 feet

**Width:**
4 lanes divided by a 4-foot median

**Clearance:**
119 feet MLW

**Date completed:**
14 February 1973

**Designer:**
E. Lionel Pavlo Design Consultants, New York

**Bridge:**
#4510900001 in Madison Parish

**Owners:**
Mississippi and Louisiana Departments of Transportation and Development

Vicksburg I-20 Bridge

Mary C. Costello

# Vicksburg Highway/Railway Bridge, US 80

*T*his Vicksburg Bridge has been responsible for many river accidents. It is considered to be one of the most dangerous bridges on the Mississippi. Checking the map, I found that the span is very close to a sharp turn in the river, which to me made the accident situation understandable. However, back home as I was reading The Amazing Mississippi by Willard Price, I found an explanation of the real reason for the bridge hazard.

What makes the Vicksburg Bridge so dangerous is that there is a strong cross current or 'set' from the right shore. All the officers are in the pilot-house to watch our captain take us through. He heads straight for a pier and apparent destruction. In the nick of time the set carries the enormous tow sliding to port just far enough to miss the pier and we pass through with plenty of room to spare.

This would not be too hard a trick for an easily maneuverable motorboat, but try it with 21,300 tons of tow stretching a quarter of a mile ahead of your steering levers!

As I stood on Look-Out Point to the right of this "dangerous" bridge, it didn't seem different from other truss bridges I had seen—a cantilever span with two anchor spans adjoining three simple trusses on the Louisiana side. A woman walked up and commented as I was putting final strokes on my bridge picture, "Isn't that an interesting bridge? That is the first time I have driven on a bridge right next to a train!"

I was astounded! I didn't know that the structure was both a highway and railroad bridge. From my side position, I could not see the train tracks or the two distinct approach ramps. I immediately moved to where I could see and redrew my sketch. After that incident, I crossed the bridges before I sketched.

On that quiet Sunday morning in Vicksburg, from my new location, I saw the black through-trusses, part of the solid concrete piers not hidden by trees, the bridge tender's office, and the steel towers supporting the girder highway and railroad approaches. I could hear the birds in the trees beside me. My mind wandered to things I had seen earlier—the small airplane that had scared me as it flew down to dust crops along the highway, the freshly picked cotton that blew along the roadside from large open carts, and the lush green of the "kudzu vine" that blanketed the trees and landscape outside of the city. Vicksburg is a very interesting place and its bridges add to its appeal.

Shortly after the bridge was completed, a deep-seated slide of the entire riverbank occurred, causing the settling of the two east piers and the first tower. A member of the bridge design team claims "...the main piers have tilted and with the jumbling of the mechanism, the bridge continues to stand today by the grace of God and a good deal of maintenance." (Ashton 1944, 6) Cars and trains have continued to cross it for 60 years since. Despite boats, "sets" and tilts, this old US 80 Bridge survives miraculously.

With another page done in my sketchbook, I drove across the bridge and remembered what the lady had said earlier. It would have been a thrill to have had a Mid-South Railroad train next to me crossing the bridge, but that didn't happen. However, I was glad there were not a lot of cars on the 18-foot-wide two-way road. It was "heart-in-mouth time" with just one or two cars to pass! I can't imagine what it was like the first day the Vicksburg Bridge opened in 1930. People rode all day toll free, back and forth! But at that time cars were narrower...and slower!

---

**Use:**
US 80 highway and Mid-South Railroad (pays to use)

**Location:**
Between Vicksburg, Mississippi and Delta, Louisiana

**Style:**
7-span cantilever through-truss* for trains and vehicles

**Length:**
Channel span - 800 feet clear
825 feet total
Total length -   8,546 feet

**Width:**
2-lane highway beside a single train track, 18-foot roadway

**Clearance:**
119 feet MLW

**Date completed:**
1 May 1930, supplanting ferry service

**Designer:**
Louis R. Ash, engineer/designer of Ash Howard Needles & Tammen Consulting Engineers of Kansas City, now Howard Needles Tammen & Bergendoff

**Toll:**
Until 1 January 1966

**Bridge:**
#...no known number

**Owner:**
Vicksburg Bridge Commission

---

* Although many of these bridges are "through" type bridges, meaning that the traffic drives under the bridge's superstructure rather than on top as a "deck" type, this bridge allows both trains and cars to travel at the same level, inside the superstructure.

Vicksburg Railway/Highway Bridge

Mary C. Costello

23

*I*t was night when I arrived in this "Port City of the Delta", as Greenville is called. The timing was unplanned, and I was a little nervous driving unfamiliar roads in the dark. However, the wide well-lighted streets and a helpful gas station attendant relieved my anxiety. The attendant directed me to the area where I found a southern-appearing motel—red brick with white pillars and lighted porch. It was a warm September evening and the people were friendly. I liked Greenville already.

The following morning the motel owner gave me directions to the bridge seven miles away. Until 1931, she said, the river flowed right past Greenville. About that time Congress decided to straighten the river's serpentine curves which created the distance between Greenville and the Mighty River.

When I arrived, I crossed a mile-long approach (68 spans) on the Mississippi side. The Greenville Bridge's through-trusses over the navigable river consist of only three spans as opposed to five at Natchez. The bridges were both built in 1940 and largely from the same plan with identically designed piers—a big economic plus for the engineers. (Ashton 1944, 32) The piers were sunk 180 feet below the water's surface in water that was over 100 feet deep constituting the bridge's major design contribution. "Each pier...cost almost as much as all six piers together cost in the Rock Island (Centennial) Bridge."(Ashton 1944, 28)

The Arkansas approach was short but high and curved. What surprised me lay around that wide curve as I exited the US 82 Bridge—a flea market identified by "Dave's Fireworks"! I stopped at the open air market and met J. K. Vick, an antique merchant and long-time resident of the area. He told me some of the bridge's history.

In the spring of 1948, the tugboat "Natchez" headed north from New Orleans with crude oil barges in tow. The treacherous current caught the barges and boat throwing them against the concrete pier of the Greenville Bridge broadside. The boat overturned and sank immediately. Tragically, thirteen of the twenty-six crew members drowned. [4]

In the 1950's from an airbase near Greenville, Vick continued, a fighter pilot tried to fly under this high Greenville Bridge. Instead he hit it and was killed.

Neither of these incidents was on file at the library, nor did anyone else to whom I spoke seem to know about them. I have since found references in books verifying the "Natchez" sinking story.

Among the most unusual features visible on the Greenville Bridge are large pipes that bow out beside the deck both at the beginning and end of the superstructure. These pipes, Vick said, run alongside the bridge road and carry utility lines that actually make the bridge profitable. The Arkansas Power and Light and the Bell Telephone Company both lease space on the bridge. When the Tennessee Gas Company, who until recently also leased space on the bridge, attempted to lay their pipelines below the water in the past, the swift current wouldn't allow them to stay down. (The fees from the utilities permitted the bridge commission to remove the toll from the bridge in 1950 and also maintain its spotless appearance.)

In his book, The Amazing Mississippi , Willard Price noted that a tow of lead worth a million dollars went down by the same pier as the "Natchez" in about 1963. In contrast to the little that was done to find the "Natchez," every effort was made to find this tow. However, because the cargo was so heavy, it sank into the soft bottom and was immediately buried in the silt forever!*

---

*Engineer Harold Sandberg, Chicago, says that at "high flood" the river bottom lowers during this time, the "Natchez" or the lead tow might be found. He claims, "When the river rises 10 feet, the (river) bottom lowers 20 feet."

**Use:**
US 82 Transcontinental Highway trafffic

**Location:**
Between Greenville, Mississippi, and Lake Village, Arkansas

**Style:**
3-span cantilever through-truss with plate-girder approaches

**Length:**
Channel span - 800 feet clear
              - 840 feet total
Total length -  9,957 feet

**Width:**
2 lanes plus narrow walkways,
24 feet total

**Clearance:**
130 feet MLW

**Date completed:**
October 1940

**Designer:**
Ash, Howard, Needles and Tammen

**Toll:**
From October 1940 to late 1950

**Bridge:**
#0.0 in Washington County, Mississippi

**Owners:**
City of Greenville

**Unique Feat:**
Money from power and telephone companies' pipelines pay for maintenance

*Greenville Bridge*

Mary C. Costello

25

# Helena, Arkansas, Highway Bridge, US 49

*T*he bridge here at Helena was a bit of a problem for me. It was hard to find, hard to see, and especially hard to believe.

To get to the Helena Bridge, I passed cotton plantations, orange-painted cotton-filled mesh carts, and a processing plant with a yellowish plume of smoke rising from its smokestack. The highway took me through West Helena before I came to Helena, an old town that saw battle during the Civil War. On 4 July 1863, Confederate troops tried to recapture it from the Union Troops but failed.

As I drove through the town, (population 9,600), school buses were letting off students. I knew I'd better hurry to find the bridge as it was getting late in the day. I drove toward the river through an opening in a concrete wall. On the other side were train tracks and people enjoying the waterfront, but I saw no bridge. At a warehouse office nearby, I was told the bridge was south of town.

The Helena Bridge stood directly opposite a Holiday Inn and a gas station. I crossed the two-lane through-truss structure, which was long, high and narrow. Though painted a cerulean blue, the superstructure in the strong sunlight looked silver. On the Mississippi side of the river I found farm fields and trees but no place to stop, so I turned around to go back. Luckily, the bridge was not busy! I was a driving hazard—going slowly and watching for a good view to sketch. Finding none, I went to the gas station for assistance. The attendant suggested I go onto the levee about halfway up the approach.

Fearfully, I did as he suggested, driving past the abandoned toll booth, watching for a break in the bridge railing, all the while hoping no one would come close behind. I found the opening and parked on top of the levee. First, I walked along the north side and then crossed to the south, where I could see just a little of the bridge's side. What I saw was mostly the portal end and the aluminum railing leading to it. From where I stood the bridge looked fairly short. I managed to make out the peaks, however, and knew I was seeing the whole bridge. I could move further over, but then the trees totally blocked the view.

Two things occurred to me as I sketched. One was that I could see no water from my position. However, if the Mississippi River were flooded, I would have seen it because highwater lines were visible on the piers in front of me. The other thought was that the large overhead "X" at its entrance and repeated throughout the through-truss made the bridge interesting.

When I received the profile drawing of Helena's bridge from the Arkansas State Highway Department, I was greatly surprised at just how long the bridge really is. The superstructure alone is 3,108 feet long—longer than the river is wide here, longer than the Greater New Orleans (3,019 feet) and the Baton Rouge Highway 10 Bridge (2,423 feet). The bridge has five spans of multiple cantilevered trusses. It was hard for me to believe that this was the same bridge I had sketched from the levee. For that reason, I'm including an extra drawing of a boatsman's view of the Helena Bridge for the reader to appreciate—as I did—its amazing length.

**Use:**
US 49 Highway traffic

**Location:**
From Arkansas to Mississippi about a mile and a half south of Helena

**Style:**
Multiple cantilever through-truss plus steel plate-girder approaches

**Length:**
Channel span - 800 feet clear
840 feet total
Total length - 5,200 feet

**Width:**
2 lanes, 26 feet total, plus a 2-foot safety walk on each side

**Clearance:**
115 feet MLW

**Date completed:**
27 July 1961

**Designer:**
Howard Needles Tammen & Bergendoff

**Toll:**
Originally charged toll

**Bridge:**
#02. in Coahona County, Mississippi
**Owners:**
Mississippi and Arkansas Departments of Transportation

Helena, Arkansas Bridge

Mary C. Costello

# Memphis, Tennessee, I-55 Highway Bridge

*T*his "Memphis-Arkansas Memorial Bridge" is old, a 1949 vintage, but it is in such good condition with fresh silver paint and classic lines, that it appears new. Modjeski and Masters, well-known bridge consultants, designed this bridge to span time. From the outside it has unencumbered, simple lines and flat-top spans connecting the four peaks. Inside is a low-arched horizontal bracing above the four lanes of traffic—seen mostly from the end or as one crosses the bridge—providing a feeling of spaciousness.

The I-55 Bridge piers are only one set out of three supporting a close line-up of bridges in Memphis. The I-55 Bridge was the last to join the distinguished group—the Frisco and the Harahan—and is the only highway bridge. Although one feels that one can almost "reach out and touch" the next bridge, they are really 150 feet apart. The adjacent bridge piers are equally spaced—in line like soldiers—to facilitate boat navigation.

This Memphis Bridge is the first bridge, as one comes up the Mississippi River from the South, with a full-size sidewalk as opposed to a safety walk for maintenance workers and stranded motorists. Since the I-55 Bridge was built in the late 40's, before the Interstate System, it may have been used by pedestrians then but not so today. Mr. W. B. Conway, an engineer and a partner in Modjeski and Masters, told me that the Interstate Highway System does not allow pedestrians or bicycles on its bridges under penalty of law. One reason is to prevent suicides. Also, Conway continued, bridges in the South are not from bluff to bluff, but often from lowland, even swampland, rising for long distances to and across the river before descending on the other side. Sometimes these bridges are more than three miles long with extreme heights, and he felt pedestrians may not be interested in walking across.

Another important point of interest on the Memphis I-55 Bridge is the style of the verticals and horizontals used. This structure has box members with evenly spaced oval holes for fastening rivets. On close look one sees the openings are covered with bird screen to prevent them from becoming pigeon havens. From land, however, these holey parts resemble tinker-toys. The box construction makes for greater strength and simple beauty and, perhaps more than anything else, gives the 1949 bridge the look of the 90's.

Because of the high elevation of Memphis's shore, (contrary to Conway's description of bridges further south) there is no need for a long approach to the I-55. The bridge "takes off" next to Crumb State Park, where I stood drawing. If I were taller, I think I could have walked over and touched the bottom chord. This low-level bridge is a change from the high bridges I had seen, especially in Louisiana. Being close and at eye-level seemed to make the I-55 a more personal structure—appropriate for a Memorial Bridge.

**Use:**
Highway traffic for 61, 70, 79 and I-55

**Location:**
Between Tennessee and Arkansas at Memphis

**Style:**
8-span bridge with multiple cantilevers, two simple through-trusses and one deck-truss span

**Length:**
Channel span -  770 feet clear
                790 feet total
Total length -    5,222 feet

**Width:**
Four 12-foot lanes and two 6-foot sidewalks

**Clearance:**
109 feet MLW

**Date completed:**
December 1949

**Designer:**
Modjeski and Masters

**Bridge:**
#79I00550101 in Tennessee

**Owners:**
Tennessee and Arkansas Departments of Transportation

Memphis I-55 Bridge

Mary C. Costello

29

# "Frisco" Railroad Bridge, Memphis

*I* stood in the middle of the railroad track to draw the "Frisco" bridge!—Dangerous? Yes, but I had little choice! With bridges on both sides of the railroad bridge there was no place I could go to see the bridge profile. However, never did I become so engrossed in my work that I forgot to be aware of what might be coming behind me. From 4:30 to 6:00 p.m. no train came.

It had just rained, and the water remaining on the black boards beside the tracks reflected the white sky. Inside the towering silver structure I could see repeated "X's" overhead and concentric rectangles below, leading the eye through the super-structure to the end where there was but a small hole of light. It was a pleasing arrangement of shapes as well as lights and darks.

The designer of the Frisco Railroad Bridge, George S. Morison, one of America's foremost bridge builders,[5] built an award winner. It was the first bridge constructed over the Lower Mississippi. When completed in 1892, its 790-foot main span was the longest railroad truss in North America and won the National Historic Civil Engineering Landmark Award. It had the greatest clearance of any bridge in existence in the U.S. When built, it was the third longest railroad bridge of its type in the world; only the Firth of Forth Bridge in Scotland and the suspension bridge across the Niagara River were longer. The Memphis Bridge became Morison's most important bridge project.

Ralph Modjeski was the chief draftsman and chief inspector of the superstructure. Reading his narrative of the Memphis Bridge, I became aware of just how much influence the Congress and War Department had on the construction of a bridge. (Today it is the Coast Guard that regulates bridges.) Congress fixed the minimum length of the Frisco channel span at 700 feet, and the height above high water at 75 feet. The engineers felt the bridge needed to be only 65 feet above high water instead of 75. In order to convince Congress, Modjeski secured the measurement of all smokestacks and pilot-houses of important steamboats that used the Lower Mississippi River and had a Congressman present them to the Assembly along with an amendment reducing the vertical clearance. The Fifty-first Congress failed to pass his bill and, as a result, the bridge was built with the 75-foot MHW clearance.

The 1888 charter from the Secretary of War required that the bridge provide for railway trains plus wagons, vehicles of all kinds, and for animal traffic. From the beginning, therefore, planks were laid next to and between the tracks to accommodate all. Wagons and animals did not use the bridge at the same time as the trains. A bridge tender controlled the bridge use.

I was almost finished with the Frisco Bridge, nicknamed after its former owner, the St. Louis-San Francisco Railway, when the sky became very dark and opened up. As soon as I left the bridge and started home to my friend's house, I heard, then saw, through the heavy sheets of rain a long freight train head across the Frisco. It traveled the very spot where I had stood moments before.

The next day when I returned to finish my sketch, the sky was clear, the sun shone brightly, and the Frisco Railroad Bridge had changed character. It had lost its drama—no more reflective puddles, no more grey sky for the black skeleton to dance before, no more sharp black railbed, ties and track. Surrounding color made the Frisco so ordinary!

---

**Use:**
Burlington Northern Railroad traffic

**Located:**
Memphis to Arkansas

**Style:**
One continuous, two cantilever and two anchor-arm spans riveted through-truss, plus one deck-truss

**Length:**
Channel span - 770 feet clear
790 feet total
Total length - 5,015 feet

**Width:**
Single track

**Clearance:**
111 foot MLW

**Date completed:**
May 12, 1892; heavy maintenance 1970's

**Designer:**
George S. Morison

**Bridge:**
#482.1

**Owner:**
BN Railroad since 1981

**Unique Feat:**
First bridge built across the Lower Mississippi River; the recipient of the "National Historic Civil Engineering Landmark Award" 1987

Frisco Railroad Bridge

Mary C. Costello

# Harahan Railroad Bridge, Memphis

*N*ever before had I seen fog roll in. It followed the river and came around the bend from the south, enveloping first the I-55 Bridge, and then the Frisco Bridge, before it hid the Harahan. The grayish white cloud moved very fast. In minutes the whole area was under its cover.

Sketching the Harahan Bridge profile from about two blocks away, as I had been doing, was difficult because of the trilogy of bridges. Picking out one bridge design from another was a challenge. Ten barges had been navigated under the three bridges and around the curve in the river just before the fog descended. A darkened sky foretold a weather change, sudden rain fell and fair-weather people made bee-lines for their cars, driving off.

I had been standing in the parking lot but dashed to my Datsun for cover. Much of what I had left to do on the bridge drawing I could do from memory. The fog made seeing the span impossible. It was extremely warm and humid in the car with no air-conditioner, but after twenty minutes the weather cleared. A man with a metal detector left his auto and started scavenging the beach once more, while two middle-aged women continued to talk in their white Ford. I made a few final pen strokes, now that the bridge skeleton had reappeared. As I watched, two trains started across the railroad bridge from opposite directions. They were so small in relation to the bridge that they appeared to be little more than two moving lines. A crash looked imminent! However, a few moments later, the trains passed on the bridge's double track.

A closer look at the Harahan Bridge was imperative. With that in mind, I drove several blocks to a fenced area next to the bridge. I parked behind a white building 100 feet from the long truss span. Albert, a crippled old black man with a cane, told me the building was a Unitarian Church.

Walking from here to the underside of the bridge, I could see the trussed beams close up. This view revealed the heavy riveted members, the now empty roadway brackets outside the railroad deck, and simple stone piers. The most unique part of this cantilever bridge is its beginning in Memphis. The first span starts on the edge of the bluff with a vertical beam. Most truss bridges begin with a diagonal (as does the Arkansas end of this bridge). Ralph Modjeski was commissioned to design this bridge by the Rock Island Lines Railroad in 1914, but needed to keep the bridge in line with the Frisco Bridge (already there and only a short distance away).[6] Since the first span of the Harahan is a short one, there is an imbalance and a tendency for a vertical reaction. To counteract that action, Modjeski weighted the massive portal end of the short span with eyebar tension members connected to the weighted abutment.

Modjeski's achievement in the Harahan Bridge was overshadowed by the famous Frisco Bridge beside it, and later, in 1944, by the I-55. If it had stood alone, the Harahan would have been recognized as one of the "greats" in American railroading.

As I picked my way around the undergrowth, mud and water under the bridge, a young man in his late teens surprised me, jumping from one level of ground to the next. He asked me directions to the I-55 Highway Bridge, then continued descending to the river, which he followed to the bridge.

Back at my car, the sun was out again. The clouds had shuffled themselves around in the sky and made room for that celestial body to show itself. I felt, "The sun's in the sky...all's right with the world!"

**Use:**
Cotton Belt & Union Pacific Railroads

**Location:**
Memphis to Arkansas

**Style:**
4-span cantilever system continuous over five piers; originally had two 14-foot bracketed roadways

**Length:**
Channel span - 770 feet clear
790 feet total
Total length - 4,973 feet

**Width:**
2 tracks

**Clearance:**
110 feet MLW

**Date completed:**
July 1916

**Designer:**
Modjeski and Masters

**Bridge:**
#121.50

**Owners:**
Cotton Belt & Union Pacific Railroads

Harahan Railroad Bridge

Mary C. Costello

# Hernando De Soto Highway Bridge, Memphis I-40

*U*nique in its design and alone in its setting is this tied-arch bridge. From Mud Island, the Memphis I-40 Bridge looks like a giant roller coaster because one sees the tandem arches as high-rolling, twisting three-dimensional skeletons. Not so from the riverside park from where I sketched. I saw only the bridge contour from there.

Named after the Spanish discoverer of the Mississippi River, Hernando De Soto, the De Soto Bridge became the center of the Memphis community's interest in September, 1986. Lights were added, emphasizing the bridge's attractive profile at night. Everyone I spoke with was very proud of the bridge and its new fame.

From the park I could see Mud Island tucked under the bridge's east end. The island flags and delicate green paint on the newly nicknamed "Bridge of Lights" added a little color to the otherwise muted scene. The concrete of the historical museum buildings on the island repeated the tan of the many bridge piers. It was late morning and the sky was overcast. "Ol' Man River" looked muddy and rough.

The Hernando De Soto Bridge is composed of two 900-foot-long tied arches. A matching double channel is unusual on the Mississippi (though found in Natchez also) and is humorously justified as follows: "...provided so that navigators had an alternate channel in case the river ever changed course." (Plowden 1974, 260) Actually, the east channel is truly the main or pilot channel (kept to a 9-foot depth) but the second or west 900-foot span is used at high water.

Distance gives an illusion of frailty to this Memphis bridge, but in crossing it one finds the span very substantial, even built to withstand earthquakes. When driving up the ramp toward the main spans of the six-lane structure, one's first impression is of its great size—width, height, and individual parts. The arches are composed of welded-steel box members (with no holes or lacing). The top and bottom chords are 32 inches square, and all verticals and diagonals are about half that size (15 to 18 inches). With the fast-moving speed on the bridge approach there is no time to dwell on these thoughts, for the next moment one is swept under the De Soto Bridge's arch entrance. With a quick glance up into the "bridge attic," one has a spectacular view of repeated horizontal strut "flooring" between lower arches, spine-like "roofing" between upper arches, and zigzag bracing or "windows" through which one sees all. The view is momentary! Traffic has carried you past the entry. All one sees now are equally spaced hangers on the bridge sides that actually support the concrete roadway; hangers that are barely visible at a distance become sturdy 3 1/2-inch diameter single cables. The arch overhead now descends before us, looking almost bony-shaped as it appears to meet the deck. As the second huge arch begins, one has another chance for the inside view of the illusion caused by repeated lines and shapes on a curve.

Memphis is proud of its most recent bridge. It has benefited from its lighted image, and the Mississippi River, if it could speak, would say to the De Soto Bridge, "Glad to have you above! You add to my beauty!"

**Use:**
I-40 highway traffic

**Location:**
Between Memphis, Tennessee and West Memphis, Arkansas

**Style:**
2-span continuous trussed tied-arch plus continuous box-girders

**Length:**
Double channel span - 870 feet clear
900 feet total
Total length - 19,535 feet

**Width:**
6 lanes with median, 90 feet

**Clearance:**
117 feet MLW

**Date completed:**
August 1972

**Designer:**
Hazelet & Erdal, Louisville, Kentucky

**Bridge:**
#79I00400001 in Tennessee

**Owners:**
Tennessee & Arkansas Departments of Transportation

**Unique feat:**
World's largest of its kind, 3,660 feet total (Plowden 1974, 260)

Memphis I-40 Bridge

Mary C. Costello

# Caruthersville, Missouri, I-155 Bridge

*T*he Caruthersville Bridge is the shape of a slipper with the toe pointing to Tennessee—an original bridge shape for the Father of Waters. However, to find the slipper profile one would have to be on a boat or a specific piece of land. For that reason my picture is an end view that a four-year-old described very candidly, "Looks like a barn."

No matter its shape, I liked this blue-green Caruthersville Bridge—the only crossing between Memphis and Cairo, 219 miles below the Ohio River's confluence with the Mississippi. Crossing the bridge, I felt "high in the sky" as I had on the Luling Bridge in Louisiana—an up-lifted feeling. The bridge looked fresh and new because crews were resurfacing it, although it was built in 1976. The Caruthersville area had waited 30 years to the day from the feasibility study (in 1946) to the bridge's dedication and opening. It was a dream become reality for local residents and ended the long-established era of motorists ferrying across the Mighty Mississippi. The great width of the 4-lane bridge, the interesting large oval holes in the huge verticals and diagonals, the airiness I felt with the spacing of the beams and still the protection from the hot sun—all made me appreciate this Tennessee-Missouri Mississippi River Bridge. It is aesthetically pleasing from the inside out.

The sense of welcome that I experienced was marked. Workmen were jack-hammering areas on the Tennessee approach when I asked for a spot from which to sketch. "Sure, just pull your car behind the barrels anyplace," was the response.

Having already crossed the bridge, I was near the bottom of the long approach, but a median forced me to drive a mile further before finding a turnaround...just a small break in the center barrier that the workers used. I wanted to be situated where I could see the bridge view showing the kingposts. Therefore, I couldn't get too close.

Alternately, I sat on the waist-high concrete wall in the center of the bridge or stood next to it. The wind was strong up there, so strong that it kept rolling a MacDonald's plastic cup uphill, bouncing the container as it did so, picking it up and dropping it again and again. This was the loudest noise I heard because of the extreme height and the distance from the workers.

Soon a yellow highway department truck came by. The driver looked and waved. The word had spread about my book, and from then on, when any of the crew drove by, they signaled a greeting. One driver even stopped his truck and talked for a minute. All of this made me feel welcome to the Caruthersville area in general and to this Tennessee-Missouri Mississippi River Bridge in particular.

---

**Use:**
I-155 highway traffic

**Location:**
Southern Missouri to Tennessee near Caruthersville

**Style:**
2-span cantilever truss with girder approaches

**Length:**
Channel span - 900 feet clear
                920 feet total
Total length -   7,102 feet

**Width:**
4 lanes plus shoulders and median divider

**Clearance:**
96 feet MLW

**Date completed:**
1 December 1976, resurfaced 1986

**Designer:**
Sverdrup & Parcel & Associates, St. Louis (now Sverdrup Corporation)

**Bridge:**
#A-1700 in Missouri

**Owners:**
Tennessee & Missouri Departments of Transportation

*Caruthersville Bridge*

Mary C. Costello

From the river it looks like a slipper...

# PART *T*WO

# PART *T*WO

## Huck Finn Territory

*B*etween Cairo, Illinois, and Burlington, Iowa, the Mighty River's character changes. The water color becomes chocolate brown from the Muddy Missouri—Lock #27 begins the stairway of locks and dams—river rocks generate a problem in the Chain of Rocks area—a 9-foot channel depth is maintained by the Corps of Engineers all the way to Baton Rouge—the limit a boat can tow is reduced to 15 barges though sometimes one extra is carried on the "hip" (beside the boat)—cities like St. Louis are right on the river's edge but suffer at times from floods—small towns, merely dots on the map, lie clustered along the river.

Though no signs of rafts with Mark Twain characters are seen on the river, one cannot help but think of Tom Sawyer, Becky Thatcher and Aunt Polly, in and near Hannibal, Missouri, with its islands, forested banks and mysterious caves. Even under the shadow of today's Gateway Arch one can often see the Delta Queen, a stern-wheeler, similar to what Huck Finn and Jim might have seen on their trip below St. Louis. Mark Twain has imprinted the area in our minds, an area that still can be identified as "Huck Finn Territory."

# Old Cairo, Illinois, Bridge, US 62

*T*he "Upper Mississippi" begins here. The Corps of Engineers has designated the navigable parts of the river as either the Upper Mississippi or the Lower Mississippi with Cairo, Illinois, being the dividing point.

My impression of Cairo from my limited time there was that it is a community of mixed cultures and nationalities in a precarious position between two rivers. Two different high levee walls protect it today from floods that ravaged it in the past—a concrete seawall on the Ohio River side and an earthen one on the Mississippi River side. The town looked less than prosperous. The personnel at the supermarket where I got milk, fruit and directions were friendly and helpful.

The Cairo motels were on the main highway, and I chose "City Motel" run by an Indian couple. Since it was after 5:00 p.m., I only glanced at my room and immediately left for the Old Cairo Bridge. The clerk in the grocery store had said it was further down US 62. Along the way, I was surprised to see a bridge to my left crossing the Ohio River to Kentucky. The Mississippi River Bridge was about a mile further south. The road angled to the right over a long approach, below which a crop of milo was growing with rust-colored heads bobbing in the breeze. I was really interested in this farm crop—new to me.

The "Old Cairo" is a truss bridge but looks a little like a suspension because it has two high kingposts resembling towers. However, instead of cables and hangers, there are chords and trusses. The US 62 Bridge curves into Missouri, where a convenience store stood on the right. I appreciated the large parking lot as a place to leave my car.

Across the highway, I "set-up." The late afternoon sun highlighted the plowed field, the right side of the green-blue trusses, and the rounded sides of many piers supporting the approach. Dark trees shaded the closer bridge parts. As I worked here beside the busy roadway, the breeze from a fast-moving truck blew my hat off, so from then on I used it to nest my camera and binoculars.

The only part of the river I could see was between the two visible piers in the water, and I was glad I was high enough to see that much. Sometimes levees prevent any view of the great river. The main piers, I later learned, were built on caissons sunken 80 feet down in dense sand (as are all the bridges in the old embayment of the South) instead of on rock.

The sun was setting and it was rapidly getting dark when I left. It was dangerous walking across the road to my car because of the number of fast-moving vehicles and effects of dusk. Going back to Cairo, I was aware of how narrow the roadway lanes are—only 10 feet in each direction. In my motel room again, I could reflect on the town that was squeezed between two rivers and two states on the southern-most tip of Illinois. Navigation-wise, this is a very important spot. The Ohio River from the east joins the Mississippi from the north at the foot of Cairo, almost doubling the Mighty Mississippi and increasing its velocity and force. The treacherous speed of the water at this point often forces barges into the piers. I recalled what Roger Wiebusch, Bridge Administrator for the Upper Mississippi, had told me about the danger to river traffic that this Old Cairo Bridge represents: "Three barges are sunken by one pier and two by the other." For the first time I felt a little depressed about a bridge.

**Use:**
US highways 51, 60 & 62

**Location:**
Cairo, Illinois to Birds' Point, Missouri

**Style:**
7-span cantilever through-truss

**Length:**
Channel span - 675 feet clear
700 feet total
Total length - 5177 feet

**Width:**
2 lanes, 20 feet

**Clearance:**
114 feet MLW

**Date completed:**
August 1930

**Designer:**
J.A.L. Waddell, Consulting Engineer, New York City

**Bridge:**
#0020005 in Illinois

**Owners:**
Illinois and Missouri Departments of Transportation

Old Cairo Bridge

Mary C. Costello

43

# New Cairo, Illinois, Bridge, I-57

*S*even miles upstream from the old span in Cairo is the "new" bridge. It was about 8 a.m. when I arrived under the Illinois approach to the I-57 Bridge. I drove through the high grass under the bridge to get to the rocky levee. It wasn't so high a dike as the ones further south nor was it sodded here. The levee gravel tended to slide as I climbed, and the vegetation which had sprung up got in my way. Before I reached the top, my hands and clothes were stained with red berry juice.

From the top, I found the bridge view was not satisfactory, so I picked my way down the embankment and drove over the span to Missouri. This bridge, built in 1978, seemed brand new, with a 4-lane concrete roadway and each box-shaped truss member designed free of holes or decoration. The downgrade of the road on the Missouri side of the bridge was rather steep and long. At the bottom I pulled onto the gravel shoulder to park. Immediately after I started walking towards the bridge, a man in a white van stopped to ask if I needed help. Of course I didn't, but I was pleased to think he wanted to assist—an example of the friendliness of the people in Cairo.* This happened at only two other places on the whole length of the river, at Fort Madison, Iowa, and at Rapid City, Illinois, by the I-80 Bridge.

The best spot from which to draw the I-57 Bridge, I found, was from the top of the hill in a cornfield next to the bridge approach. Luckily, the field was harvested, so only a few husks remained. It was cloudy, cool and very windy. I couldn't see much of the profile of the bridge, but I knew that the center had a round top and the end spans were flat. Later, when I received a picture of the bridge profile, it confirmed that there is an arch over the main channel with welded box-shaped hangers. These box-like road-suspenders are hermetically sealed against water and moisture-laden air, saving expensive painting inside. The top of the arch has "K-shaped" bracing to minimize the number of members, said Mr. Sandberg, President of the Board of Alfred Benesch and Company, designers of the bridge.

I really liked the fresh blue-green color and the giant "X" bracing inside the superstructure. This shape was repeated again and again, giving the illusion of a pointed archway as one enters and crosses the bridge.

As far away as I was from the Mississippi, I could still see the water between piers and trees. The distant trees this morning in Cairo were hazy layers that looked the color of the bridge. The sun was not even able to glow through the solid whitewashed sky. The only sounds were the crickets and the cars coming and going.

Back at my Datsun, I unpinned my keys from my slacks, as was my habit, and gladly got out of the crisp wind.

---

* I had to practice pronouncing "Cairo" (Ka'ro) like the syrup, not like the capital city of Egypt.

**Use:**
Interstate 57 traffic

**Location:**
Alexander County, Illinois to Mississippi County, Missouri

**Style:**
3-span continuous truss with a center span designed as a tied arch

**Length:**
Channel span - 804 feet clear
821 feet total
Total length - 4085 feet

**Width:**
4 lanes, 59 feet total

**Clearance:**
111 feet MLW

**Date completed:**
July 1978

**Designer:**
Alfred Benesch & Company, Chicago, Illinois

**Bridge:**
#0020022 in Illinois

**Owners:**
Illinois and Missouri Departments of Transportation

*New Cairo, Illinois, Bridge*                    *Mary C. Costello*

45

# Thebes, Illinois, High Railroad Bridge

Some bridges are special because of their history or style, and some are special to me because of what happened when I saw them for the first time. The "Thebes" is special for both reasons.

When I arrived at the Thebes Bridge, it was midmorning and the sandy shore was sloping to the river with boulders big enough to use as a chair. The spot was shaded by large trees behind. The bridge, a block away, was completely in view except for the approach arches on the Illinois side (the side on which I stood). I was delighted.

As I was about to begin drawing, my attention was diverted to the houseboat on my right. I thought it was a boat that people lived on but found it was a landing-flat for a river dredge sitting about a mile downstream. The dredge was clearing out the river channel, as the channel was too shallow here. Since 1896 the law requires, for the sake of barges and large boats, that the river be at least nine feet deep. A man on the "flat" said that visitors were invited onto the dredge, called "The Potter," but it wasn't until a part of the crew came that I decided to go with them.

I was fascinated by my ride in the fast motorboat sent out by "The Potter," as well as my tour of the larger boat, seeing and discussing its giant vacuum-cleaner process of dredging. In addition, my unexpected lunch on the dredge and, finally, my return trip under the bridge, passing next to its sturdy stone piers, all made for an exhilarating prelude to sketching.

It was difficult to concentrate on my work when I got back. A long freight train crossed the Thebes—long enough to span the entire bridge and more beyond. I was wishing it could have been a steam locomotive; nevertheless, this fast-moving diesel freight silhouetted against the sky was a spectacular sight.

The Thebes Bridge[1] is known for its strength.

Given titles such as "The Steel Monster" and "The Monster Connecting Link," it was severely tested when it was first built in 1905 by 33 coupled steam locomotives that came to an abrupt halt (as abrupt a halt as trains can make) in the middle of the bridge. This was repeated several times on each of the two tracks. The bridge withstood the torture without a tremble.

Built from high cliffs on both sides of the river and on solid rock in the bottom of the river, "the last solid rock bottom on the Mississippi River southward to the Gulf of Mexico,"(Hente 1987, 6A) the bridge has not settled significantly in over 90 years.

Two interesting facts have appeared in articles about the Thebes Railroad Bridge. One is that during World War II it was guarded against sabotage. (W. B. Conway of Modjeski and Masters informed me that all Mississippi River railroad bridges were so guarded during World War II.) The other is that in the mid 1920's, when the automobile was becoming popular, "wings" were added to the bridge to allow a road to be built on either side. However, since the Cape Girardeau Bridge was completed about that time (1928), the "Thebes vehicular road" was never constructed.

Because of its remarkable strength and endurance as well as my memories, I have dubbed the Thebes "super-special."

**Use:**
Union Pacific and Cotton Belt Railroad traffic

**Location:**
Thebes, Illinois to Scott City, Missouri

**Style:**
5-span cantilever through-truss with 5 or more 65-foot concrete deck-arch approaches

**Length:**
Channel span - 651 feet clear
               671 feet total
Total length - 24,816 feet or 4.7 miles

**Width:**
2 tracks

**Clearance:**
104 feet MLW

**Date completed:**
April 1905; ferries transported entire trains previously between Missouri and Illinois

**Designer:**
Ralph Modjeski and Alfred Noble

**Bridge:**
#121.50

**Owners:**
Union Pacific and Cotton Belt Railroad

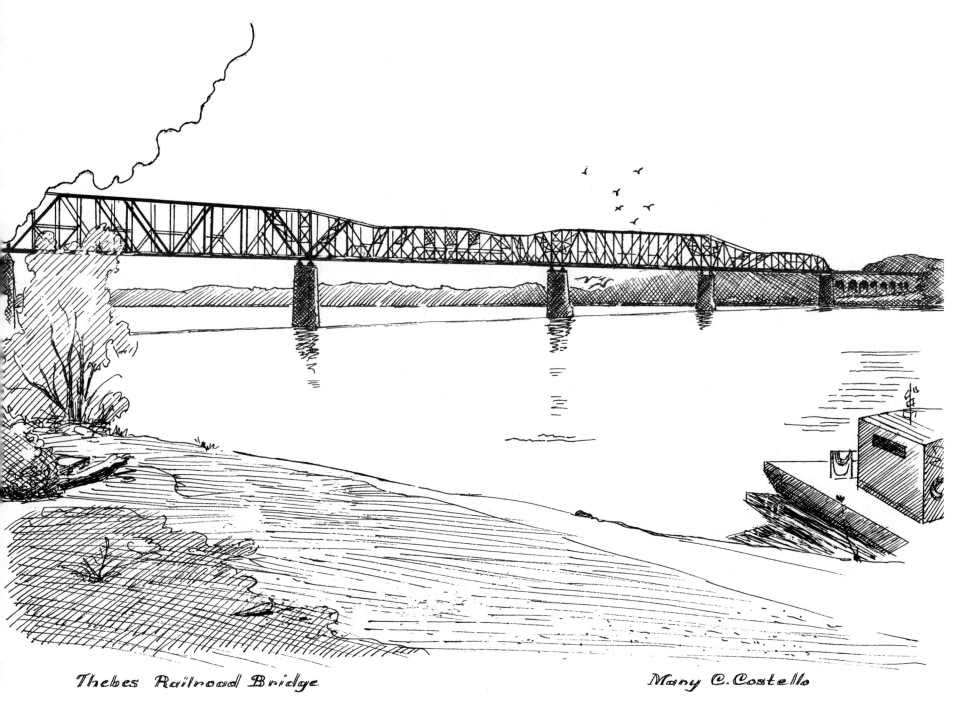

*Thebes Railroad Bridge*

*Mary C. Costello*

# Cape Girardeau Highway Bridge, Missouri

*I*t isn't often that a dog plays a part in a bridge's history, but Lucky, a small shaggy dog mostly cocker spaniel, was a part of this bridge almost as much as its toll-takers. From November, 1951, until its toll-free state in June, 1957, Lucky was the bridge's mascot. It was during an ice storm at about midnight that the dog headed across the ice-coated bridge from the Illinois side. She was bumped by a car and almost pushed off the bridge before making it to the toll-booth, where she scratched to get in. From then on she was the guard dog and friend of the bridge, often receiving gifts from regular bridge-crossers.

The financial history of this bridge is not the usual one. Instead of the gala opening followed by fifty to one hundred years of stockholders making money as hoped, within three and a half years the new bridge was going bankrupt. After its opening bankruptcy papers were filed, the bridge was sold at auction to a champion golfer named Stranahan for less than half the original building costs. In 1935 he sold it to the Ozark Bridge Company, who kept it for 11 years. During this time, southern Illinois improved its roads. They had been gravel and dirt—not inviting to visitors. The bridge company cleared a million and a half dollars and then put the bridge on the market one day. Officials of Cape Girardeau found out about it quite by accident, and hastened to form a group to buy the bridge. "Cape Special Road District" was formed to prevent the bridge from being condemned or closed. Two sets of bonds were issued to complete the transaction. In June, 1957, when the bonds were paid off, the bridge became free. By then, 2,321 vehicles were crossing the bridge daily. It had become a success, but no toll meant changes in the life of the toll-takers and the dog Lucky.

The attractive tollhouse which was Lucky's home for five and a half years was a building with columns and reliefs. Day and night, eleven different men over the years took their 6-hour shifts in the small room on the Missouri end of the bridge. On 29 June, 1957 all this came to an end. There was no need for toll-takers or a mascot anymore, so Lucky went to live with Harry Rabe, one of her bridge masters, where she stayed until she died about ten years later.

Although the fancy tollhouse was no longer there in September, 1986, when I arrived, the entrance arch for the bridge was. It is a unique bit of architecture. The squared portico over the west ramp of the bridge has a large crest in relief with Art Deco style columns on the sides, typical of the late 1920's. The decoration is composed of Winkle Terra Cotta similar to what is on the Missourian Building, built in 1925 when the bridge plans were being formulated.

The next morning I received permission to park and trespass on the St. Vincent's Evangelization Center property. I walked alongside the bridge approach arches under which, on the opposite side, I could see a group of wonderful old brick homes of 1890 and early 1900 vintage. Because of the trees, I continued down the terraced hill of St. Vincent's grounds to Water Street to view and draw the silver trussed bridge. Built for the Model-T car, the Cape Girardeau Bridge is so long and narrow it is a wonder that Lucky survived to become the important and interesting part of Cape Girardeau history that she is.

**Use:**
Missouri Highway 74 to Illinois 146 and 3

**Location:**
Between East Cape Girardeau, Illinois to Cape Girardeau, Missouri

**Style:**
2-span continuous truss plus six humpback truss spans

**Length:**
Channel span - 460 feet clear
                      670 feet total
Total length - 4744 feet

**Width:**
2 lanes, only 20 feet wide

**Clearance:**
104 feet MLW

**Date completed:**
September 1928, replacing a ferry

**Designer:**
Harrington, Howard and Ash, Consulting Engineers, Kansas City

**Toll:**
Until June 1957

**Bridge:**
#002007 in Illinois & K-948 in Missouri

**Owners:**
Illinois and Missouri Departments of Transportation

Cape Girardeau Bridge                    Mary C. Costello

49

# Chester, Illinois Bridge, Missouri 51

*L*ittle did I know that Popeye, the Sailor Man, would be in this book. Chester, Illinois, was the home of Elzie Crisler Segar, the cartoonist who created Popeye. Overlooking the river, the park next to the bridge is dedicated to Segar and displays a life-size statue of the spinach-eating, bulbous-muscled, pipe-smoking character of the popular comic strip of the 1920's and 30's.

The Bridge's Popeye Park provided a few benches, a convenience unusual for me. But try as I might, I couldn't stay seated; trees and bushes got in my way. Standing, I could bob around for a better view. So stand I did.

According to the librarian in Segar's hometown, a freak wind (some people say a tornado) destroyed the Chester Bridge center span in 1944, just two years after it was completed. Waldo McDonald, a citizen of the small Illinois town and toll-taker for the bridge, was playing in a dance-band the night it happened. When he drove home in the early morning hours, he couldn't get across. "The bridge was gone!" he told his father the next morning. His dad didn't believe him until he went to see for himself. Waldo was right. The bridge was gone.—The new span was rebuilt with the same continuous truss and peaked center.

The two spans on either side of the Chester Bridge through-trusses are called deck-trusses, being below the deck, and are deeper over the piers where greater strength is needed.

I felt right at home when I clearly heard a train rumble by the lower part of the steep cliff on which the park is located. In contrast to the train sounds, only by looking out at the river would one know that the towboat, "American Heritage," was quietly gliding by on the Mississippi, pushing its many barges in the late afternoon sunlight.

Finished with my work, I spoke to the toll-takers, whose tiny house is located in the center of the Chester Bridge roadway. While making change for the 90-cent toll, the two money-collectors informed me that they had had a robbery once during which a toll-taker, Frank Gagnepain, was killed. Besides the victim's name I found no other details.

A parking place off to the side of the bridge approach is for bridge-employee cars and for anyone visiting the park. Visitors can see Popeye and get an overview of the lovely Mississippi scene from here.

The bridge keepers were extremely cooperative. I was embarrassed when the tollman detained a city official, who was paying toll, to ask him questions for me. I'm sure the people in line, trying to get home for supper, were not very happy. In fact, if they could have had Popeye's strength, it would have been too bad for the toll-taker...or for me!!

**Use:**
Illinois 150, 3 & Missouri 51

**Location:**
Between Chester, Illinois, and Perryville, Missouri

**Style:**
2-span continuous truss bridge with deck trusses on the sides

**Length:**
Channel spans - 2- 650 feet clear
2- 672 feet total
Total length - 2826 feet

**Width:**
2 lanes

**Clearance:**
109 feet west, 103 feet east MLW

**Date completed:**
1942, rebuilt in 1946 after wind damage

**Designer:**
Sverdrup and Parcel and Associates

**Toll:**
90 cents in 1987

**Bridge:**
#0796001 in Illinois

**Owner:**
City of Chester

Chester, Illinois Bridge

Mary C. Costello

51

# Jefferson Barracks Highway Bridges, Missouri, I-255

*B*arred to pedestrians and bicyclists and viewed by motorists only head-on, the 1984 Jefferson Barracks Bridge could not be seen in its true beauty except from the river. Most routes for profile views were blocked by trees or "No Trespassing" signs. A young state employee led me, in her Missouri highway pickup truck, to a suitable parking area, from which I followed a rugged path to a clearing marked "Hard Hat Area" and a tool shed nestled against a jagged limestone cliff. Before me was the giant-sized simple arch bridge. There was nothing heavy about its appearance—no trusses, no triangles, no "X's"—just the equally wide brown girder crossing the river on concrete piers with the 180-foot-high tied arch. Even the 17 horizontal struts (overhead connectors on the arch) are simple straight members equally spaced and located where the suspenders attach to the deck.

What surprised me was the second set of piers, looking like hollowed dominoes lined up for a fall. I had crossed the bridge, but the solid railing hid the view.

In 1989 a second and identical span was to have been completed on these previously-built piers. However, the crane that was putting the last piece of the huge arch in place dropped it. In falling, the massive piece damaged another bridge section and ended up in the river. Luckily, the men waiting to bolt the piece in place were able to hang on and were not hurt. The bridge part was eventually fished out of the Mississippi and the damaged part refabricated. A year later the bridge was safely completed and dedicated. Both Jefferson Barracks Bridges now carry three lanes of traffic in each direction with the fourth used as a breakdown lane.

The arch is slightly parabolic, with more of an arc in the middle than at the ends, to make better use of the strength per ton of steel. The hangers that are almost invisible from a distance are really 2 1/8 inches in diameter with a breaking strength of 269 tons and are hung in clusters of four. Harold Sandberg, principal designer of the span, in order to make the construction more aesthetically appealing, hid the top end of the suspenders in the horizontal struts and the bottom end in the deep 12-foot I-sections of the tied arch. The new JB Bridge is painted even though it is built completely of weathering steel two or more inches thick. That mix of steel and copper requires no painting, but to prevent overhead rust from the piers and to keep the color uniform, the bridge has a low gloss brown paint which appears to have a reddish cast from a distance.

Perhaps the most interesting feature for me is that this arch superstructure is like a house within a house. Because the tubular arch rib and its horizontal struts are 5 1/2 feet deep with no trusses inside the skin of steel, inspectors and painters can walk freely within the Jefferson Barracks Bridges. Human activity can be going on inside, while traffic crosses outside.

Suddenly the sun shifted and reflected off something in the distance. To the north, a bright object glistened above the trees. It took me a second to realize that it was the Gateway Arch in downtown St. Louis. What a wonderful sight!...almost edifying! It gave me a sense of place.

**Use:**
I-255 and US 50

**Location:**
South of St.Louis, Missouri, northwest of Columbia, Illinois

**Style:**
Single tied-arch with welded plate-girder approaches

**Length:**
Channel span - 850 feet clear
910 feet total
Total length - 4029 feet

**Width:**
4 lanes, 54 feet total

**Clearance:**
110 feet MLW

**Date completed:**
May 1984 & July 1990; replaced first span—1944 continuous truss

**Designer:**
Alfred Benesch Company of Chicago
Harold Sandberg, principal designer

**Bridge:**
#0670020 in Illinois

**Owners:**
Missouri and Illinois Departments of Transportation

**Unique feat:**
Longest tied-arch bridge on the Mississippi and among the longest in the world. Received the Structural Engineers Association of Illinois award—"Most Innovative Structure"

Jefferson Barracks Bridge

Mary C. Costello

# MacArthur Railroad (Highway) Bridge, St. Louis, Missouri

*P*robably the only free parking spot in downtown St.Louis is directly under the double-deck MacArthur Bridge. With almost everything in the metro-area commercialized, it was a pleasure finding such a spot. It is a high piece of land next to the river, between the on-land piers of the bridge. Located at the south end of the brick-paved levee, it was completely unimproved—no concrete, gravel or even grass. Other people seemed to find it a place from which to enjoy the river, to fish, people-watch or just relax. I talked to a retired man who comes here several times a week to "keep up on what is going on." I found this location one of the most exhilarating of my travels.

From under the giant double-decked bridge, I watched and waved to five trains going overhead on the "MacArthur." I visually followed the "Sarah Elizabeth" towboat pushing fifteen barges upstream under bridge after bridge, and I was enchanted by seeing the giant "Gateway Arch" perform its magic of turning from silver to gold as the sun hit it, and then to sky-blue and grey when the sun went behind the clouds. (It was sometimes hard to determine which was sky and which was the large steel sculpture) I became emotionally involved in a farewell party and launch of a 70-year old Russian-born gentleman who was about to fulfill a lifelong dream of sailing "The Great River" to New Orleans. He had a younger man, possibly his son, with him and lots of friends waving farewell.

The Douglas MacArthur Bridge history is truly unusual. St. Louis was host city for the 1904 World's Fair, a big event for the river town. However, the only bridges in existence then were the Eads Railroad/Highway Bridge and the Merchants Railroad Bridge, whose tolls for crossing, according to St.Louis officials, were excessive. After the fair, the city decided to build its own "free" bridge. Pier work began in

December of 1909 and the three bridge channel spans were completed in 1912. However, the money ran out before the approaches were built. Three elections were held, and with each election the bond issue to raise money for the bridge was defeated, delaying the completion date longer.

> During the interval...the Municipal Bridge lay idle, except for limited use by pedestrians. A board walk with hand rails was laid on the railway deck, and passes issued to responsible persons desiring to cross the river. An average of one hundred persons crossed the bridge daily during a period of three or four years. (Rolfe & Cannon 1922, 181)

The deck extremities were completed in January of 1917 and the highway bridge was immediately used up to expectations; but because "of strained relations existing between the city and the combination formed by the railroads," (Ibid, 167) trains did not make full use of the bridge until 1935. (Glaser: telephone conversation)

Popularly, the "St. Louis Municipal Bridge" was known as the "Free Bridge," even though in 1932 a fee of ten cents a car was charged, the money going for relief during the "Great Depression." In 1942 the bridge was officially renamed the "Douglas MacArthur Bridge" after the famous World War II General.

The highway deck eventually deteriorated but the city didn't have the money to repair it. Therefore, since 1981 the bridge has been used only for trains. A 40-foot highway section was removed in 1989, making the upper deck unusable forever. This was done before the City of St. Louis swapped the MacArthur for the Eads and the Terminal Railroad became the MacArthur's new owner.

---

**Use:**
Trains on lower deck, upper highway deck closed in 1981

**Location:**
St. Louis, Missouri, to East St. Louis, Illinois

**Style:**
Double deck 3-span humpback truss

**Length:**
Channel span - 647 feet clear
             677 feet total
Total train deck -   18,261 feet
Total wagon deck - 9,785 feet

**Width:**
2 tracks (lower deck); 30-foot road and 6-foot sidewalks (upper deck, unused)

**Clearance:**
110 feet MLW

**Date completed:**
January 1917 (highway); 1928 (some trains used); 1935 (full use)

**Designer:**
Boller and Hodge, New York

**Toll:**
Until 1973

**Bridge:**
# none

**Owner:**
Terminal Railroad Association as of 31 August 1989

**Unique feat:**
The second longest railroad bridge in United States (Huey P. Long in New Orleans is first)

MacArthur Highway-Railway Bridge

Mary C. Costello

# Poplar Bridge, St. Louis, Missouri, US 66

*If* one word were to describe the Poplar Bridge in St.Louis concerning its design, it would be "simplicity." Its purpose was to allow a maximum of vehicles per day to cross the Mississippi River without cost and without unnecessary superstructure so as to harmonize with the Gateway Arch and the historic Eads Bridge upstream. This orthotropic deck plate-girder bridge design satisfied all those needs, carrying 110,000 cars per day. Its protective coated bituminous road surface was laboratory-tested before being used. There is nothing unnecessary or left to chance in the Poplar Bridge plan.

The blue-green steel girders of the Poplar Bridge gently arch over the main channel though otherwise they are straight. This eight-lane structure next to downtown St. Louis serves a number of highways—US 66, I-55 and I-70—and has cloverleaf approaches in both St. Louis, Missouri, and East St. Louis, Illinois, making its aerial view much more complicated than its profile.

If one word were to describe the Poplar's safety, I am told it would be "abominable." I had been warned by relatives and strangers alike, "If you don't have to cross it, don't!" On this trip, however, I'm afraid I did not always do what people thought safe for me. My goal was to cross each bridge if it were crossable.

I chose Sunday to do this "popular" bridge sketch in order to avoid as much traffic as possible. I had added the last shading to the drawing and needed a break. This I took by driving over the beautiful Eads Bridge. However, I couldn't find the "on" ramp from East St. Louis to return on the Eads.

I had not intended to defy my friends' warnings about the Poplar Bridge nor my cousin Betty Sipchen's admonition about going into East St. Louis at all. My intent was to turn around and go right back. However, fate took me past a sign pointing to another bridge—the I-70; which one this was I didn't know since there were many.

Unprepared for this change and not knowing exactly how to get to the approach, I headed into the business district of East St. Louis. Further down the almost vacant street was a Gulf Station. It had a number of customers, so I pulled in and parked off to one side. I locked my doors as I got out, thinking all the time of Betty's warning, "Don't go, even in broad daylight!"

I went to the door of the gas station, hoping I could get change and directions inside, but the door wouldn't open. A woman in an attractive black and white silk tunic-top dress came behind me and said, "You can't get in. All the places are locked up over here." She went to the open window and I followed. A man behind me was trying to make conversation with her. I got change and directions to the bridge approach just a block down the street.

I hurried back to my Datsun where, by now, a gang of boys had collected. It was near the air-pump and some of them had bikes, but mostly they were just socializing. I didn't look at them; I just got into my car and drove off toward the bridge.

When I got there, I realized this was another "No, no!" The I-70 Bridge was the "accident-prone" Poplar Bridge. My heart was in my mouth, but the lanes were many and wide, and traffic was light at supper hour on a Sunday. I zipped across with no difficulty and, thankful for my safety, headed for the Sipchens to tell my tale.

**Use:**
US 66, I-55 & I-70 highway traffic

**Location:**
Between St. Louis, Missouri & East St. Louis, Illinois

**Style:**
5-span orthotropic plate deck girder

**Length:**
Channel span - 580 feet clear
600 feet total
Total length* - 2175 feet

**Width:**
8 lanes & median, 111 feet total

**Clearance:**
97 feet MLW

**Date completed:**
November 1967

**Designer:**
Sverdrup & Parcel & Associates

**Bridge:**
#0820004 in Illinois or A-1500 in Missouri

**Owners:**
Missouri and Illinois Departments of Transportation

**Unique feat:**
1968 award winner for "Most Beautiful Bridge." First orthotropic deck plate-girder bridge designed in the United States.

* Length does not include approaches because of the great number of them.

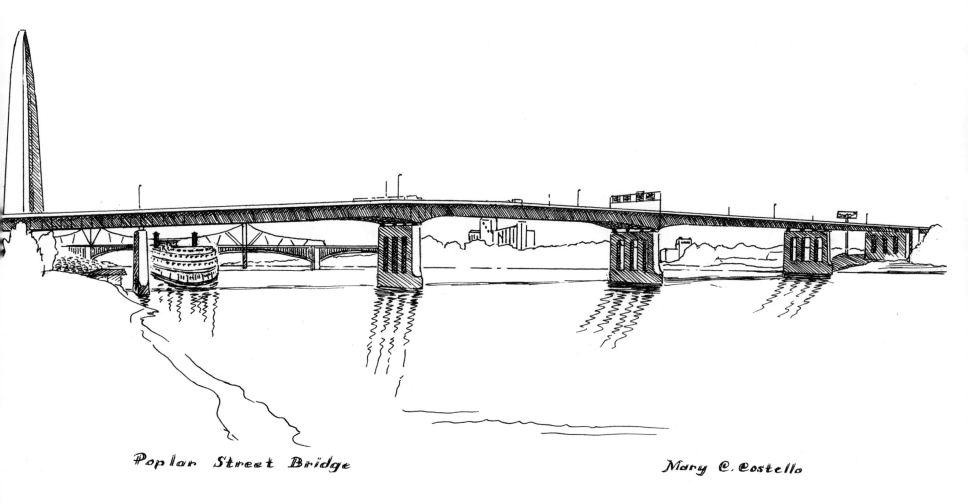

Poplar Street Bridge

Mary C. Costello

# Eads Railroad/Highway Bridge, St. Louis

*T*he Eads Bridge is a standing monument to its designer, James Buchanan Eads. It is the oldest bridge on the Mighty River and has seen more than 120 summers and winters. Contrary to some people's belief, it was not the first bridge ever built across the river, but it was the first bridge in St. Louis and is the oldest bridge now existing on the great waterway. The bridge's beauty, innovations and survival rate are all tributes to Eads, who not only dreamed and planned the bridge but also promoted and engineered it.

James Eads was born in Lawrenceburg, Indiana, in 1820 but moved to St. Louis as a boy. There he learned to know and love the Mississippi River. He walked along the river-bed, learning the current and soil formations, invented the diving bell, and raised sunken steamers for their cargo. It was Eads who suggested to President Lincoln the use of ironclad ships during the Civil War and then designed seven ironclad steamers, building the first in just 45 days. (One of these, the "Cairo," is on display in Vicksburg after being at the bottom of the river for over 100 years.) Among engineers Eads is best known for a series of jetties he designed at the mouth of the Mississippi. However, most people know Eads for this beautiful three-span deck-arch bridge that they may have crossed either by car, by train before 1974, or by light rail starting in 1990. "James Buchanan Eads is the only engineer in the Hall of Fame." (Steinman 1953, 35)

Captain Eads did more than build an unprecedented bridge in 1874. He overcame tremendous odds—fighting tuberculosis all his adult life and strong opposition to his plans by others. The best engineers of his day said his bridge plan wouldn't work.

With the Eads Bridge came many innovations. "It was the first large scale use of steel in bridge construction, the first use of the pneumatic caissons in the founding of large piers, the first use of hollow tubular chord members and the first use of high-strength structural steel as a bridge material." (Steinman & London 1981, 4:537) Eads used no falsework in the building of this bridge. Instead, starting from the completed piers, he gradually extended the construction out from both sides until the steel work met in the middle. This method of construction is called cantilever, new to America in 1867, when Eads began the bridge. When it was time to insert the last piece of metal, the steel was one and one-eighth inches too long. The workmen tried to shrink the steel by using ice, but that wasn't enough. They knew Eads had arranged for a half-million dollar loan if the arch was completed by 19 September. However, Eads was in Europe for his health at the time. At 10 p.m. on 17 September they called him, feeling he would have the answer, and he did. He had designed and manufactured some adjustable parts to insert for just such an emergency. The workmen made the deadline, and Eads received the loan.

On 2 July 1874, the bridge was finished and fourteen heavy locomotives lined the approaches to the lower deck as thousands of people jammed the upper deck. It was hard to believe that three steel arches could hold seven hundred tons of moving weight. The steam engines moved over the tracks while the crowds shouted. "The Eads" was a success and is today in full use.

---

**Use:**
Vehicles on top deck, US 460, and as of 1990 'light rail' traffic below

**Location:**
Between downtown St. Louis, Missouri, and East St. Louis, Illinois

**Style:**
3-span steel trussed-arch bridge, (each span over 500 feet), with stone-arch approaches

**Length:**
Channel span - 300 feet clear*
520 feet total
Total length - 4,014 feet

**Width:**
4 lanes plus sidewalks on each side, 50 foot total

**Clearance:**
79 feet MLW

**Date completed:**
July 1874

**Designer:**
James Buchanan Eads

**Toll:**
50 cents

**Bridge:**
#14 on railroad, 0829929 in Illinois

**Owners:**
City of St. Louis (upper deck), Bi-State Transit Authority (lower deck owners)[2]

**Unique Feat:**
Oldest bridge still in use on the Mississippi River. First use of high-strength steel as bridge material. In 1898, first bridge ever to be pictured on a United States postage stamp.

---

* The big difference between the usable channel span and total span width is due to the low overhead clearance of the arch.

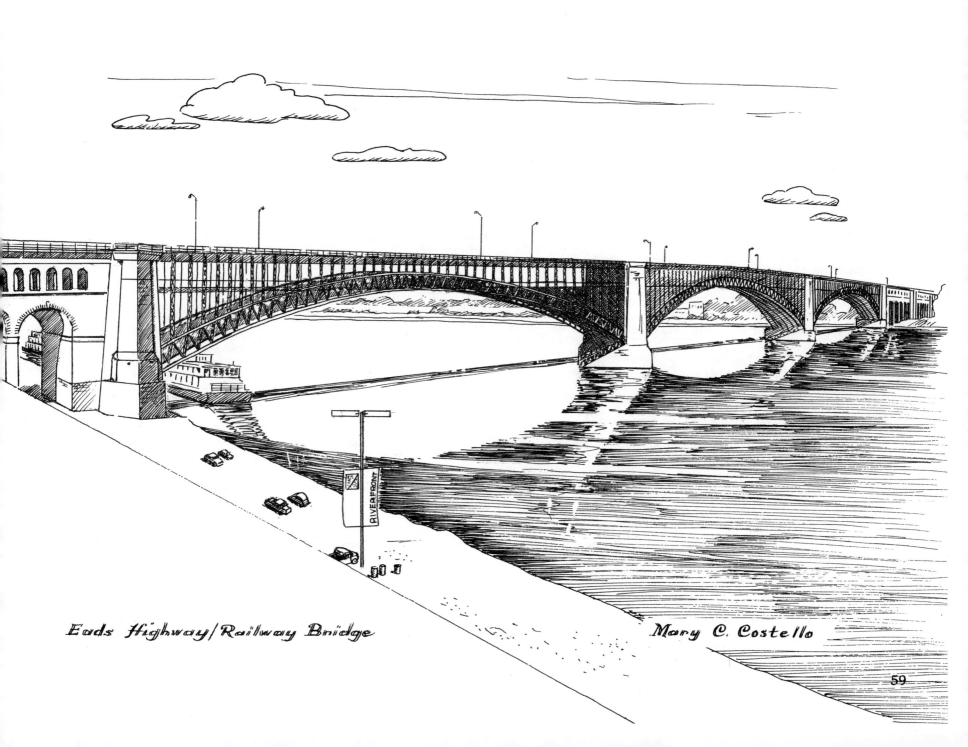

Eads Highway/Railway Bridge

Mary C. Costello

59

# Martin Luther King Bridge, St. Louis, US 40

*N*ext to the Eads Bridge but looming above it is the Martin Luther King Bridge. Built in 1951 as the Veterans' Memorial Bridge, it was a life-saver to the downtown area. The first span constructed since the MacArthur Highway/Railroad Bridge in 1917, the Veterans' Bridge helped relieve the ever-growing traffic on the other St. Louis bridges. It eased congestion on downtown streets and provided easy access to downtown St. Louis for Metro East area shoppers. This toll bridge was profitable until 1967, when the Poplar Bridge was built as a free bridge. For years after that, the city of East St. Louis, that owned the bridge, was not able to meet the bond payments or keep up with repairs. The bridge was literally "falling down" from lack of maintenance. Today the Missouri and Illinois Departments of Transportation are the new owners, and rehabilitation work has been completed.

Driving over the bridge late on a Sunday afternoon, I encountered few other cars compared to the average peak hour traffic on weekdays of almost 1200 cars. I found the road to be rough. Numerous blocking barrels and a sign even warned people to avoid the outer lane. (All of this has changed with the renovation completed since.) The bridge was not fancy like older truss bridges but used trussed beams in the overhead struts. Renamed after the late Martin Luther King, the bridge dominates the Eads Bridge with its superstructure. The Warren truss zigzags from the top to the bottom chords, except where the suspended span connects, and at the kingposts there is angled bracing halfway down, in an arc like a rising sun above the deck.

The piers are concrete but of a different design, resembling the old-fashioned collapsible cup stretched open and inverted. The bridge piers are, however, square instead of round.

In reading about how the bridge was built, I was interested to learn that each half of the suspended span was cantilevered out from the cantilever arm to the middle—481 feet erected without support (not a record at the time, but close). The halves were then joined with a jacking device in both the top and bottom chords at the ends of the cantilever arms. This method was cheaper, though slower, than floating in the suspended span, but could be done only if the members were strong enough to permit it. Apparently the Martin Luther King (then the Veterans') Bridge had such strength.

My parking spot in St. Louis was to the left of the Martin Luther King Bridge when facing the river. It was pay-parking, using the honor system. I didn't have the four quarters required for the slot and there were no arrangements for a dollar bill, so I held off paying but parked next to other possible non-paying customers. When I finished an hour later, there were two young men in the entrance who stopped me. "Did you pay?" they asked. When I said I hadn't and explained why, they announced, "Well, now it will be two dollars." I told them I didn't have two dollars, which was the truth. I had only one. "Have a good day!" they responded smilingly as I left.

My next encounter with people of the area was at the other end of the King Bridge. When I arrived at the toll booth, I paid 40 cents with my remaining change and asked about turning around to go back. They said I could make a "U-turn" right there and need not pay for the return trip. I think both of these incidents speak well for the kindness and consideration of the people of the area. I applaud these St. Louis folk.

**Use:**
US 40 and 66 highway traffic

**Location:**
Between St. Louis and East St. Louis

**Style:**
3 spans cantilever truss plus 2 spans of deck trusses

**Length:**
Channel span - 940 feet clear
963 feet total
Total length - 7000 feet

**Width:**
4 lanes, 40 feet total

**Clearance:**
96 feet MLW

**Date completed:**
January 1951; new deck, paint, and decorative lighting in 1989

**Designer:**
G.A.Maney & Associates, Chicago; Sverdrup Corporation designed "rehab" work

**Toll:**
40 cents, removed in 1987

**Bridge:**
#0826001 in Illinois, A-4856 in Missouri

**Owners:**
Illinois and Missouri Departments of Transportation

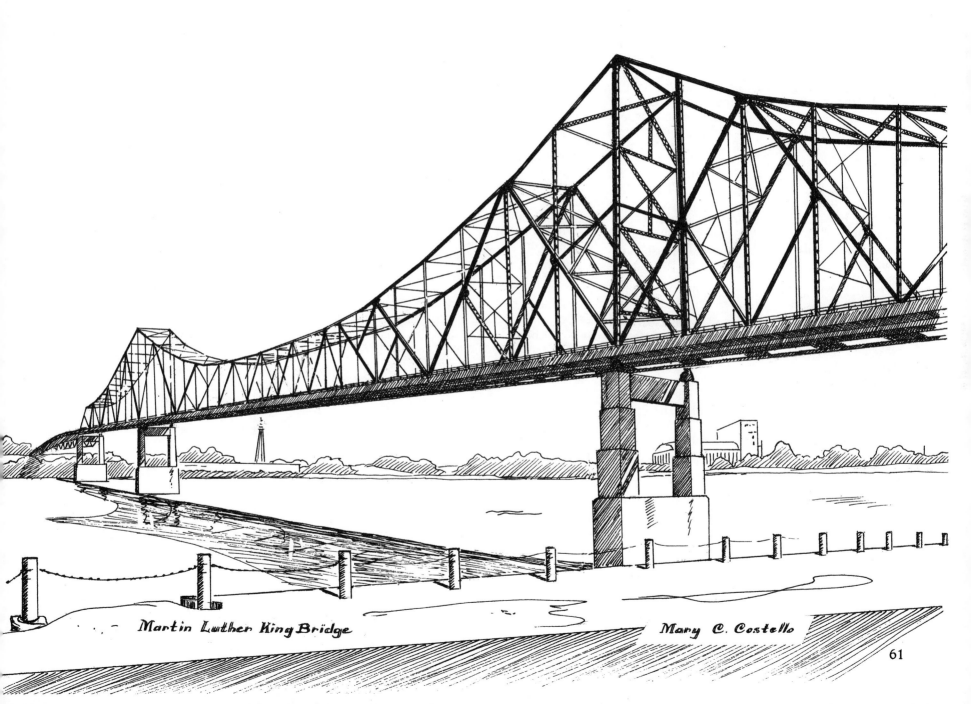

Martin Luther King Bridge

Mary C. Costello

61

# McKinley Highway (Railroad) Bridge, St. Louis, Missouri

*T*he McKinley Bridge was "the pride of the town" in 1910, just nine years after President William McKinley was assassinated. However, contrary to popular belief, the bridge was named not after the late President of the United States but after the president of the Illinois Electric Traction System, William B. McKinley, who commissioned Ralph Modjeski to construct it. Since its early years, the bridge has fallen from its high pedestal. Because of passage of time, lack of money and, consequently, little maintenance, the bridge today is more like "the great disgrace." "It gives a bumpy ride but is structurally sound!" said Roger Wiebusch, U.S. Coast Guard Bridge Administrator. Though a new deck and improved approaches would be a great help, there are no such plans as of this writing.

This camelback bridge is two miles north of downtown St.Louis. When first built, it could handle both railroad and automobile traffic—trains inside the truss superstructure, and cars outside on bracketed roads. Now only vehicles can use the span.

At the time I traveled the McKinley Bridge, I knew none of its history and drove the Salisbury Road approach, making the curve onto the bridge with the road empty in front of me. I came to the steel superstructure on the bridge and saw both the outside and inside roadways. The tracks seemed to be breaking out of the blacktop and I wasn't sure which way to go, so I stopped. A car with two men in it came behind passing around me. I could see the men were laughing at my indecision. I followed them under the truss structure but avoided the tracks. Coming back, I tried the outer roadway and found it was a grid deck partially filled with what appeared to be orange-colored asphalt.

At the Venice, Illinois, end of the span, I paid the toll each way. Venice needs the money for its bridge debt (14 million in 1984).

Back in St. Louis, the best view I found for sketching the Modjeski's third Mississippi bridge design was in a "guarded" manufacturing company lot. The uniformed watchman gave me permission to sketch from there. I stood on the grassy levee that was perhaps 10 to 12 feet high. I could see the four sturdy limestone piers, an unusual, stubby, flat-roofed boat, white sand on the Illinois shore, and a lot of white foam in the water on the far side of the river. I could hear furnaces from a foundry roaring behind me. The bridge itself appeared to be green, but the approaches were painted black, with supports on the ground of steel instead of concrete or stone. Each span of the bridge was a "humpback" shape with Petit or simple subdivided Pratt trusses.

What appeared most unique on the McKinley Bridge was an upside-down arched truss below the deck on the Illinois side of the river. It reminded me of a squirrel hanging by its feet.

**Use:**
Originally for trains and cars, now only vehicles travel Illinois Highway 3

**Location:**
St. Louis to Venice, Illinois

**Style:**
3 simple through-truss spans with bracketed roadways outside

**Length:**
Channel span - 500 feet clear
                517 feet total
Total length -   6315 feet

**Width:**
4 lanes, 2 inside and 2 outside the superstructure

**Clearance:**
90 feet MLW

**Date completed:**
November 1910

**Designer:**
Ralph Modjeski

**Toll:**
50 cents, formerly 30 cents

**Bridge:**
#0606002 in Illinois

**Owner:**
City of Venice, Illinois

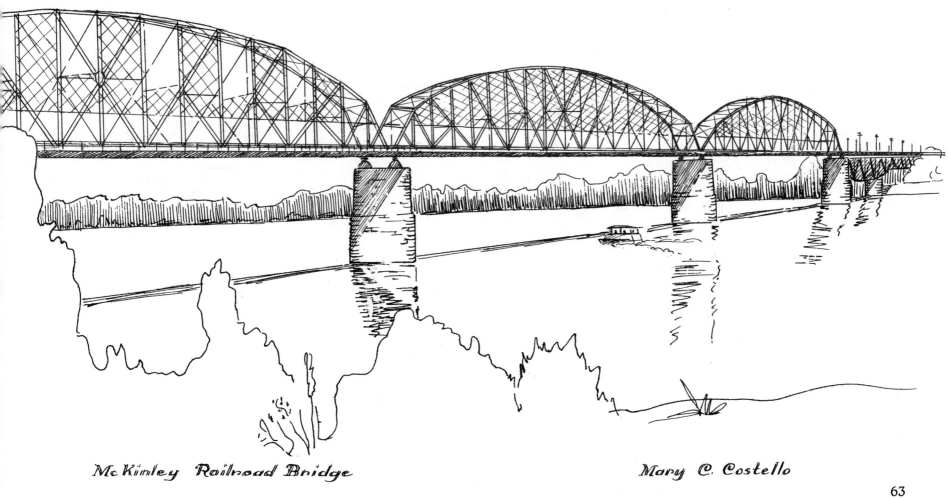

McKinley Railroad Bridge

Mary C. Costello

63

*I* drew the bridge from "Hobo Heaven." It had all the essentials: the "rails," the river, seclusion, a spot for a fire and room to rest. I had taken Ferry Street across tracks and ruts, over a big hump in the road and more tracks to the river. There was unmistakable evidence of hobos—the remains of a bonfire, broken bottles, a potato chip bag and some logs—all on lumpy-bumpy, somewhat grassy ground. It was a narrow strip slightly hidden by medium-sized trees and undergrowth. Gravel edged the river several feet beyond bigger trees. Through an opening in the branches I could see the bridge. It started on my left but crossed in front of me for an almost perfect view.

Shortly after I arrived, a fisherman came but moved further upstream, while a man in an old truck fished a quarter of a block downstream. It was a good day, a Sunday morning in September, with plenty of sun and warmth.

Surprisingly, the ground seemed to be on a level with the river's surface. "The Mississippi must be getting high," I thought. Then for the first time in the south, I noticed the water was dirty with tree trunks, branches, and containers. Besides the trash, it was slimy and smelly, apparently from stagnant water near the shore, but "Ole Man River" was flowing very fast just a few feet out. I had not encountered this combination of debris and stench the whole trip until now, nor did I find it afterwards. I could hear crickets and outboard motorboats. A coal barge traveling upstream made considerable noise after going under the bridge; with motor running at high speed, it churned up lots of foam.

As I surveyed the area, a switch engine started onto the Merchants' Railroad Bridge from the Illinois side, very slowly, lights flashing. It backed up and immediately a long, three-diesel-engine freight crossed from the Missouri side. I thought they were sharing the same track but there are two tracks on the bridge.

This Merchants' Railroad Bridge was the second constructed in St. Louis, in 1890, sixteen years after the Eads. (Its design was almost duplicated by the McKinley Bridge in 1910.) The Merchants' Bridge has three humpback spans, four limestone piers, three deck trusses at each end and metal bents on the ground. Designed by E. L. Corthell and George Morison (Morison's first over the Mississippi), the Merchants' Bridge is a pin-connected Pennsylvania truss, funded by St. Louis railroad entrepreneurs and businessmen. Its elevated approaches were the first in St. Louis, since the Eads Bridge's trains entered a tunnel after crossing the Mississippi. The elevation eliminated the need for trains to go underground—a great advantage for passenger trains. Instead of I-beams, the Merchants' Bridge uses "trussed beams" for all verticals, and metal rods for diagonals because they are lighter and more cost-efficient. The casual observer may not notice these differences, but this combination makes the bridge fancier or more fragile-looking, depending on the angle from which it is seen.

When I finished drawing, I noticed a partially sunken barge on the other side of the river. It didn't seem to bother or be bothered by all the river action. It was an observer like me.

At 11:10 I ate my lunch in the car watching the river and wondering when the stick I threw into the Mississippi at Lake Itasca two months ago had gone past here.

---

**Use:**
Trains only

**Location:**
Between St. Louis and Madison County, Illinois

**Style:**
High 3-span through-truss with deck-truss approaches

**Length:**
Channel span - 505 feet clear
518 feet total
Total length - 3100 feet

**Clearance:**
Double track

**Height:**
83 feet MLW

**Date completed:**
1890; raised overhead bracing in 1988 for freight container "double-stacks"[3]

**Designer:**
George Morrison & E. L. Corthell

**Bridge:**
#10

**Owner:**
Terminal Railroad Association of St. Louis

**Unique feat:**
"First curved-chord truss bridge erected over the Mississippi" (Fraser 1988, 267)

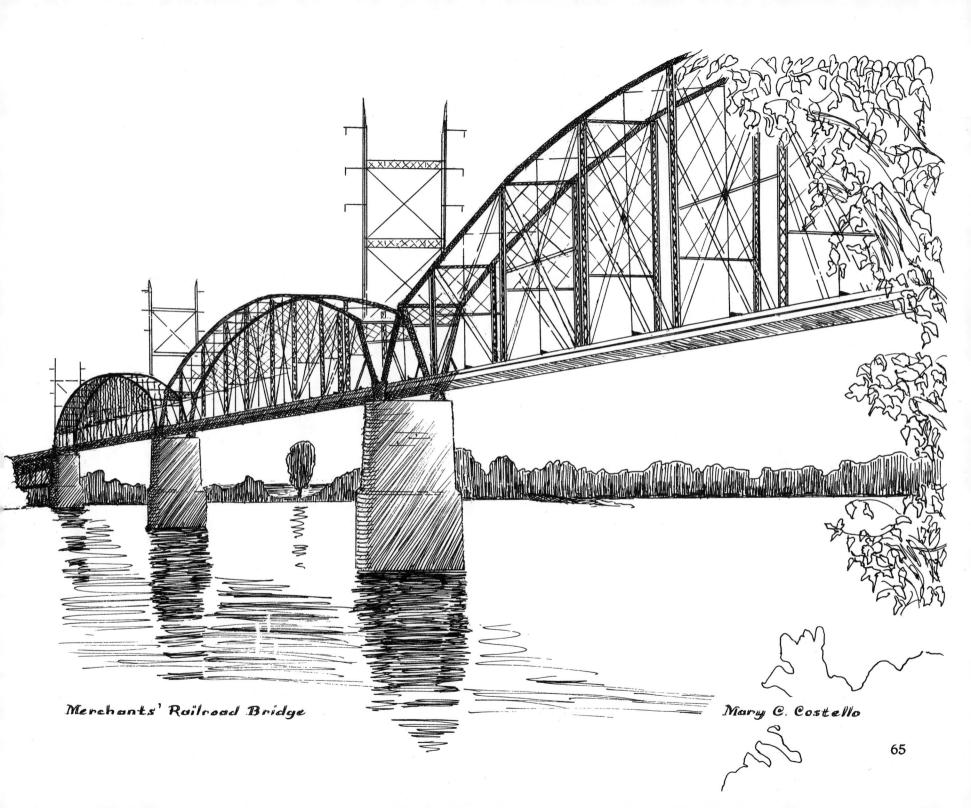

Merchants' Railroad Bridge

Mary C. Costello

65

# Old "Chain of Rocks" Bridge, St. Louis

*T*he story of the "Chain of Rocks" starts with this bridge. A toll span built for a private concern in 1929, the Chain of Rocks Bridge was a money-maker and a much needed northern St. Louis crossing of the Mississippi. In 1939, the city of Madison, Illinois, at the bridge's eastern end, took ownership and for years continued to make a profit despite a dangerous curve in the bridge. Today the span is closed and is for sale or rent. What happened in the interim or "the rest of the story" follows.

The name "Chain of Rocks" comes from a rock problem in the Mississippi River north of St. Louis. Roger Wiebusch, Bridge Administrator for the Upper Mississippi, says, "The main channel had a backbone of rock that made it treacherous at low water." This fact, coupled with a meandering channel, created a need for a safer route for boats to travel.

Therefore, in the late 1950's, a straight 47-mile canal was built to bypass the twisting river channel from Oldenburg to Granite City, Illinois. At the same time, a new straight bridge was constructed slightly to the north. These two changes—a new bridge and a new river-route—led to the demise of the Old Chain of Rocks Bridge.

Just looking at the "old" truss bridge from a slight rise in the park across the street, I was ready to say that the "Old Chain" was five spans long. However, after finding the Illinois entrance, (the Missouri approach was well-hidden), I found that behind the trees were many more spans—fifteen truss spans in all.

To walk onto the bridge from the Illinois approach, I was forced to climb two mountains of clay (put there on purpose to deter such action). Between them was a long approach with jungle-like growth encroaching on the roadsides. Getting over the last rise of dirt would have been bad enough normally, but this Sunday morning it was drizzling rain. I picked and slid my way down the last hill, hanging onto the bridge rail near the bottom. Then I noticed the inner bridge. Someone had had a graffiti party! Colorful messages of love and friendship with years and dates sprayed on the floor, railing and rusted superstructure. One said, "Do not spray-paint this bridge!" Area residents use the bridge as "both a dump and as a place to take a Sunday stroll." (Weiss 1986)

After walking eleven spans, I came to the Mississippi's edge. From here I had an unobstructed view to the north of the I-270 Bridge. To the south I could see two small, stone "castle-like" buildings in the river, which I found were the St. Louis Waterworks Intake Tower and Metering Station. Walking further, I could see how dangerous the old bridge had been. A sharp turn, called a "dogleg," begins after the long double main-channel truss spans. It would be almost impossible to see what might be coming around the bend. Big trucks would have to go into the other lane to negotiate the turn.

The day was windy, cold and damp. Finished sketching, I was glad to leave this green monster. The abandoned bridge and its setting made me feel lonely.

In its old age this Missouri-Illinois bridge has "made it into pictures." A 1981 movie entitled "Escape from New York," starring Curt Russell, Andrea Bardow and Ernest Borgnine, was filmed on this "Old Chain of Rocks Bridge." If the bridge must go, at least it has had its day of glory.

---

**Use:**
Unused since 1970, formerly US 66

**Located:**
Between north St. Louis and Unincorporated Madison County, Illinois

**Style:**
Continuous steel truss

**Length:**
Channel span - 680 feet clear
                        700 feet total
Total length - 5350 feet

**Width:**
2 lanes, 40 feet total

**Clearance:**
93 feet MLW

**Date completed:**
October 1929; closed February 1970

**Designer:**
Edward B. Fay, civil engineer

**Toll:**
1929 toll—5 cents per person in car

**Bridge:**
# none

**Owner:**
City of Madison, Illinois, since 1939

**Unique Feat:**
12th longest continuous truss span in the world.(Steinman 1981, 547)

Old Chain of Rocks Bridge

Mary C Costello

# Single Chain of Rocks Canal Bridge, Madison County, Illinois

*If* a person could view this bridge from the air, he or she could tell that the Canal Bridge is on the Old Chain of Rocks Road and was, therefore, an important part of the Old Chain of Rocks route. Unless one were going to Chouteau Island located between the bridges, travelers on US 66 in the past would have crossed both spans.

The Single Chain of Rocks Canal Bridge was designed by Sverdrup and Parcel as a single humpback-truss span, 465 feet end to end, totally spanning the canal. On either side are three deep deck-trusses, deeper at each pier, lending a "scalloped bottom" appearance. Beyond the trusses on either end are six more spans supported by concrete bents, which diminish gradually to the heavier abutment.

Until the New Chain of Rocks Bridge opened in 1967, the "Old" team of bridges served the community faithfully, although I can imagine people wishing for the new span because of the dangerous dogleg on the old main-channel crossing.

With the Old Chain of Rocks Bridge closed, the inhabitants of Chouteau Island and local fishermen are now basically the only users of the Single Canal Bridge. As many as thirty people a day can be seen fishing off a series of sheet-steel circular cells filled with rock and topped with concrete, along the Mississippi River bank of the island. These are part of a low-water dam created to maintain the water level in the canal.

I questioned why the Corps of Engineer figures indicate a total channel span of 465 feet but a clearance of only 348 feet. Study of the Canal Bridge plans answered my question. The canal bed slants on both sides, making 58 feet on either side unusable at times by large-boat navigation.

From 1948 until 1967 (when the I-270 Bridge was complete), the Old Chain of Rocks and this Single Canal Bridge were the closest link between Illinois and north St. Louis. This Canal Bridge carried traffic to and from the old main-channel bridge. Those were the "good old days." Now the Single Canal Bridge is relaxed into semi-retirement. No wonder it looks so attractive in its fresh coat of paint.

This Warren truss Canal Bridge rises over the earthen dike on the east, the first of three canal bridges, unpretentiously passes over the canal, and starts a downward trend beyond the western levee. On this sunless autumn day the Single Chain of Rocks Canal Bridge was just another value of gray in the clouded sky.

**Use:**
Local traffic, formerly US 66

**Location:**
Between unincorporated Madison County and Chouteau Island, Illinois

**Style:**
1-span simple steel through-truss

**Length:**
Channel span - 348 feet clear
465 feet total
Total length -   2530 feet

**Width:**
2 lanes

**Clearance:**
84 feet MLW

**Date completed:**
August 1948; new grid deck 1990

**Designed by:**
Sverdrup and Parcel and Associates

**Bridge:**
# none, not on highway system

**Owner:**
Illinois DOT

Chain of Rocks Single Canal Bridge

Mary C. Costello

# New Chain of Rocks Bridge, Old Channel, I-270

*W*hat can I say after I say—"I saw it"? Modern as this bridge may be, with no superstructure to draw, to study, or to describe, I had little involvement and was somewhat disappointed seeing the I-270 Bridge for the first time. The one thing that kept me on task while sketching was the realization that there were nineteen piers under the long silver girder.

However, the very reason for my let-down feeling is a great boon for the bridge builders, city fathers and taxpayers. There is no superstructure to pay for, to keep up or to have endangered men's lives in its construction over this always dangerous Mississippi.

Constructed across the main Mississippi River channel north of St. Louis, the I-270 Bridge was designed for highway traffic with no concern for navigation beneath. The "New Chain of Rocks Bridge" has only a 36-foot clearance at low water and much less at high water. Large boats and barges travel the canal about three miles to the east. Rocks hinder navigation on the main channel, ironically referred to as the "back" channel because it is no longer the primary waterway.

The New Chain of Rocks Bridge has two lanes of traffic in each direction, straight across the wide Mississippi River. For safety's sake, it has a concrete median barrier to keep oncoming traffic on the opposite side, and a 3 1/2-foot-high parapet including a pipe railing on the river side. Travelers must forego viewing the river's beauty while crossing this bridge.

Today the sky dominated the river scene. From the deck of the "Old Chain of Rocks Bridge," I viewed both the bridge and fluffy, finger-like clouds as they grayed the heavens above. Away from tall buildings and free of superstructure, the I-270 Bridge allows skyscape views like those seen in open countryside.

A new bridge is planned after the year 2000, to be built parallel to the present span. In the meantime, the I-270 Bridge over the Old Channel is to be rehabilitated with a new deck and repairs to the piers in 1995 and '96.

**Use:**
Highway I-270

**Location:**
North St. Louis to unincorporated Madison County, Illinois

**Style:**
Continuous steel plate-girder

**Length:**
Channel span - 220 feet clear
243 feet total
Total length - 5414 feet

**Width:**
4 lanes with 4-foot median, 27 feet in each direction

**Clearance:**
36 feet MLW

**Date completed:**
January 1967; in the 90's, planning a new span

**Designer:**
Sverdrup and Parcel and Associates

**Bridge:**
#0600035 in Illinois, A-890 in Missouri

**Owners:**
Illinois and Missouri Departments of Transportation

I-270 New Chain of Rocks Bridge

Mary C. Costello

# Twin Chain of Rocks Bridges over Canal, I-270

*A*lthough looking like a confused spider web from the side, these dual bridges are really carefully planned. The reason for the deranged appearance is that the bridges, side by side and alike, have staggered beginnings. The southern-most bridge, or eastbound roadway, starts 50 feet west of the other bridge because the crossings are at a 60-degree rather than 90-degree angle to the canal below. Looking through from one bridge to the other, one does not line up verticals and diagonals as a person normally could do with like-bridges. As one travels across either span, however, one can pick out the simple Warren truss design of the spans.

As with many of the Mississippi River bridges, these twins are cantilever truss spans. Cantilever bridge construction originated in India, where "planks of wood, weighted down by abutment stones, were projected from two banks. Each plank extended a little farther until a single piece was enough to connect the two projections." (Steinman 1981, 531) Today's cantilever bridges are more complicated but the principle is the same—based on balance and counterbalance. From the abutment to the main pier, the "anchor arm" acts like the weight or rocks in India. From the pier, the "cantilever arm" is constructed gradually to the center with nothing underneath, like the ancient planks. Cantilever arms from each side support the last piece or "suspended span" in the center. The suspended span can be installed as a single unit built elsewhere, floated to the spot, raised from the barge to the proper height and connected with large pins. (Another less expensive method is to build the arms out from either side to the middle and install the last link or single piece as the ancient Indians did. Recognizing a slight change in the Warren truss pattern, I believe the former method was used for the Canal Twins.)

The cantilever type construction allows for more flexibility and is not so rigid as a "continuous truss," which looks somewhat similar.

Before the Chain of Rocks Canal was dug to make a safer traffic lane than the rocky Mississippi main channel, this area was a slough. The workmen cut the canal 350 feet wide. They dug 25 feet deeper than the surrounding area, resulting in an average water depth today of 18 feet. Riprap keeps the sloping canal sides intact. Since the piers were built 480 feet apart, they are located in riprap. Therefore, the water near the piers (for 65 feet) has a sloping bottom, but is adequate depth for any vessel on the Mississippi except possibly at very low water. Lock and Dam 27, built at the lower end of this canal, controls the water depth.

These Chain of Rocks Bridges have the distinction of being twin bridges over the only canal on the great twisting Mississippi Riverway. This thought passed my mind as I watched the blue-green twins celebrate their birthday by having a four-tier tow resembling a huge birthday cake pass under them.

**Use:**
I-270 traffic

**Located:**
North of St. Louis, over the canal, 3 miles east of the main channel bridge

**Style:**
3-span cantilever truss

**Length:**
Channel span - 350 feet clear
                    480 feet total
Total length -  1992 feet

**Width:**
2 lanes, 32 feet total

**Clearance:**
84 feet MLW

**Date completed:**
October 1964

**Designer:**
Sverdrup and Parcel and Associates

**Bridge:**
# none

**Owner:**
Illinois Department of Transportation

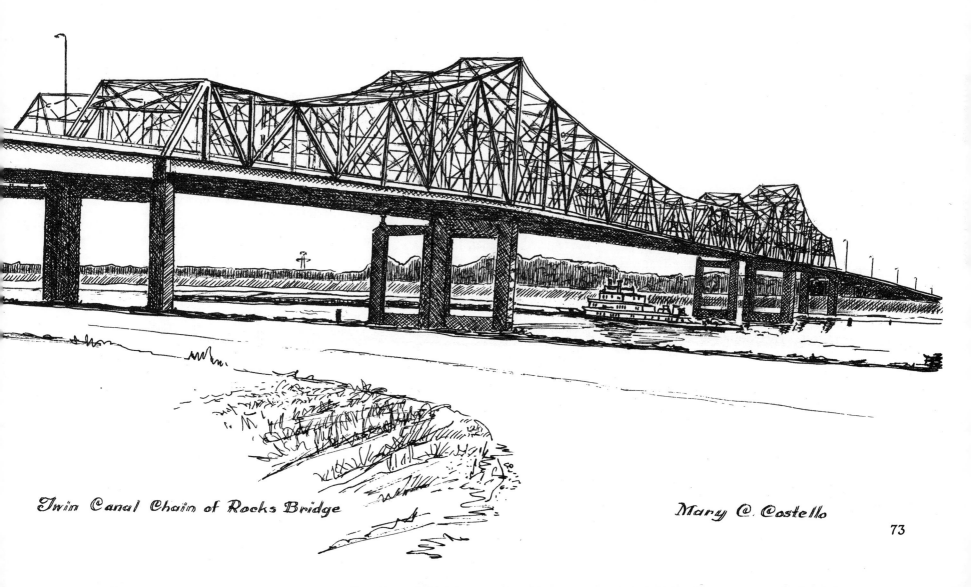

Twin Canal Chain of Rocks Bridge

Mary C. Costello

73

# The "Clark Bridge," Alton, Illinois, US 67

*T*he famous explorers, Lewis and Clark, in 1804, left St. Louis to find a water route to the Pacific. Their discoveries gave the US claim to the Oregon territory. In their honor there are two bridges opposite Alton, Illinois, bearing their names, one over the Missouri and the other over the Mississippi River. Interestingly enough, the original bridges were completed within 5 days of each other. The two spans are traveled one after the other with only the Missouri Point between. They are often mistakenly spoken of as though they were one. Since the Lewis Bridge does not cross the Mississippi, it is not included here.

The "old" Clark Bridge was a silver camelback through-truss completed in 1928. I interviewed one of its builders, Howard Boren, a former steel worker who, like a spider in a web, climbed around on its verticals and diagonals, at age 22, earning 90 cents an hour. Now his bridge is gone.

The "new" Clark Bridge, completed in 1994, is entirely different—a four-lane cable-stayed span. As we crossed, my cousin Bill and I saw two golden teepees—at least that's how the fan-like cables appeared over the middle of the roadway. Unlike the other Mississippi River cable-stayed towers, Alton's bridge has irregularly shaped pylons (cruciform above the deck and octagonal below it) extending from river bottom to a total height of 250 feet. The cables are in two planes supported by a common saddle. There is only one other in the world with this cable construction and that is in France. Gene Muller was designer for both bridges.

For the old through-truss span, surveys began in March 1927 and the bridge was completed and ready in June of the next year—no doubt a record for a major bridge. The new Clark Bridge, on the other hand, was discussed and planned starting in 1985 and took nine years to complete.

Each cable on the Clark Bridge is a bundle of epoxy-coated steel yarns (7 wires form a strand). One contains anywhere from 19 to 46 strands. The cable is enclosed in a polyethylene sheath or pipe pumped full of grout (cement without coarse aggregate) then wrapped in yellow tape to reduce heat absorption.

Alton's business district overlooks the Clark Bridge. From the town's high location, getting onto the US 67 Bridge is easy. "The Clark" spans train tracks and a high earthen dike before the Mighty River.

"Today there are nearly 100 cable-stayed bridges the world over. Only 25 are in the U.S.," according to John Harms, project manager with Hanson Engineers Incorporated. The Mississippi River now can boast four such designs—one at Luling, Louisiana; one at Burlington, Iowa; one at Quincy and now one at Alton, Illinois. The Clark Bridge designers achieved elegance and grace as well as strength and economy. The very design reduced costs because wide pier foundations are not required. (Freitag 1991, 4)

The entire river scene in Alton has changed since 1989. Then there were two bridges and an interconnected Lock and Dam. Now the Alton Burlington Northern Railroad Bridge and the old Lock and Dam #26 are gone. A new locking system has been built[4] just two miles downstream and only the new beautiful Clark Bridge remains in "Bluff City."

---

**Use:**
Highway 67 traffic

**Location:**
Alton, Illinois to St. Louis County, Missouri

**Style:**
Cable-stayed bridge with two towers

**Length:**
Navigation span - 665 feet clear
756 feet total
Total length - 4620 feet bank to bank

**Width:**
2 traffic lanes in each direction plus a 10-foot breakdown-and-bicycle lane on each side.

**Clearance:**
66.8 feet MLW

**Date completed:**
5 January 1994; previously a two-lane 8-span steel through-truss built in 1928; before that a ferry was used

**Designer:**
Hanson Engineering Incorporated, Springfield, Illinois, with Figg and Muller, Florida, as consultants

**Toll:**
None now, but there was a toll on last bridge from 1928 until 1956

**Bridge:**
#060-0255 in Illinois and A4278 in Missouri

**Owners:**
Illinois and Missouri Departments of Transportation

**Unique feat:**
One of two bridges in the world with "saddle-designed" pylon for carrying the cables; won "Eminent Conceptor Award" from Consulting Engineers Council of Illinois in 1995

The Clark Bridge, Alton, Illinois
Mary E. Costello

# Gateway Western Railroad Bridge, Louisiana, Missouri

*T*he only railroad bridge that Mark Twain mentioned in his Life on the Mississippi was the Louisiana, Missouri, Bridge. Arriving at the bridge before dawn, Twain said, "There was a railway bridge across the river here well sprinkled with glowing lights, and a very beautiful sight it was." (Twain 1917,428) This was in 1882, twenty years after he had retired as a riverboat captain and was on a steamboat deck as a tourist. Twain was obviously impressed with the first bridge here.

Coming to the spot in town where the train tracks crossed the highway, I knew I was close, but the bridge was still not in sight. An entrepreneur, selling honey by his van along the roadside, said the only way to get close to the bridge was to walk a block out on the tracks. So I did.

When I stepped between the ties, the white rock or ballast, inside and outside the track, slid, and my foot with it. This made walking slow and tedious. For that reason, I walked as much as I could on the ties themselves. The track out to the bridge was curved and seemed long. I reached the bridge about 3:30 p.m. The best view was to the left side of the train tracks down an incline. Here I could see at least a little more than just the end of the bridge. I was standing in foot-high weeds to take my photos and start my sketch.

The guard-pier in the center of the main channel turnspan that usually helps to guide boats and protect the bridge itself was not there, and the guide fence closer to me was in bad condition. This was a bone of contention between the railroad and Coast Guard since these protective devices had been knocked out or washed away. These have both been repaired by now with a piling fence and guard cells. For me, however, the scene was more picturesque before repairs were made.

Besides the white-looking swingspan near the Missouri shore, there are eight spans making up this Louisiana, Missouri Bridge—five small, one very large, close to the Illinois side (probably the raft span*), and two other in-between sizes. The rest of the bridge is a dark grey color, somewhat rusty. The horizontal boat clearance for the main channel is 195.4 feet, a record for quite a few years until the Fort Madison Bridge was built in 1928 with a 200-foot horizontal clearance. The heights of the spans show the great variety of sizes.

The date 1898, marked on the top of the Missouri entrance, was an enlightening bit of information. The first bridge here was built in 1873. A diagram of that bridge in General Warren's book of early crossings shows the bridge to have had a different configuration but the same number of spans.

In 1945 the railroad got a permit to rebuild parts of the present bridge. According to Howard Boren, after World War II the American Bridge Company built three new spans for the bridge, two short and one long. "They took the old spans out and floated the new ones into place," Boren said. (He knows because he worked on it.) The Louisiana, Missouri Railroad Bridge has changed hands many times since the Louisiana and Missouri River Railway Company built the original 1873 span. This is a bridge with a long and fascinating history.

No trains came as I sketched the GW Railroad Bridge. I returned by the same route to the "Honey Man" who was watching my car.

---

\* The raft span is not a technical term but refers to the former need to provide large spans able to pass wide log rafts.

**Use:**
Trains of the Gateway Western Railroad

**Location:**
Between Louisiana, Missouri and Illinois

**Style:**
8-span through-truss plus a 446-foot swingspan

**Length:**
Channel span - 195 feet clear
446 feet total
Total length - 2150 feet

**Width:**
Single track

**Clearance:**
16 feet MLW

**Date completed:**
1898; original bridge 1873; in 1945, 3 spans were replaced

**Designer:**
E. L. Corthell

**Bridge:**
#02744, Coast Guard assigned

**Owner:**
Gateway Western Railway

**Unique feats:**
Mark Twain wrote about this bridge in Life on the Mississippi; the 1873 span was one of the first fifteen bridges on the Mississippi

Chicago, Missouri and Western Railroad Bridge
Louisiana, Missouri

Mary C. Costello

# "Champ Clark" Highway Bridge, Louisiana, Missouri

*W*hen this Missouri bridge was being built, Howard Boren, then a twenty-two-year-old steel worker, climbed around on the trusses and chords as agile as a cat. His job involved catching red-hot rivets in a can and then pounding them into place to secure bridge parts together. A man, 50 feet below on the deck of a barge, heated the rivets at a forge, and with long-handled tongs and a quick aim would throw the molten slug to him.

For Howard, one day stands out especially. The day after Labor Day in 1927, as Boren and Eddie Engel, another worker, were perched on the framework, the falsework that supported their section of the metal gave way. They both fell 30 feet into the water, and Engel was killed. Boren suffered only a knee and ankle injury. He was taken to the hotel to be treated. "There were no hospitals in this town in those days," said Boren, at age 82. "I was laid up for two and a half months before going back to work.[5] The falsework was sent to Milwaukee to be repaired, which took six to eight weeks." (Another man who normally would have been "on the steel" that day had had a dream that something would happen, so he hadn't gone to work.)

Riverview Park is high above the Champ Clark Bridge. From it one has a panoramic view of the river area with the bridge as the center of interest. The blue-green of the "camelback" (a descriptive term used by Boren), was one of its most striking features, though some people I met found the color ugly. Opposed to the vivid blue of the water and sky, the distant hazy-blue horizon and the varied greens of the trees, I felt that the bridge was a tie—a blending of the surrounding hues.

The bridge was named Champ Clark after a "favorite son" who was Speaker of the U.S. House of Representatives and came from Bowling Green, a Missouri town close to Louisiana, Missouri.

Noteworthy features of the Champ Clark Bridge concern its design. All five spans are alike with Petit trusses. The very center has an X with a bull's-eye-like steel cover where the diagonals intersect.

The pier structure is unique. The outer edges appear to be long cylinders with two plastic cups slid over them (bottoms out and upside down), with one stopping at the top and the other half way down. The result is a most unusual shape.

The people in Louisiana, Missouri, were relaxed and easy to talk to. A young realtor and his wife stopped pushing their two-year-old on the playground swing to tell me of "the man who fell from the bridge and lived to tell about it." Then, at the end of my sketching, two couples drove up to talk. One of them had an aunt, Louise Allison, who was a friend of Eads, designer of the very famous St. Louis Bridge by the same name. The older couple felt nostalgic, seeing the familiar bridge and their former two-story white framed home next to the park. They were headed for St. Louis and asked me to call when I arrived safely at my destination.

It was a delightful experience seeing the Champ Clark Bridge and meeting the friendly people. I can imagine the pride the citizens at the bridge-opening ceremony felt looking down on their new highway bridge from this bluff. Unexpectedly, though, that day they had an additional daredevil display. Someone dove off the new Champ Clark Bridge center span into the Mississippi River!

**Use:**
Highway US 54

**Location:**
Between Louisiana, Missouri, and Pike, Illinois

**Style:**
5-span through-truss

**Length:**
Channel span - 300 feet clear
                405 feet total
Total length -   2287 feet

**Width:**
2 lanes

**Clearance:**
65.9 feet MLW

**Date completed:**
June 1928

**Designer:**
Harrington, Howard and Ash

**Bridge:**
#0759900 in Illinois, K-932 in Missouri

**Owners:**
Missouri and Illinois Departments of Transportation

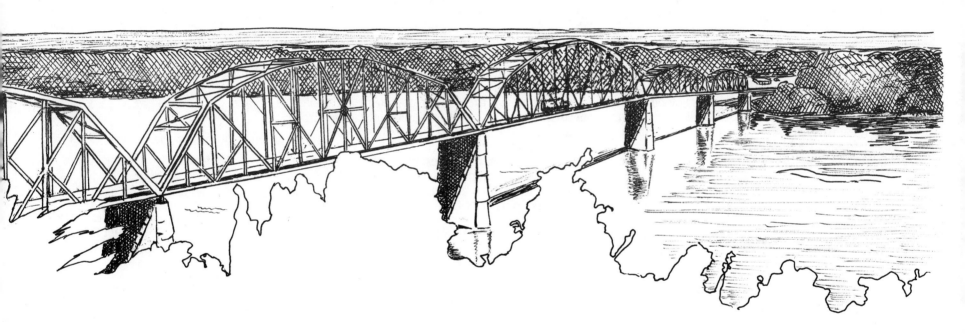

Champ Clark Highway Bridge

Mary C. Costello

# Mark Twain Memorial Bridge, Hannibal, Missouri, US 36

*P*resident Franklin Delano Roosevelt dedicated the previous highway bridge in 1936 at the foot of Cardiff Hill, made famous by Mark Twain in <u>Tom Sawyer</u> and <u>Huckleberry Finn</u>. In his dedication speech, FDR described the town as world-famous because of Twain's writings and compared the "drowsing little white town" of the Twain past to the "metropolis" of 1936 in northeast Missouri. The President saw the bridge as another step in this progress. It was a big day in Hannibal, as 75,000 people attended. Forty homing pigeons were released and flew with messages to Denver, Pittsburgh, St. Paul and New Orleans—all on a very hot 4th day of September.

Almost fifty years to the day later, I stood on the rough gravel parking lot opposite the last truss span in Hannibal to sketch the Memorial Bridge. On that chilly morning the high silver-colored steel looked golden in the sun. The open trusses and horizontal struts appeared to be filigree in this bracelet-like highway crossing the Mississippi. Only a single yellow-tinged tree on the close shore broke the continuity of the scene.

Fourteen years after my visit, a new bridge had been built and was about to be dedicated. President Clinton was invited to the opening but could not attend. The old span, with two humpback through-trusses flanked by a longer continuous truss, was narrow and overtaxed with traffic not able to meet the needs of the 21st century. Now the new Mark Twain Memorial Bridge is four times wider than the 1936 span and close to 2000 feet longer. It is composed of only one humpback through-truss and six girder spans in the water and about 20 more outside of the water. The piers themselves are in the configuration of a giant "W" connected at the top and bottom. This span is almost four times wider than the previous bridge. Interestingly the construction crew built the bridge using moored barges in the river as their base of operations. The girders are made of weathering steel painted a brown color in the area 10 feet from the piers. The reason for this is that this steel forms a rusty weather barrier which in time will match the brown paint used.

The unique features of this Mark Twain Bridge are that it is designed to withstand earthquakes and impacts from barges and ice floes up to 15 inches thick. Also the brochure from the dedication entitled, "Mark Twain Memorial Bridge, Dedicated September 16, 2000," says that "a new type of pavement/weather sensor, known as Road Weather Information System, will provide data in wintertime. If there is ice on the deck or approaches, or salt is needed on the pavement, maintenance can tell from a computer miles away. The DOT, therefore, can better control people's safety, which is one of two factors uppermost in the designer's plan. The other factor is better traffic flow. It appears both are attained with 12-foot lanes, 10-foot and 6-foot shoulders, plus a 3-foot wide median having a concrete barrier.

It teases the imagination to think what Samuel Clemmons might do with Huck Finn and Tom Sawyer in this new setting.

**Use:**
Interstate 72

**Location:**
Between Missouri and Illinois at Hannibal, closer to the railroad bridge than the 1936 span

**Style:**
A single humpback through-truss with six steel girders over the water and 20 more over land

**Length:**
Channel span - 600 feet clear
- 640 feet total
Total length - 4,490 feet

**Width:**
4 lanes plus 10-foot outer shoulder and 6-foot inner shoulder, total 85 feet

**Clearance:**
62 feet MLW

**Date completed:**
September 2000; replaced 1936 two spans of humpback through-trusses flanking one continuous truss; 1871 railroad bridge had a deck added for wagons and eventually cars, used until 1936

**Designer:**
Sverdrup Civil Incorporated

**Toll:**
On previous bridge until 1941

**Bridge:**
#A5054 in Missouri; #075-0151 in Illinois

**Owners:**
Missouri and Illinois Departments of Transportation

Mark Twain Memorial Bridge, Hannibal

Mary C. Costello

81

# Norfolk Southern Railroad Bridge, Hannibal, Missouri

*H*ats off to a dedicated bridge worker! Bill Stout, Hannibal drawspan operator, was under great tension when I visited his bridge. He was doing three things at once: communicating with a train engineer by two-way radio, talking to a riverboat pilot by telephone, and working on files on the computer monitor—while I watched. When things quieted down, he announced he had some papers to give to the engineer on the approaching train. The words "give to" fascinated me.

About 60 feet from where we stood was a high limestone cliff. In this sheer facing is a tunnel opening (excavated 1870) from which emerged the Norfolk Southern train. We stood next to the track, on the ground in front of the operator's house[6] between the bridge and the concrete arched tunnel opening. As the ten-mile-per-hour train passed, Bill simply handed the papers to the brakeman who had come out of the cab, walked beside the diesel engine inside a railing, and down some steps to reach for the rolled sheets. These were new orders, Stout told me. "He will give a copy to each of the train crew."

It was a busy place, this entrance to the bridge. "Gandy Dancers" had just finished working on the tracks here in front of the bridge operator's house. Tourists and residents alike were passing in cars on the 15-foot-wide road parallel to the river that crossed the tracks in front of the tunnel. They stopped only when the gate was down for the train. Another train came from the opposite direction, but no boats went through while I was there for Stout to need to open the swingspan.

The history of the Hannibal Railroad Bridge goes back to 1871. That original bridge, according to Warren's <u>Bridging the Mississippi River Between St. Paul and St. Louis</u>, had piers made of stone from the neighboring bluffs and from Joliet, Illinois. The original drawspan, turned by a steam engine, was wrought iron, as were the rest of the spans; the top chord, however, was made of cast iron. Trains and wagons traveled on the same level, but trains could not cross if vehicles were on the bridge, and vice versa. The bridge had no sidewalks.

"The river at this point is one channel, narrow and deep," said Warren in 1878. About a half mile above here, is one of the narrowest points on the Mississippi River (a quarter of a mile wide) and a "noted crossing place for Indians in their day!" (Warren 1878, 122)

There were three different height spans on the 1888 bridge but Stout informed me that the first three spans on the Illinois side were new and alike. Since then, Stout has retired and the bridge has been transformed to a lift-span with the required towers on either side. This lift-span was built across the Tennessee River in 1960 at Florence, Alabama. No longer needed there, it was reconditioned and floated up the Tennessee to the Ohio and then the Mississippi River to Hannibal.

One of the most interesting features surrounding this bridge is the 250-foot tunnel. Although there is another Mississippi River bridge with a tunnel at its end or beginning (Dubuque), the "people-activity" here seemed greater and therefore more exhilarating.

**Use:**
Norfolk Southern Railroad Trains

**Location:**
Hannibal, Missouri to East Hannibal, Illinois

**Style:**
Lift-span and 5 through-truss spans with a girder span between

**Length:**
Channel span - 400 feet clear
406 feet total
Total Length - 1584 feet

**Width:**
Single track

**Clearance:**
20 feet MLW or 61.48 feet when lifted

**Date completed:**
December 1993; former swingspan 1888; original bridge 1871

**Designer:**
Modjeski and Masters

**Bridge:**
#DH514.45

**Owner:**
Norfolk Southern Railroad

**Unique feat:**
Location of one of the first fifteen bridges listed by Warren

*Norfolk Southern Railroad Bridge, Hannibal*

*Mary C. Costello*

83

# Quincy Memorial Bridge, Quincy, Illinois, US 24

*B*irds, the sun and a cowboy on horseback played a part in my visit to the Quincy Memorial Bridge.

I was in Kesler Park along the Mississippi River sketching the colorful teal-blue truss bridge, when a large number of small black birds flew up from the river below. On the western horizon, at the same time, were hundreds of black specks which sped toward the park and turned out to be birds identical to those I had just seen (red-winged blackbirds, I believe). If they had practiced, their timing could not have been better. They all then followed the river south. It was a spectacular scene I shared with three girls in their late teens standing thirty feet from me. It was their loud "Ohhhhhh" that initially drew my attention.

As I continued to sketch the world's 20th longest continuous truss bridge (Steinman & London 1981, 547), Mother Nature put on another show with her red-orange sun slipping toward the horizon. The fireball cast a multitude of warm colors on horizontal clouds in the lower sky, making it difficult to concentrate on Quincy's old highway bridge.

With darkness approaching, I finished sketching the long girder end of the structure. The bridge itself is so long (3000 feet) that there were four different style piers. The three supporting the superstructure are square columns with a solid web between. Added to the square shafts are decorative cuts front and back, and thicker concrete at the bottom, tapered where attached. The rest of the 33 piers are two simple columns joined in different places as they diminish in height.

The next day on the way from my motel in West Quincy enroute to my work for the day, the early sun cast strong dark truss-shadows on the narrow two-lane deck and blinded me so that driving was dangerous. Only a hastily contrived map sun-shield kept my vision of the bridge roadway from being totally obstructed. Only then could I appreciate the low overhead lattice strut between the vertical beams. At each crossing of the steel there was a button of blue, the color of the rest of the bridge.

Back in Quincy again, I looked for a better location from which to photograph the bridge. A block up on Maine Street, I stopped in a parking spot and turned to see what I thought was a city sculpture of a cowboy on horseback with a lasso, silhouetted against the clear blue sky. I was impressed! Later I found I was seeing the back of the Marlboro Cigarette advertisement.

**Use:**
US 24 Eastbound traffic from Missouri

**Location:**
Between West Quincy, Missouri, and Quincy, Illinois

**Style:**
2-span continuous through-truss with 35 simple girder spans

**Length:**
Channel span - 617 feet clear
            628 feet total
Total length -  3512 feet

**Width:**
2 lanes, 24-foot total

**Clearance:**
63 feet MLW

**Date completed:**
May 1930

**Designer:**
Strauss Engineering Corporation, Chicago, Illinois

**Bridge:**
#0010019 in Illinois

**Owners:**
Missouri and Illinois Departments of Transportation

Quincy Memorial Bridge

Mary C. Costello

# Quincy "Bayview" Highway Bridge, Quincy, Illinois

*T*he "reverse hourglass design tower" bridge in Quincy is one of a kind. Although not the first cable-stayed bridge in the country or even on the Mississippi, it is the first to be built of this hybrid or composite design, according to Dr. John Kulicki, chief designer of the bridge for Modjeski and Masters. The Bayview span is the first to combine cables with steel and precast concrete. The Luling Bridge, north of New Orleans, is an all-steel bridge with three cables per side as compared with seven in Quincy.

When I first saw the Quincy Bridge in September of 1986, it was not complete. The last section of the roadway and much of the 160 miles of individual cable were not installed as yet. I sketched the bridge anyway, fascinated by its design, the first of its kind I had seen. A young workman who had noticed me from the 270-foot-high tower stopped after he got off work to see what I was doing. When I told him that this was the first "suspension bridge" I had seen like this, he quietly explained that it was a "kind of suspension" known as a "cable-stayed" bridge. The cables themselves go directly from the tower to the deck at a diagonal instead of supporting the roadway from hangers attached to them.

Quincy's Bayview Bridge "fan pattern" cables are "five-inch bundles of wires coated with epoxy, a material that has not been used before for this purpose and is constantly being checked,"[7] said the young man. He added proudly, "It's the only one in the world!" (Since then, other bridges have installed them.)

Besides the cables, however, there are two other innovative features. One is the concrete deck and steel girder combination arranged to share the weight of vehicles on the road. There are 60 steel-plate girders (thirty pairs), each 60 feet long and six feet deep. The numbers are rather impressive.

The concrete slabs were poured a half-mile away and "cured" for six months before being installed, a procedure which prevented them from shrinking on the roadway after installation.

The other unusual feature of the Bayview Bridge has to do with the strength of the towers or "pylons." The steel rods inside are arranged in three directions. The rods were placed fore and aft as well as sideways before being covered with concrete. This eliminated the need for larger, more expensive towers that would not be so sleek and trim in appearance.

There were two puzzling questions for me: "How did the men get up and down the tower to work on it?" and "Why does the final construction look so different from my drawing?" Bill Nash, from McCarthy Construction, St. Louis, answered my first question on the telephone. The workmen rode from the bridge deck in crane-baskets up and down the 182-foot towers.

My second question was answered by information from the Illinois DOT. In order to maintain stability to the towers while cantilever construction was going outward from them and to help anchor the cables, temporary steel head frames were added to the tower tops. These crossbar workdecks I saw and sketched. Once these head frames were removed, the bridge presented a different appearance.

This Illinois-Blue painted bridge was planned with the aid of a computer, engineer-checked by computer, and is now monitored by computers.

Looking like a ship rigged for sail, the beautiful new Bayview Bridge has begun a journey that could last 100 years.

---

**Use:**
Westbound traffic leaving Quincy, Illinois on US 24

**Location:**
Between Quincy, Illinois and West Quincy, Missouri

**Style:**
Cable-stayed bridge with concrete towers and steel girder approach spans

**Length:**
Channel span - 870 feet clear
900 feet total
Total length - 4511 feet

**Width:**
2 lanes plus shoulder, 46 feet

**Clearance:**
60 feet MLW

**Date completed:**
22 August 1987; closed 17 July 1993 for several months during the flood and flood repairs

**Designer:**
Modjeski and Masters

**Bridge:**
#0010068 in Illinois

**Owners:**
Illinois and Missouri Departments of Transportation

**Unique feat:**
First cable-stayed bridge in the United States with composite steel girder and concrete slab configuration. (Witte 1986 42) First bridge in the world to utilize an epoxy coating on the individual cables that make up the cable-stays. Winner of American Institute of Steel Construction Award (AISC) for 1989 in the "long span" category

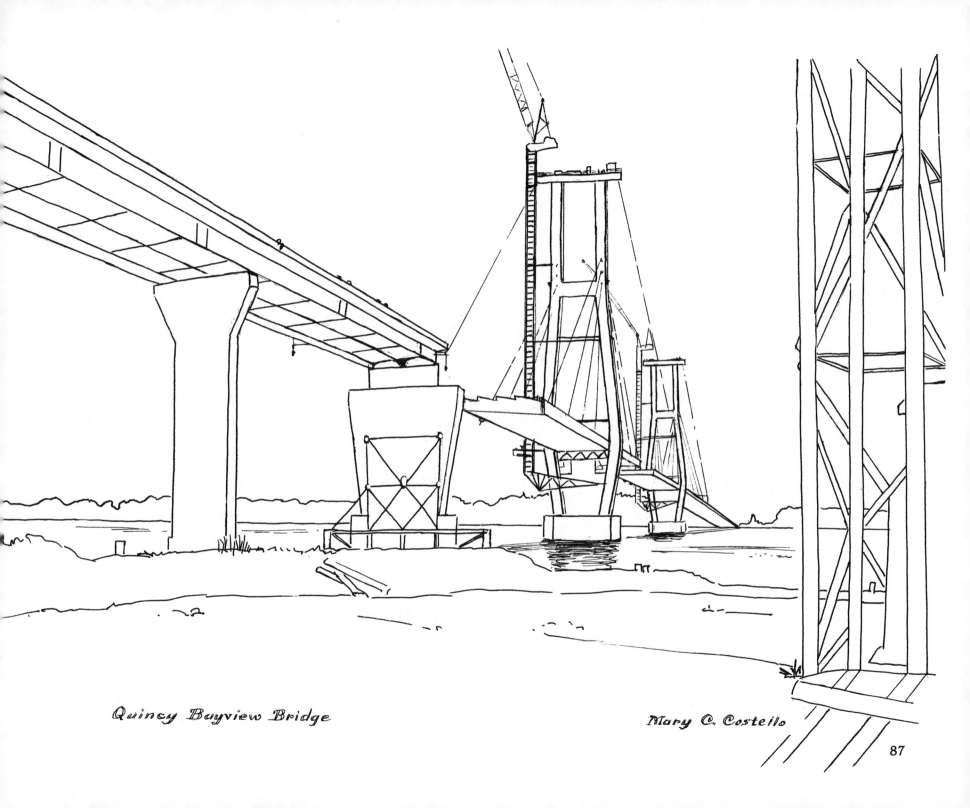

Quincy Bayview Bridge

Mary C. Costello

87

# Burlington Northern Railroad Bridge, Quincy, Illinois

*Is* Quincy's Railroad Bridge a moveable lift-bridge? No, it is not, though it looks like one. Instead, this BN Bridge is fixed in position with only one span built high enough for large boats and barges to pass under. The greater length of the bridge has what looks like a "skirt" of trusses. This railroad bridge, designed by Howard Needles Tammen and Bergendoff, with trusses both above and below the train tracks, is unique. Nowhere else on the Grand Old Mississippi is there this combination of a single through-truss with deck-trusses forming most of the remainder of the long bridge.

The original railroad bridge in Quincy was constructed in 1868, five hundred feet south of today's span. It had a moveable drawspan with 16 fixed through-trusses made with Phoenix-rolled posts. Thomas Curtis Clark designed the Whipple truss bridge, one of the first all-metal bridges on the Mississippi River.

In 1897, the general manager of the CB&Q announced that a new bridge was on the drawing board to replace the 1868 structure, designed by R. J. McClure, consulting engineer for the "Q." This bridge was built on the original piers but with fewer spans and a Pratt design. Two major changes were made—brackets were added on each side to support a wagon road, and a "loop" was made near Quincy. The loop was to allow trains to stop at the new depot without backing up. All projects—the reconstructed bridge, the loop, wagon road and depot—were completed by July 1899. The attached wagon roads were used until 1930, when the new Quincy Memorial Highway Bridge was completed. The Lower Bay Bridge was removed about 1944.

A bridge-tender was not on duty at all times on the 1899 railroad bridge, but an operator was provided to open the swingspan if advance notice was given (St. Louis Division Engineer 1940, 28). The turnspan for the early bridges was placed second from the Missouri shore. On the present bridge the channel span is near the Illinois shore. The Corps of Engineers helped to develop this channel change (500 feet above the old bridge) for safety reasons and to speed barge traffic on the river. The old bridge piers were badly damaged from being hit so often.

As I viewed from Quinsippi Island Park, Quincy's grey-colored railroad bridge silhouetted against the sky, I could hear a train approach. This unseen train's "clickety-clack" taunted me until the engine broke through the trees. It was an 82-car freight with three diesel engines. Once it passed the single through-truss, it was in the open with blue sky to accentuate its shape. Diesels are not so thrilling as steam engines, it is true, but nevertheless fascinating for their power, strength and suggestion of days gone by.

The Quincy Bridge, built in 1960, belongs today to the Burlington Northern Railroad and is a simple Warren truss design. In the evening light the BN Bridge took on the fanciful appearance of a long black animal with a decorative body of double zigzags interspersed with fine X's. The piers were the many sturdy black legs of an animal walking on the water, head lifted and tail vanishing into the Missouri tree line.

**Use:**
Burlington Northern trains

**Location:**
Between Missouri and Illinois at Quincy, Illinois

**Style:**
One fixed steel through-truss, seven deck-trusses and short deck-girder spans at the ends

**Length:**
Channel span - 300 feet clear
339 feet total
Total length - 5500 feet

**Width:**
One track

**Clearance:**
63 feet MLW

**Date completed:**
1960; originally 1868, 500 feet further south; rebuilt in 1899 with "loop" and wagon roads on sides

**Designer:**
HNTB Consulting Engineers

**Owner:**
Burlington Northern Railroad

**Bridge:**
#262.44

**Unique feat:**
1868 span was one of the first fifteen bridges across the Mississippi

*Quincy Burlington Northern Railroad*

*Mary C. Costello*

89

# Quincy Bay Railroad Bridge, Quincy, Illinois

*T*hree thousand feet of embankment with train tracks both separate and unite this Burlington Northern Railroad Bay Bridge and the main channel bridge in Quincy, Illinois. The bridge is a girder span over Quincy Bay, a back channel of the Mississippi.

On this cold but sunny November day the bridge looked attractive with its tall, solid, tapered piers of concrete designed with pointed ends facing the river's flow. This configuration is necessary to keep eddies from forming as the river hits the piers and also breaks up the ice floes. Most bridge piers have extra concrete added at the bottom with a point for this purpose, but here the pointed shape continues for the total height of the bridge supports.

Across the top of these approximately 50-foot-high visible structures are ten-foot-deep plate-girders in white. This alone is unique since most railroad bridges are painted black. On the south side of each pier, telephone lines cross the back channel on short multi-crossbar poles.

Before 1960 the earlier CB&Q Railroad Bridge crossed the Bay in a location further south, at right angles to the stream. In order to do that, the train tracks made a 45-degree turn as they approached the river. In designing the present route, Howard Needles Tammen and Bergendoff have straightened the approach and crossed the Mississippi backwater obliquely.

The crisp, late afternoon fall sun gave the bare trees and 30-year-old concrete piers an orange cast against a light blue sky and rich cerulean blue water. The severity of the bridge angles and whiteness of the bridge girders were in direct contrast to Mother Nature's soft-appearing trees, river curves and bank indentations. There was no question, the Quincy Bay BN Bridge reigned over the scene.

**Use:**
Burlington Northern trains

**Location:**
3,000 feet east of the main Mississippi River Bridge, across Quincy Bay

**Style:**
7-span deep plate-girder

**Length:**
Channel span - 90 feet clear*
105 feet total
Total length - 707 feet**

**Width:**
One track

**Clearance:**
50 feet MLW

**Date completed:**
1960; 1868 original bridge, a swingspan, was rebuilt 1899; earlier spans located 1,980 feet further south

**Designer:**
HNTB, Howard Needles Tammen and Bergendoff, Kansas City

**Bridge:**
#261.57

**Owner:**
Burlington Northern Railroad, formerly the CB&Q Railroad

* approximate measurement
**excluding approaches

Quincy Back Channel Railroad Bridge

Mary C. Costello

91

# The Quincy Bay Park Bridge

*A*fter the new Quincy, Illinois, Railroad Bridge was built in 1960, the Chicago Burlington & Quincy Railroad gave the old railroad span and the railroad's portion of the lower Bay Island to the community for development as a public recreation area. As a part of the recreational activities of Quincy's Park District in the late 60's, a miniature train ran across the bridge on narrow-gauge train tracks. The train with riders chugged along a total of one-and-a-half miles one way on Quinsippi Island. It continued running until about 1984. Since then, the tracks have been removed and sold along with the train. Today the bridge is used solely for vehicular travel to the park and the marina.

This old Quincy Railroad Bridge is much closer to the water than the newer railroad span 1,980 feet to the north. The park bridge is a deep plate-girder construction with five solid stone piers, interspersed with timber-pilings apparently used by the railroad to shore-up the bridge's outer edges. The center pier is much bigger than the rest since it originally supported a swingspan. I found the most interesting part of the bridge to be its abutments. Like the piers, the abutments are of rough stone the height of the road, with the girders butting against them. What is so unique is that in each of these end supports there is an attractively centered round-arch almost as tall as the short piers. However, each arch opening is partially filled by ground from the angled embankment on which it is situated. In addition to aesthetic reasons, the purpose of this attractive architectural addition would seem to be to relieve pressure on the abutment at high water by allowing a place for floodwater to escape.

It is hard to believe that in 1868 the Bay Bridge had a central tower over which hog-chains hung to support a drawspan. Instead of being turned by machine power as the main channel turnspan, however, this drawspan was turned by hand (Warren 1878,119). Trains crossed the deck-truss on cast iron upper chords with truss sections below ten feet wide and ten feet high in the Bollman pattern.

The present Quincy Park Bridge deck is only wide enough for a single lane of vehicular traffic with a 20-mile-per-hour speed restriction. Motorcycles are forbidden. When I crossed the span, cars straddled the the sunken railroad ties still visible from the narrow-gauge train track. Pedestrians on the bridge's sidewalks are protected from cars by a low steel rail on the traffic side and on the bridge's outer edge by a high braced chain-link fence. The Quincy Bay Park Bridge is a sturdy span with a fascinating history, still serving the community.

---

**Use:**
Single-lane vehicular traffic to Quinsippi Island

**Style:**
Plate-girder with 10 spans (counting wooden and stone piers)

**Location:**
At Front and Cedar Streets across Quincy Bay, Quincy, Illinois

**Length:**
Channel span - 80 feet clear*
                 - 100 feet total*
Total length -  650 feet*

**Width:**
One-lane road with two sidewalks originally a single-track bridge

**Clearance:**
10 feet MLW *

**Date completed:**
1899; original 1868 was a turnspan

**Designer:**
R.J.McClure, consulting engineer for CB&Q, did main span and, I believe, the Bay Bridge also

**Bridge:**
#261.80 (as a railroad bridge)

**Owner:**
Quincy Park District

---

* approximate measurements

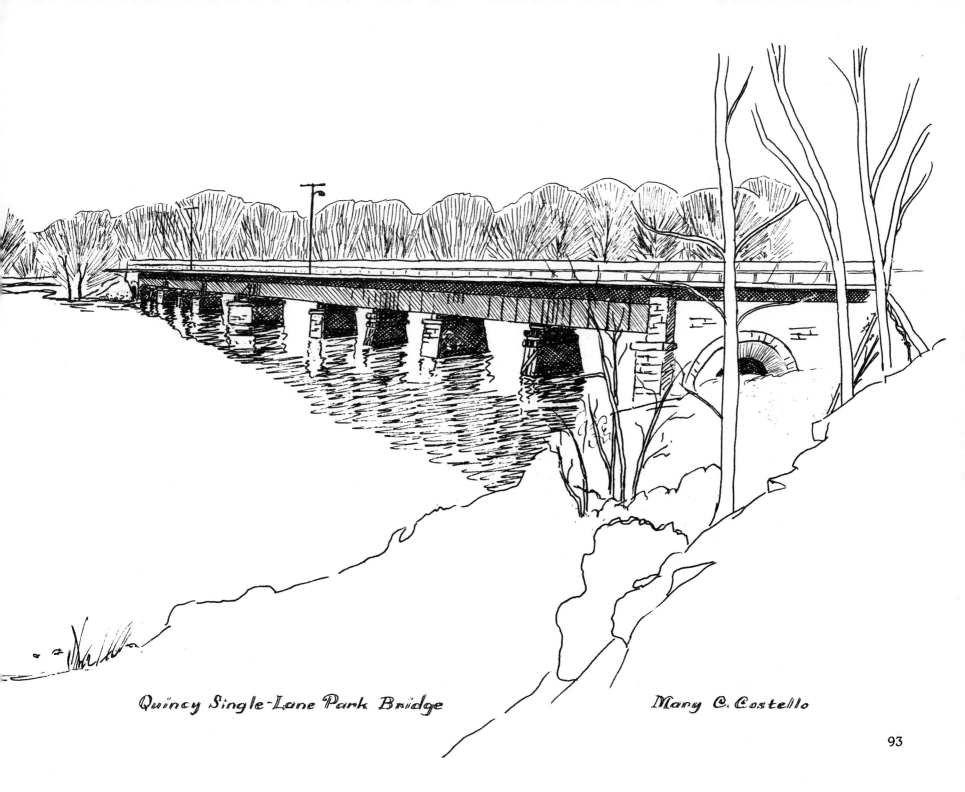

Quincy Single-Lane Park Bridge

Mary C. Costello

93

# Keokuk/Hamilton Highway Bridge, US 136

*T*he American Bald Eagle helped decide the site of this Keokuk-Hamilton Bridge. The health and well-being of our national bird were given great consideration before and during the building of this new Keokuk Bridge. This endangered species has a winter feeding ground near-by in the timber area between Hamilton and Warsaw. For that reason, the Illinois Endangered Species Protection Board examined each of the eight sites chosen for the new bridge with an eye to which location would disturb the favored birds the least.

According to the 22 November 1985, issue of The Daily Gate City, Keokuk's newspaper, the Protection Board said on 11 July 1980, that after studying the impact of the bridge on the wintering habits of the bald eagle, the present bridge site was the "best possible" one. In August of the same year that location was officially chosen.

The law stated that any work disturbing the bald eagle's habits is forbidden between the 15 November and the 1 March. In 1984, however, the mild winter allowed the bald eagle restrictions to be relaxed. This put the new Keokuk-Hamilton bridge work nearly five months ahead of schedule. Therefore, the bridge opened in November of 1985 instead of July of 1986, as originally planned.

The new Keokuk/Hamilton Bridge is toll-free, financed 80% by the federal government and 10% each by Illinois and Iowa DOT's. The first three Iowa piers are located in the former Victory Park along the Mississippi River and assume the shape of "double-T's." The next 11 piers are what I call "he-man" piers because they look like a strong man with arms holding up the roadway. Pier 4 is on the river's edge and Pier 5 is at the guide wall, the approach to the longest lock on the upper Mississippi. The bridge curves above this area, and there is a 200-foot-wide navigation channel below. After Pier 6, the remaining piers progress straight

toward Illinois.

Several months after the bridge was started, Pier 5 was redesigned so as not to disrupt barge traffic through the old bridge's swingspan more than was necessary. It has a protection cell around it and a fender projecting out from it. On Pier 5 also is the river-gauge showing the water depth in easy-to-read numbers, noted mostly at times of flood and drought.

As I looked up from below, the bridge's rich teal-blue steel girders were separated from the lighter blue of the sky by a white metal railing and white light-posts. The curve of the bridge as it leaves the Iowa shore is accentuated by this white railing.

It was a pleasure driving over the wide four-lane bridge. Well-planned, it has a 34-inch concrete median and a concrete barrier to protect the pedestrian or biker from auto traffic. In addition, there is a steel parapet on the outside.

Keokuk residents can certainly be proud of this "humane" bridge. It has taken into account not only the safety of drivers but also the needs of walkers, bikers and local wildlife, with the unexpected benefit of providing for those traveling on foot a tree-top-level view of the eagles.

---

**Use:**
Local & US 136 highway traffic

**Location:**
Between Keokuk, Iowa and Hamilton, Illinois

**Style:**
15-span steel plate-girder

**Length:**
Channel span - 200 feet clear
275 foot total
Total span - 3,340 foot

**Width:**
4 lanes plus 8-foot walkways & 34-inch median, 64-foot total

**Clearance:**
67 feet MLW

**Date completed:**
November 1985

**Designer:**
Howard Needles Tammen & Bergendoff

**Bridge:**
#5603.6Sl36 in Iowa
0340062 in Illinois

**Owners:**
Iowa and Illinois Departments of Transportation

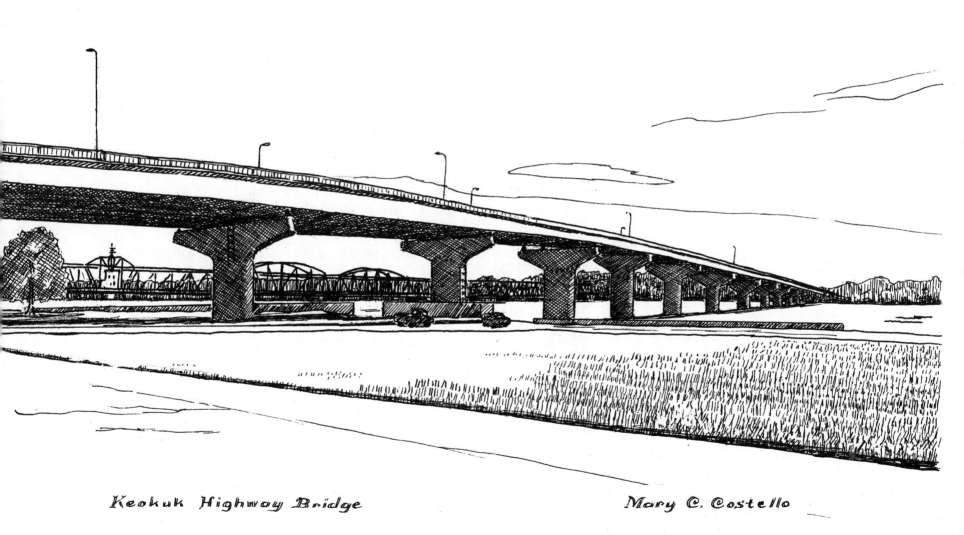

Keokuk Highway Bridge

Mary C. Costello

# Keokuk Railroad (Highway) Bridge

*H*orses and buggies traveled on either side of, and probably on, the railroad track of the first Keokuk Bridge, a swingspan truss. Open for traffic in November 1870, the whole bridge including sidewalks was "floored over at the same level,the top of the track being about 1 inch above this floor." (Warren 1878, 114) The sidewalks were on the outside of the trusses. Thus everyone was provided for on this first-of-a-kind bridge. (Hannibal had a road next to the tracks but it was built in 1871; Rock Island's 1872 span had trains above and road below; and Eads has a road above and trains below, finished in 1874.)

Interestingly enough, the draw of the original Keokuk Railroad Bridge was moved by a small steam engine on a turn-table, or it could be turned by hand. This first bridge was promoted by New York's Andrew Carnegie (Keokuk and Hamilton Bridge Company) and built by the Keystone Bridge Company.

The Keokuk Bridge was located "on the tail of the Des Moines Rapids," which made the water fast and dangerous for navigation. On 4 November 1881, the steamboat "War Eagle" became unmanageable in the current and swung against the Keokuk Bridge, taking out the span and damaging the boat. As a temporary repair to the bridge, a wooden "covered bridge" was built. It filled the span vacancy (90 by 16 feet) and was used for two years. When the steel span was replaced in 1883, the covered bridge was saved and placed in position at Lima, Illinois, where it eventually burned down. (Bickel Collection 1932)

The Des Moines Rapids is no longer a problem because Lock and Dam #19 was built in Keokuk in 1911[8] with private funds. The dam raised the water level above the rocks and slowed the river current.

In the early 1900's, horses and buggies and autos not only had to watch for barge and boat traffic but train traffic as well. All shared the rail section of the bridge. The train engineer was often frustrated because he had to wait for a signal if the bridge was being used.

To avoid sharing one deck, an upper highway deck was added to the Keokuk Bridge in 1916, when it was rebuilt on the piers from the first bridge. Designed by Ralph Modjeski, the second deck was of Douglas fir planking with wooden paving blocks and a wooden sidewalk.

"Streetcars used the train tracks of the bridge to cross to Hamilton and Warsaw, Illinois, until about 1927," said Robert Miller, curator at the George M. Verity Riverboat Museum.

In 1941, the city of Keokuk purchased the bridge from Andrew Carnegie, and in 1942 extensive renovations were undertaken. Then in 1957, a steel grid highway deck replaced the wooden floor, bringing it up to more modern standards, although it still has the original limestone piers quarried at Mt. Mariah on the Illinois riverfront.

Cliff Buriton, former tolltaker, recalled memorable events on the bridge (Rockhold 1985). There was one birth while a mother waited for the swingspan. Cliff saw two suicides and two attempts in his eight years on duty. He remembers four fatal accidents and many fender benders. For safety reasons he, for one, was glad to see the new highway bridge built, relieving the Keokuk Railroad Bridge of that extra burden.

Today "The Wonder of the Nineteenth Century" Bridge still serves the Keokuk Junction Railroad, which makes daily trips[9] across it and can glory in a long and significant history.

---

**Use:**
Originally vehicles and trains, now just Keokuk Junction Railroad

**Location:**
Between Keokuk, Iowa and Hamilton, Illinois

**Style:**
10 through-truss spans and a swingspan

**Length:**
Channel span - 158 feet clear
            380 feet total swing
Total length - 3500 feet

**Width:**
2 train tracks

**Clearance:**
25 feet MLW

**Date completed:**
September 1916 on original piers; original bridge built November 1870; major renovation 1942

**Designer:**
Ralph Modjeski, 1916 & 1942

**Toll:**
10 cents first, 50 cents until highway closed November 1985

**Bridge:**
# none

**Owner:**
City of Keokuk

**Unique feats:**
1870 span was first "official" railroad/highway bridge and one of the first fifteen spans on the Mississippi River

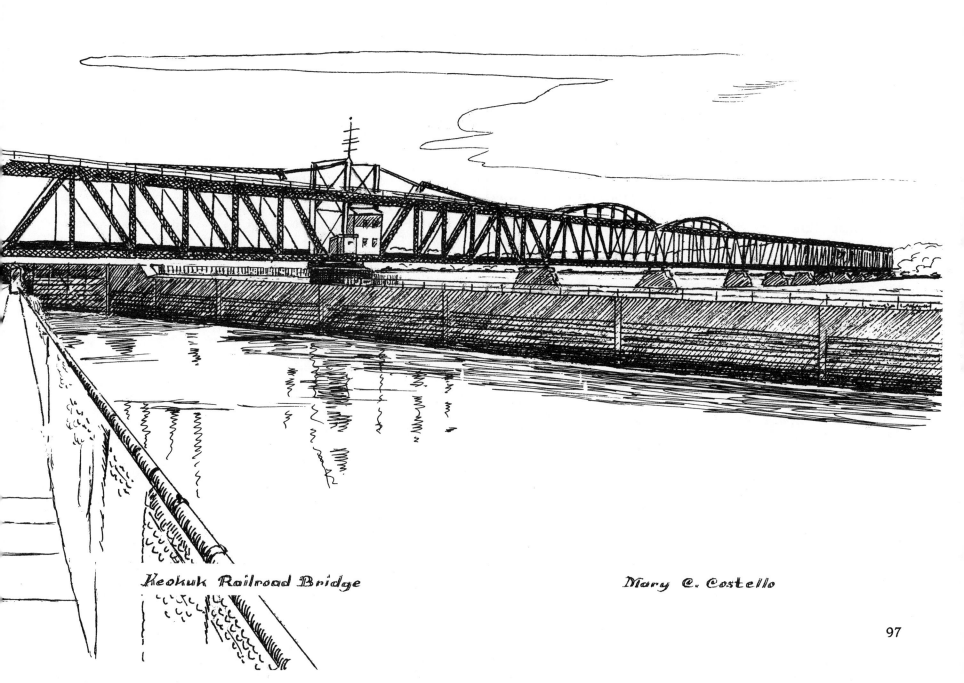

Keokuk Railroad Bridge                    Mary C. Costello

# Santa Fe Highway/Railroad Bridge, Fort Madison, Iowa

*F*ort Madison's gargantuan swingspan, 525 feet long, built in 1928, is the second longest swingspan in the world. Until the Suez Canal Railroad Bridge was built in 1965, the Santa Fe Bridge at Fort Madison was the longest ever built. Besides its great length, the swing is also a double-decker, carrying cars on the upper deck and trains on the lower. It is literally two bridges, with independent approach locations and designs, and different headroom and decks—a concrete highway deck and creosoted timber railroad deck. Uniquely after long side-by-side approaches, the highway swings over the tracks on an upper deck at the truss spans.

Because of the small clearance between the bridge and the water level (only 10 feet at high water), "the bridge must be opened for practically all river craft from barges to pleasure yachts. Barges and other large water vessels have precedence over all types of bridge traffic, including passenger trains," said T. R. Adams, former Santa Fe Assistant Trainmaster-Manager.

The Santa Fe Railroad owns the Fort Madison Bridge, which crosses the river to Illinois. Amtrak trains cross daily from Chicago. Despite being the only Mississippi River crossing for 20 miles, the Santa Fe Bridge has been known to close in the spring to allow clean-up when May flies hatch. These short-lived insects come from the bottom of the river and solidly coat the bridge, which becomes very slippery because of the bugs' oiliness.

When a boat captain gives one long whistle blast or contacts the bridge by radio, requesting the bridge be opened, the railroad dispatcher is notified and railroad signals are set to stop trains. Next, here in Fort Madison, the highway traffic light and a loud siren are activated to warn drivers, before highway barriers are lowered. Finally, the swingspan is opened. I was surprised to hear the shrill siren sound carried over the water as I sketched more than a block away. However, when I was ready to cross the Fort Madison Bridge, I was not detained by any river craft. I enjoyed the drive. All the beams are solid and simple with a row of fine-gauge steel zigzags as horizontal struts overhead. The only interruption in my blissful drive was a jog in the road at the east end of the Baltimore truss superstructure. This bend marks the point at which the highway deck separates from the railroad deck underneath and starts the descent to ground level.

The Chicago, Santa Fe and California Railroad advanced money for the first Fort Madison Bridge completed in January, 1888. On 1 June 1900, the Atcheson, Topeka and the Santa Fe Railroad became full owner of the bridge. This first single-track structure also served as a wagon bridge, with a 10-foot-wide wooden roadway bracketed onto the sides of the superstructure. Toll for a horse and buggy to cross this first span was 25 cents. In 1919, the Leisy Brewing Company's wagons, weighing six tons loaded, were regularly crossing the bridge. This was too much weight for the stringers, so a load restriction of 5,000 pounds and a six-mile-per-hour speed limit were enforced.

Forty years later, a new bridge was needed to carry greater loads and one that would provide a double track. This second span, still standing, was built north of the old bridge. The mammoth bridge has a pivot pier 47 feet in diameter. Turning machinery with four driving pinions, independently operated by four individual motors, act as one in moving Fort Madison's giant bridge swingspan.

---

**Use:**
Highway 61 and the AT&SF Railroad traffic

**Location:**
Between Fort Madison, Iowa and Niota, Illinois

**Style:**
Double-decker swingspan with 5 through-truss spans, plus deck-girder (railroad) and through-girder (highway) approaches

**Length:**
Channel span - 200 feet clear
530 feet total
Total length - 3347 feet

**Width:**
2-car-lanes wide above and two-train-tracks wide below

**Clearance:**
12 feet MLW

**Date completed:**
July 1928; original bridge 1888

**Designed by:**
Santa Fe engineer A. J. Robinson's office, overall; American Bridge Company, the superstructure

**Toll:**
25 cents

**Bridge:**
#5663.2S002 in Iowa, 0349902 in Illinois

**Owner:**
Atcheson, Topeka & Santa Fe Railroad

**Unique Feat:**
Second longest turnspan in the world but longest and largest on the Mississippi River; Amtrak "Superchief" crosses daily to Chicago and Los Angeles

*Fort Madison Railroad-Highway Bridge*

*Mary C. Costello*

99

# Burlington Northern Railroad Bridge, Burlington, Iowa

*W*hen the Mississippi River is frozen, would you consider walking, riding a car, or taking a train across on the ice? In the winter of 1855-56 people did the latter. They rode the CB&Q trains across the 2,100-foot-wide river at Burlington. For 13 years, the Chicago, Burlington and Quincy Railroad had provided a ferry service for both freight and passengers across the river until the ice formed; after that people had to wait until the spring thaw. However, when Mother Nature produced unusually thick ice on the Mississippi in 1855, tracks were laid on top, and trains crossed.

It wasn't until 1868 that a bridge was built at Burlington. It was a single-track, moveable span portrayed by the newspaper as "the Magnificent Iron Bridge," the first all-metal bridge, antedating the Dubuque and Quincy spans by only a few months. The 13 August 1868 was a memorable day in Burlington described as follows: "The bridge swung slowly and gracefully into position with no greater force than a few men at the lever—indeed, one man was able to move the massed body of metal a part of the way..." (Maffitt 1968, 7)

The real test of the strength of the Whipple truss bridge consisted in running two locomotives and two cars of railroad iron—190 tons altogether—onto the east span to sit. Then the heavy load was moved at a speed of eight miles per hour and "the center of the bridge settled two and nine-sixteenths inches... When the train passed off, it instantly rose to within one-sixteenth of an inch of where it stood before the test was applied." (Ibid.) Deeming the performance a success, a cannon boomed nine times in honor of each of the nine bridge spans.

In 1892 George Morison designed a major renovation of the Burlington Railroad structure. The bridge was given an entirely new superstructure, the piers and floor were widened to accommodate a second track, and two west truss spans were replaced by two 70-foot deck girders on new piers. In 1930 heavier trains and more powerful equipment (such as double-header engines) called for a general strengthening of the bridge.

The Burlington Northern Railroad Bridge is still in good shape almost 100 years after reconstruction. This can be attributed to the tender loving care given it, including the continuous testing, inspection and replacement of worn parts.

From the backyard of a mansion-turned-apartment on a high bluff, I saw the swingspan bridge through dripping trees and a light mist. It is one of few bridges on the Mississippi with Whipple trusses, an archaic truss configuration that was almost obsolete in 1892 when replaced. In describing this double system of triangulation, I feel as though I am back in geometry class. Each end of the six fixed spans is an equilateral triangle with an obtuse triangle beside it. The long side of the obtuse becomes one side of an inverted isosceles triangle. There are four of these inversions overlapping one another across each span. The result is a complicated pattern with a center diamond and a number of X shapes.

Morison completed the new BN Railroad Bridge superstructure with no fuss and with uninterrupted train service. The townspeople of Burlington followed his lead—with no ceremony and little newspaper coverage at its completion!

**Use:**
BN Railroad and Amtrak

**Location:**
Between Burlington, Iowa and Illinois

**Style:**
Swingspan with 6 through-trusses and 2 girder spans

**Length:**
Channel span - 153 feet clear
             362 feet total
Total length -    2237 feet

**Width:**
2 tracks

**Clearance:**
21 feet MLW

**Date completed:**
1892 rebuilt; original bridge 1868; made heavier 1930

**Designed by:**
George S. Morison 1892 rehab; Max Hjortsberg designed the original 1868 bridge

**Bridge:**
#204.66

**Owner:**
Burlington Northern Railroad

**Unique feats:**
The 1868 span was the first all-metal bridge and one of the first fifteen bridges on the Mississippi River

*Burlington, Iowa, Railroad Bridge*

Mary C. Costello

# "The Great River Bridge," Burlington, Iowa, US 34

*T*wo unique aspects of the Great River Bridge are its asymmetry and its single tower, the highest on the river. With anticipation I drove US 61 to Burlington to see the new bridge! It was going to be a homecoming for one friend in the car. We were to stop at her brother's first, but before we rounded the corner several miles northwest, we saw the bridge. The tower rose high above the river and trees on the hilltop. The season was autumn and colorful, the looming tower giant and white.

No sun, no blue sky, only a white canopy of clouds and light rain greeted us at the bridge. Here I was struck again with sizes. The old MacArthur span—Burlington's first highway bridge still in place only 75 feet upstream from the new span—was diminished by the new construction, like an adult next to a toddler.

The old MacArthur Bridge had been good to the city of Burlington. Named after A. J. MacArthur, a townsman who had had the foresight to fight for construction of the bridge despite rivermen and others who couldn't see its potential, the bridge proved to be a great success. Serving from 1917 until 1993, with only a $187,000 initial investment, the bridge in 50 years brought in almost 10 million dollars with a clear profit of over $4.5 million for the city coffer. Therefore, in 1988, making the decision to build the new bridge was like forfeiting a gold mine for the city fathers. The new structure would have no tolls, nor would it be city-owned. The MacArthur Bridge crews collected toll up until the 1993 flood, even receiving nearly 4,000 tolls from cement Ready-Mix truck drivers working on the new bridge construction. The old truss span walkway, until it was closed for safety reasons, made a perfect grandstand for city folk watching the construction.

The new and unusual single "H" tower on this cable-stayed bridge extends about 320 feet above flood stage, the tallest on the Mississippi, with Quincy, Illinois' towers reaching 182 feet, and Luling, Louisiana, and Alton, Illinois' attaining 250 feet. The hollow inside of the tower has ladders, landings and baskets for connecting and maintaining the cable jacks. The bridge engineers at Sverdrup state that the single pylon design was the result of planning for the particular location and the Interstate 34 interchange, not for its beauty.

Sixty-two cables were assembled, cut to predetermined lengths, and threaded on huge spools in the vacant Rutherford Potato Co. building on Burlington's riverfront, then were delivered as needed to the site. Each stay is epoxy coated and is made in a different thickness, depending on its place on the bridge. When the cable stays were installed, each had to be heated to at least 70 degrees to keep the plastic coating from cracking.

Much more of this new span was prefabricated—the cofferdam frames for each pier, 65 pre-stressed concrete girders for the Illinois-side, precast deck slabs which were the base for the shallow 6-foot-thick deck, and even the pre-connected framework of steel girders for the Iowa side. With self-erecting tower cranes and modern technology in planning and measuring distances, bridge building has changed. It wasn't necessary in Burlington in the 1990's to throw hot rivets as was done in earlier bridges (Champ Clark Bridge in Louisiana, Missouri #36). But with the elements to fight—the Arctic winds, freezing water, floods and sometimes intense heat, bridge building is still not easy. The Burlington Bridge is surely something to be proud of, especially at night, with pinpoint light beams reflecting on all exposed cables, accentuating their handsome fan shape.

**Use:**
US 34 highway traffic

**Location:**
Burlington, Iowa to Gulfport, Illinois

**Style:**
Asymmetrical cable-stayed girder bridge

**Length:**
Channel span - 644 feet clear
                660 feet total
Total length - 2,796 feet

**Width:**
5 lanes, 3 east and 2 west, 86 feet total, no walkway

**Clearance:**
60 foot MLW

**Date completed:**
Early 1994, initially opened to traffic 4 October 1993; replaces a 1917 cantilever truss constructed from parts of 5 different bridges

**Designed by:**
Sverdrup Civil Inc., near St. Louis

**Bridge:**
#2964.3S034

**Owner:**
Iowa-Illinois DOT

**Unique feat:**
Only single-tower asymmetrical cable-stayed bridge on the Mississippi River. Also has the highest tower on that great waterway, at 320 feet.

The Great River Bridge, Burlington, Iowa          Mary C. Costello

103

# PART THREE

# PART THREE

# The River Turns

The Mississippi River makes many changes of direction along its course, but at Muscatine and through the Quad-Cities* it turns east-west for more than 40 miles, confusing those convinced of its north-south pattern.

Bridges in the third section of this book cover the area from Muscatine through Lansing, Iowa. Along the southern Iowa/Illinois shores there is great beauty in the oaks and maples during all seasons but, with relatively low banks in the spring, there is always the fear of floods. At Dubuque and north along the Iowa/Wisconsin shores, the river is transformed. Here the artistry of the Rhine in Germany is recreated. Most Iowans don't know, maps can't show, and words cannot describe the view. From the low river valley, rising to a culminating height of 1,000 feet of limestone on the tip of Iowa shores, and 100 feet higher on the Wisconsin bank, the river bluffs are ruggedly sheared,then wooded and spectacular, with a variation of height and color. The river itself splits into so many channels with so many islands that from above it looks like broken ice on a stream just after a thaw. Many small Mississippi streams or sloughs thus formed near populated areas created the need for additional bridges. However, it was not the small but rather the large spans that required the engineering ingenuity and creativity—cantilever trusses, suspensions, simple trusses, steel arches, and girders—a special design for each area's needs.

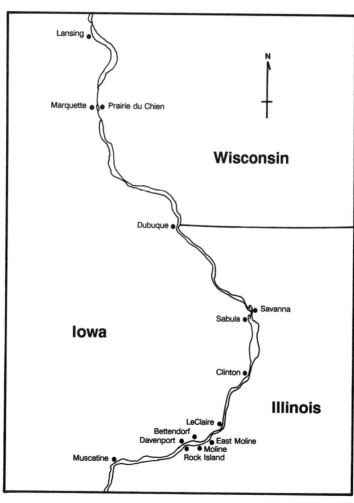

* Four Mississippi River towns make up the Quad-Cities—Moline, Rock Island and East Moline, Illinois, and Davenport, Iowa. (World Book 1991, 5:42) Because population changes have taken place since this title was coined, many people in the area consider that Bettendorf, Iowa, has replaced East Moline, Illinois. A more recent grouping—the Quint-Cities—includes both Bettendorf and East Moline.

"*I* used to have nightmares about the old bridge," said Louise Jesson, who grew up in Muscatine but now lives in Bettendorf. "I remember the turn in the bridge road, and the sidewalk had boards missing or holes in it. Kids would cross on a dare."

Although people felt quite nostalgic about the former Muscatine "High Bridge," the reality was that it needed replacement. Therefore, on 2 December 1972, the new bridge was completed ahead of schedule, and on the following April 5th the old span was "blown into history," as the Times-Democrat headlines read. It cost $45,000 more to destroy it in 1972 than it did to build the bridge ($148,000) in 1881.

The September morning sun shone on the pale green superstructure just as I was about to sketch the new Muscatine Bridge. It had been chilly and foggy till now. I could hear leaves flapping on the trees in front of me and the brakes of trucks stopping on the toll bridge below. From high on the Mark Twain Lookout I could see the whole single-truss-span bridge. It was strikingly simple. What I noticed on closer examination was the deep steel plate girders on either side of the spiney truss flanked by concrete girders, reflecting the sun, and continuing into the trees.

Two kinds of concrete piers support the bridge. The five major piers consist of two columns connected at the top and bottom, resting on a larger base. The approaches have adolescent-looking T's for piers.* The Chicago, Rock Island and Pacific Railroad tracks run parallel with the river under the bridge but provided no excitement while I was there.

Driving over the two-lane bridge, with the heavy curved overhead struts creating an arch the full length of the span, I felt a sense of security and closeness, secure the way I feel in a house built by my son, and close like a baby in a cradle. The repetition of large oval holes in the vertical and diagonal beams on the sides of the span created a very pleasing visual texture, and their cast shadows added to the pleasure. It was a feast of beauty. Muscatine can indeed boast of its Norbert Becky Bridge, named after one of its prominent citizens.

---

* Most engineers call these piers "hammerheads."

**Use:**
State Highway 92 traffic

**Location:**
Muscatine, Iowa to Illinois

**Style:**
Single through-truss span with two 250-foot steel deck-girders on each side and concrete girders the rest of the way

**Length:**
Channel span - 500 feet clear
              512 feet total
Total length -    3018 feet

**Width:**
2 lanes plus a small shoulder and one sidewalk

**Clearance:**
64 feet MLW

**Date completed:**
December 1972

**Designer:**
Sverdrup & Parcel & Associates

**Toll:**
Free now; 50 cents until July 1987

**Bridge:**
#7075.7S092 in Iowa, 0819910 in Illinois

**Owners:**
Iowa and Illinois Departments of Transportation

Norbert Becky Bridge, Muscatine

Mary C. Costello

# I-280 Bridge, Davenport, Iowa to Rock Island, Illinois

*I*t was October, 1986. The Quad-Cities were in the grips of the first fall flood in 105 years and the second worst in the area's history, when I began sketching this I-280 Bridge. The river had receded a foot or more; and yet the large numbers on the pier indicated that the depth was 45 feet, about 3 feet above normal.

The river was lapping the ground 8 feet from where I stood. South Concord had been cleared of most of the Mississippi mud, but the front lawns of the houses behind me were like quicksand. A gentleman resident arrived while I was working. He said that a week before, the water was up to the mailboxes and as high as the basement windows.

The beautiful tied-arch bridge structure looked no less beautiful with the rushing flood water reaching high on its legs. The entire bridge is designed with aesthetics in mind. It has but a single 569-foot arch whose parts—two gigantic ribs and equally mammoth horizontal struts—are all tubular or boxed. On either side of the center span and along the entire length of the bridge, are plate girders of one width, color and design, giving great continuity.

The concrete piers are simple yet out-of-the-ordinary. Each pier consists of four square pillars, interestingly spaced closer in the middle and tapered. The piers on either side of the main channel differ. They are shorter, heavier and straight. The pier cap and base this day appeared to be equal in size because of the high water. Normally the base is visibly more than twice as deep as the cap.

I saw only one motorboat braving the Mighty River. The angry water, traveling at twice its normal speed, no doubt frightened most boaters, as well it should.

When the bridge was first completed in 1973, the Quad-City residents were asked to choose the color for the bridge. A survey was conducted through the newspaper; the choices were interstate blue, interstate green, international airways orange, or a combination of interstate blue and yellow. The last set of colors won. The long horizontal girder and connecting bars overhead are painted blue with the arch itself yellow.

On an arch bridge like this the roadway is held up under the arch by "hangers." The 14 double steel rods or cables on each side are not very pronounced in appearance but are very strong in reality.

Using a little imagination, a viewer might visualize the sturdy overhead struts as "clothes hangers" without hooks. Stacked, their points meet at the top of the arch. The bottom or last section of the horizontal strut is in the shape of a capital "A" with the center bar extending up like wings.

The only part of the I-280 Bridge of which one is aware when crossing is the heavy blue "winged-A" overhead at each end of the span. With the 55-mile-per-hour speed and seemingly great height of the bridge above the water, one almost feels as if one is in the air. Even with the Mississippi flooded there is more than a 50-foot clearance below the I-280 Bridge. Perhaps "The MacDonald Arch Bridge" (as the Illinois DOT staff at Dixon have dubbed it) is one of the safest places to be at flood time, and certainly the bridge offers a most spectacular view (if one has time to look). Too bad there are no sidewalks.

---

**Use:**
Interstate Highway 280

**Location:**
Between the west edge of Davenport & Rock Island, Illinois

**Style:**
Single steel tied-arch bridge with 13 plate girder spans in Iowa and 14 on the Illinois side

**Length:**
Channel span - 500 feet clear
519 feet total
Total length - 4193 feet

**Width:**
4 lanes plus wide shoulders

**Clearance:**
62 feet MLW

**Date completed:**
October 1973

**Designer:**
DeLeuw, Cather & Company, Chicago

**Bridge:**
#8209.7S280 in Iowa, 0810106 in Illinois

**Owners:**
Iowa and Illinois Departments of Transportation

I-280 Bridge, Davenport

Mary C. Costello

# Crescent Railroad Bridge, Rock Island, Illinois

*T*he Crescent Bridge was one of my most enjoyable bridge visits. I had spent an afternoon in Davenport attempting to get to the Crescent Bridge by climbing an embankment and walking out towards the river on the tracks. When I realized that the steel rails were being used (I had been led to believe that they were not) and that the ground below was changing to wooden trestles high above Mississippi marshes, I turned around. The next day in Rock Island I was more successful. After asking several people directions to the bridge, I finally came to steps that ended at the crescent-shaped span.

I stood next to the bridge entrance where an embossed plaque on either side gave many of the vital statistics about the curved structure. From this spot I noticed that the three truss spans on this side of the turnspan were different from the four on the other side. Those spans on the east were flat-topped and those on the west were curved. The best I could find for a reason was that "Bet-A-Million" Gates (John W.), who helped finance the bridge, changed the design. There is no proof of this, ."..but it is not the result of an accident," said Peter Ehmen. Ehmen did say that when fire destroyed the trestles on the Rock Island approach, it was less expensive to eliminate them completely and ground-fill under the track. Ninety-eight percent is the original bridge.

Just as I started sketching, two people came along. One was Bengt VonRosen, an architect and close neighbor of mine in Davenport. VonRosen had come to draw the bridge also. He sat on a rock below me and we both did our thing—he in marker and I in pen.

The second person to arrive was the 3 p.m. relief drawspan operator. I proceeded to ask him questions. After a few minutes, he said, "The person you need to talk to is Pete Ehmen. He has been on this bridge for almost 40 years. Come out with me and I'll introduce you."

Without hesitation I put my things together and followed, watching his feet instead of the cracks between the railroad ties, because the movement of the water made me dizzy. There was only one train track and no railing on the bridge. We walked three and a half spans (almost to the center of the river) before we arrived at Ehmen's office. After the formalities, Ehmen informed me that he had a 3:30 appointment, but that I could call him the next day on the bridge. "You know you couldn't pay some people to come out here," were his final words before I headed back alone.

On firmer ground I breathed a sigh of relief, and my heart slowed down while I took a closer look at the bridge. The colorful red and yellow fall weeds at my feet hid some of the span's laced portal beams—common on older truss bridges. Just beyond and below are very deep cross-girders supporting the track.

When I called Peter Ehmen the next day, I asked about the bridge being closed so much. "That was my idea," he said. "Since there are more boats these days than trains, I suggested keeping it open and closing it only when a train comes."

Questioned about how many trains a day there are, Ehmen answered, "About six a day cross, mostly to Alcoa. They cross at night; that is why people don't see them."

Now when I hear the lonesome train whistle echo in the night, I imagine the Crescent Bridge closed and the bridge operator at his job.

---

**Use:**
Davenport, Rock Island and Northwestern Railroad; Soo and BN Railroads pay to use

**Location:**
Between West Davenport, Iowa and Rock Island, Illinois

**Style:**
7 through-trusses and a swingspan

**Length:**
Channel span - 197 feet clear
            221 feet total*
Total length -   2383 feet

**Width:**
Single track

**Clearance:**
26 feet MLW

**Date completed:**
8 January 1900

**Designer:**
C. F. Loweth

**Bridge:**
#149

**Owner:**
DRI&NW, called the "DRI Line"

**Unique feat:**
By terms of the articles, neither the DRI&NW Railroad nor the bridge can be sold. ("Bet-You-A-Million" 1966, 3D)

---

* half of swingspan length

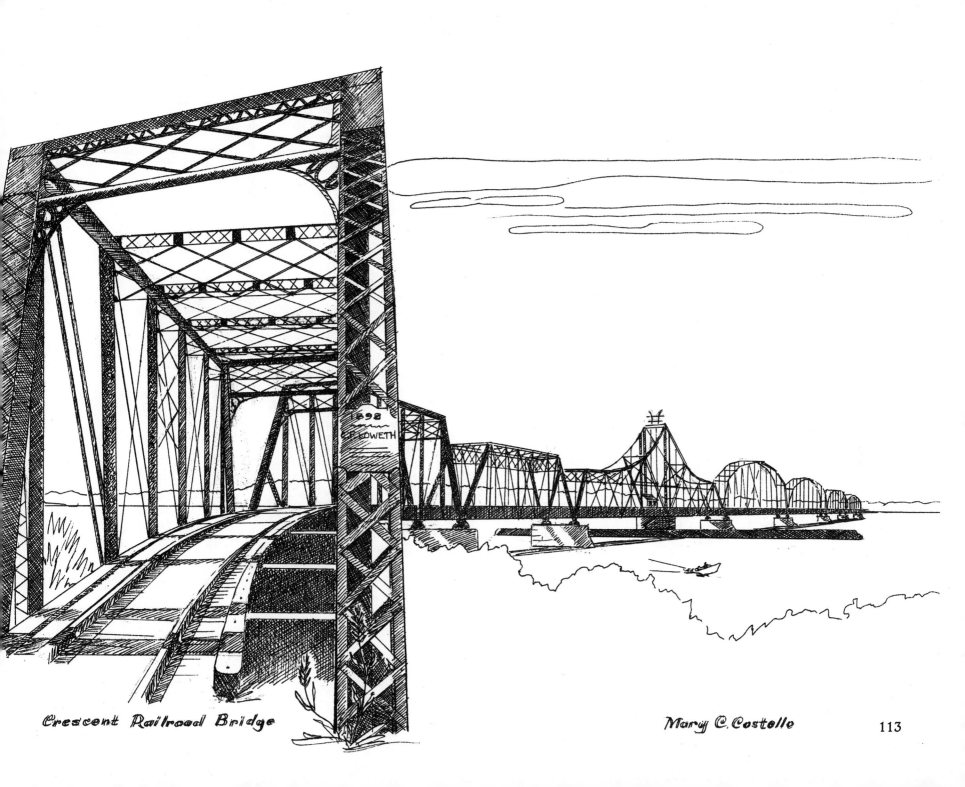

Crescent Railroad Bridge

Mary C. Costello

113

# Centennial Bridge, Rock Island, Illinois

*T*he Centennial Bridge is a strikingly beautiful and graceful series of arches, the only bridge of its kind on the Mississippi. It was called by a national publication "One of the notable bridges of the world." ("Centennial..." 1966, 3D)

Besides being photogenic (displayed in every kind of weather because of its beauty), the Centennial Bridge is strong. Bridge engineer/author D. R. Steinman explains, "An arch bridge... will carry a much greater load than the same strip of metal placed flat on two supports."(Steinman 1953, 14) The Rock Island Bridge, however, is made up of more than just arches; it is a "tied arch" construction, as we've seen in Memphis and St. Louis, as well as in Davenport's I-280. The Centennial Bridge, completed in 1940, has five arches held together at the bottom, like the string on a bow, making each arch-span independent of all others. "The use of a heavy steel tie eliminates the need of massive pier construction to resist the thrust of the arch ribs," said R. N. Bergendoff with AHNT. (Bergendoff 1940, 15)

On the Centennial Bridge there are only two different span lengths—three 395-foot spans and two 540-foot spans—even though there is an illusion of more variety from any view. The ribs are silicon steel in box sections, and the hangers that hold up the deck are unique—rigid H-beams, having maximum slenderness for the 95-foot maximum length needed. Each box comprising an arch is 4 feet wide and either 6 or 8 feet tall, depending on the span size.

The overhead bracing is an "open web" in zigzag channels between the vertical contours of the arch ribs. In contrast to the frail appearance of the center bracing are the single-plane large plate-girder portals. These two impressive flanged X-beams add to the beauty of the first four-lane bridge across the Mississippi.

The Centennial Bridge, originally named the "Galbraith Bridge" after the mayor, was soon changed by Mayor Robert P. Galbraith to reflect Rock Island's 100th year as a city. Resting on either limestone rock or hard blue shale, the bridge piers are only 15 to 30 feet below pool level, according to Ned Ashton, chief designer. The Rock Island span was one of the first and few non-federally-funded bridges. Toll is still collected, to pay the initial cost as well as for repairs and approaches. Originally the toll was 10 cents, raised to 25 cents in the 1980's, and to 50 cents in 1991 to help cover the multimillion dollars needed to bring the bridge up to modern standards.

On 4 September 1988, the contour of the beautiful Centennial Bridge's five arches was lighted at night for the first time. Lights! River! Action! was the theme of the drive and did more for the Quad-Cities than make them swell with pride. The lighted Centennial drew the Quad-Citians together and may become their "Gateway Arch."

So futuristic is the Centennial Bridge design that in 1983 its profile was used as a logo for the National Bridge Conference in Pittsburgh, Pennsylvania. According to his daughter, who currently lives in Davenport, designer Ned Ashton felt this bridge was his most important contribution to bridge design.

The day I arrived to sketch the Centennial Bridge was such a wonderful fall day that everyone was out fishing, chatting, or driving along Biederbecke Drive, raising clouds of dust that covered me and my sketchbook. Hot air balloons added a colorful touch above the Centennial — a bridge "silver" in color when the sun is high but "golden" at sunset.

---

**Use:**
US 67 highway traffic and local traffic

**Located:**
Rock Island, Illinois to Davenport, Iowa

**Style:**
5-span box through tied-arch

**Length:**
Channel span - 515 feet clear
540 feet total
Total length - 4,639 feet

**Width:**
4 lanes plus two sidewalks and 2 1/2-foot steel median

**Clearance:**
64 feet MLW

**Date completed:**
12 July 1940; previous crossing by ferryboat "Quinlan"

**Designer:**
Ned Ashton, chief designer with Ash, Howard, Needles & Tammen (AHNT)

**Toll:**
50 cents as of 1991

**Bridge:**
#8200.0S067 in Iowa, 0819905 in Illinois

**Owner:**
City of Rock Island

**Unique feats:**
Only multiple tied-arch bridge on the river; the first 4-lane bridge across the Mississippi

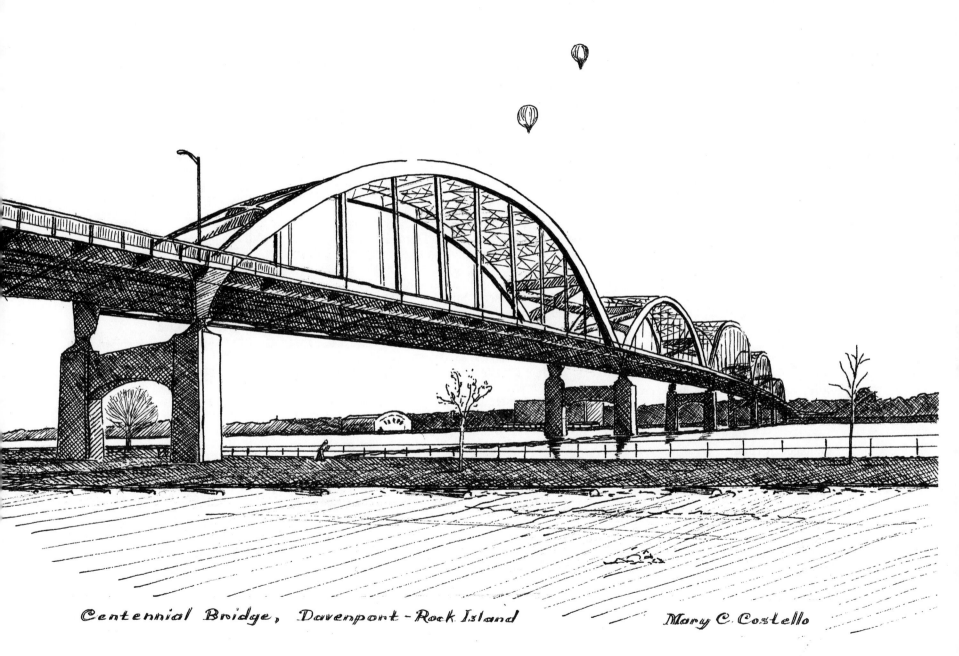

Centennial Bridge, Davenport-Rock Island                    Mary C. Costello

# Rock Island Arsenal Railroad/Highway Bridge

*A*s early as 1828 William C. Redfield of New York City published a pamphlet in which he envisioned Rock Island, Illinois, as the best location for building a railroad bridge to the Far West. On 21 April 1856 the event came to pass—the first railroad bridge to cross the Mississippi River was completed to Davenport, Iowa. It was not the first bridge, but the first "railroad" bridge, to cross "Ol' Man River." The Rock Island Bridge probably has more written about it than any other bridge on the Great River. It has survived litigation, ice and wind, sabotage attacks, and growth as times and trains changed. First built by the Chicago & Rock Island and Mississippi and Missouri Railroads,[1] the four different Rock Island Railroad Bridges are briefly described as follows:

1856-1866  First railroad bridge, private enterprise; flat-top Howe truss with Burr Arch outside, wooden structure with iron hardware, painted white; single narrow-gauge track, longest swing-span in U.S. (286 feet); steamboat "Effie Afton" hit and set bridge on fire 15 days after bridge completion.

1866-1872  Built on same piers, Howe truss with curved top chords, mostly wooden but heavier and higher; black, fire-retardant benite treated; single track; ice and wind damaged in 1868.

1872-1896  New flat-top iron bridge built two blocks downriver; U.S. Government and CRI&P owned; double deck (single track above and wagon-way below); double intersection Pratt (Whipple) construction, higher and stronger.

1896-today  Ralph Modjeski designed, built of steel on same piers; 3 feet higher and stronger; 2 train tracks above and, in early years, double streetcar tracks plus cars below; originally government and railroad owned.

Except for four occasions, the Rock Island Railroad Bridges have been in continuous service since 1856.[2]

Though name-dropping may not be well thought of in all social circles, in "Rock Island Arsenal Bridge-talk" it can be very impressive. U.S. Engineer, Lieutenant Robert E. Lee, surveyed the Rock Island-Davenport area in 1837—Abraham Lincoln visited the bridge in 1856 and used Lee's surveys in preparing for his defense of the railroad bridge company after the "Effie Afton" accident, perhaps Lincoln's most important law case—Antoine LeClaire, founder of the city of Davenport, donated the land for the bridge on the Iowa shore and turned the first shovelful of dirt[3]—Henry Farnam was chief engineer of the first bridge—General T. J. Rodman, Arsenal Commandant, designed the first plan for the 1872 bridge.

Today's Arsenal Bridge has five riveted Baltimore through-truss spans attached to the swingspan and two smaller Pratt end-spans. The 366-foot-long turnspan is one-of-a-kind, pin-connected truss that moves in a full circle (360 degrees).

While I visited the bridge's upper-deck house, Charles Fisher, head operator at the time, opened the swingspan three times for boats and a barge going through Lock and Dam #15 located below the span. There was a bouncing sensation and a great deal of noise as the huge gears in the pivot pier meshed. In the bridge-house all visible mechanisms were immaculately clean and neatly painted. "In the winter, when the river is not open for traffic, my crew and I tear down all the machinery. We clean and repair everything," said Fisher, then a 38-year veteran bridge operator.

The Rock Island Railroad Bridge set the precedent for all Mississippi River bridges. Although the Father of Waters divided the country into East and West, this first railroad bridge began the "trussing" procedure — binding the nation together with hundreds of bridges to follow.

**Use:**
Arsenal employees, local vehicular traffic and the Iowa Interstate Railroad

**Location:**
Between the Rock Island Arsenal, Illinois and Davenport, Iowa

**Style:**
Double-deck bridge with swingspan and 7 through-truss spans

**Length:**
Channel span - 110 feet clear
183 feet total*
Total length - 1,850 feet

**Width:**
2 car lanes (lower deck) and 2 train tracks (upper deck), plus 6-foot sidewalks outside trusses

**Clearance:**
23 feet MLW

**Date completed:**
December 1896; original April 1856 (for other dates see copy)

**Designer:**
Ralph Modjeski, designer/engineer

**Bridge:**
#0819903 Illinois, #1822 Government

**Owner:**
U.S. Government

**Unique feats:**
First railroad bridge and second bridge across the Mississippi River; Abraham Lincoln defended it in court

*Half the total swingspan

Government Bridge, Davenport to Rock Island Arsenal          Mary C. Costello

# Sylvan Slough "Viaduct" Bridge, Rock Island, Illinois

*I*t was a hot 31st of July and the Rock Island fire department was testing its hoses. The high arc of water with its mist filtering down to the river fogged my view of the south end of the Sylvan Slough Bridge popularly called "the Viaduct." What I saw, through and around the falling spray, were seven plate-girder spans painted black, but the concrete parapet with its one heavy pipe rail above, in silhouette, made the girder appear higher. The spans are not unique or beautiful but the view was one I hadn't observed before. Like most people, I had previously seen only the inside of the short bridge span while driving across it. The piers attracted my attention. Every other pier is stone construction the width of the bridge, gradually extending out front and back like a slide to an icebreaker pointed front. In-between piers are rectangular concrete slabs whose bases are pointed facing upstream. Because the water was low, rocks were exposed at the base of some piers.

Dr. Robert Bouilly, former historian for the Rock Island Arsenal, told me on the telephone: "In 1863, the city of Rock Island, with Bailey Davenport (son of Colonel George Davenport) as mayor and head of the city council, built a wooden bridge from the Rock Island shore, near today's 24th Street, to the island. Bailey Davenport was aware that the U.S. Government was going to build a Confederate prison on the island and that Rock Island places of business could benefit by doing business with the government." This they did.

The Federal Government purchased the Sylvan Slough Bridge from Rock Island in 1868, and almost immediately the structure collapsed from an ice gorge which also carried it away. As a result, a second Sylvan Slough Bridge that matched the 1872 main channel span was constructed in the same location. It was a flat-topped double-intersection Pratt (Whipple) through-truss bridge, with wrought-iron Phoenix columns and top chord but cast-iron caps and feet. This second Sylvan Slough Wagon Bridge was 600 feet long with four equal spans. Because the bridge looks so square and solid from the end, some people have mistaken the truss bridge drawings for a covered bridge. This 1868-69 bridge, for wagons and foot passengers, was 22 feet wide with two 6-foot walks outside of the chords. The floor and foot walks were oak planking.

Today's third bridge has no overhead structure, only steel girders below. Although improved over the years with a concrete deck, low concrete railing and paint, the Sylvan Slough Bridge is basically the same as when it was built in 1907. Ralph Modjeski designed and supervised construction and at that time added the straight piers between the stone ones, reducing the span length by half, thus permitting the use of girders.

Singing crickets, humming cars and rushing water from the hose were all that I heard on that hot 100-degree morning, until the fireman's hose sprung a leak. The tending fireman whistled sharply for help, but his buddies were talking and didn't hear. After securing the hose the best he could, he ran down the high embankment to shut off the water himself. That concluded the testing. Now the bridge was more visible, but I had already completed my sketch.

---

**Use:**
Arsenal employees and local residents

**Location:**
Between the city of Rock Island and Arsenal Island over Sylvan Slough

**Style:**
Plate-girder bridge

**Length:**
Channel span - 82 feet c.to c.*
Total length - 603 feet

**Width:**
2 lanes, 24-foot roadway, one 5-foot walk

**Clearance:**
22 feet MLW

**Date completed:**
1907; original 1863 bridge destroyed by ice; rebuilt in 1868-69

**Designer:**
Ralph Modjeski

**Bridge:**
#0819904 in Illinois

**Owner:**
U.S.Government

---

* Distance is from the center of one pier to the center of the next.

Sylvan Slough "Viaduct" Bridge

Mary C. Costello

# Sylvan Slough Railroad Bridge, Rock Island,Illinois

*I*n his <u>History of the Rock Island Arsenal</u>, Colonel Flagler referred to this bridge as "the beginning of the first railroad bridge across the Mississippi River." The Sylvan Bridge, as it was called, originally built in 1854, crossed what is today known as the Sylvan Slough, from Arsenal Island to the city of Rock Island. It consisted of three fixed spans of Howe trusses, 150 feet each. This first slough bridge was similar in construction to the fixed spans of the first main channel bridge. "Here there was no draw span because the (slough) channel was closed to navigation by a dam at its head. Both spans and piers on this side were of somewhat lighter construction." (Nothstein 1956, 8)

In April 1868 ice carried away the wooden railroad bridge (as it had the Slough Wagon Bridge). The first Sylvan Slough Railroad Bridge was replaced by an elevated span of iron in or about 1870. The United States Government was at this time relocating the Chicago and Rock Island Railroad Bridge on the lower end of the island, which island in 1862 was legislated as an Arsenal. Therefore, the angle of the short slough-crossing (a part of CRI Railroad) changed. The new bridges were in a straight line with each other instead of curving inland on the island as they did before 1872. The date is earlier for the Slough Bridge because this smaller span was completed first.

The 1894 or third Sylvan Slough Railroad Bridge had six spans instead of five. The outer ones were 75-foot deck plate-girders and the two center spans were 150-foot trusses.

In 1924 the fourth Sylvan Slough Railroad Bridge (the present span) was constructed with six through plate-girder spans each 105 feet long, plus one 75-foot deck plate-girder on the north end. Ten staggered hex-shaped piers carry this load. This span does not match the main channel Arsenal Bridge, although both are black.

The first bridging of the Mississippi at Rock Island was by private enterprise, but since 1872 the railroad bridges (including those over the Sylvan Slough) have been in joint ownership between the Chicago, Rock Island and Pacific Railroad and the U.S. Government. However, when the "Rock" went bankrupt, the government bought the railroad's share and became sole owner.

In order to photograph the Sylvan Slough railroad bridge, I drove under the Viaduct Bridge to the Rock Island Waterworks. Here is where firemen earlier had been testing their equipment. I got bridge directions and a drink of water to prevent dehydrating, as the temperature was 100 degrees that day.

The gentleman at the Waterworks told me I had two choices: drive up onto the levee and back all the way out, or take a back road. Backing up on the narrow levee didn't appeal to me, so I chose the latter approach. The road was gravel or, more accurately, two tracks with high weeds between. At a 90-degree turn in the road I stopped, walked up the dike and found that I was right at the bridge with its tapered-hex concrete piers.

I stood on an old concrete abutment with protruding rods while I sketched. Pigeons were enjoying the privacy and coolness of the underside of the bridge. Except for a few fish jumping out of and into the water, everything was calm on the Sylvan Slough.

**Use:**
Iowa Interstate Railroad since 1985

**Location:**
Between the city of Rock Island and the Arsenal over Sylvan Slough

**Style:**
6-span through-girder with one deck-girder and a sidewalk

**Length:**
Channel span - 105 feet c. to c.*
Total length -   602 feet total

**Width:**
Two tracks, one each for east and west traffic

**Clearance:**
22 feet MLW

**Date completed:**
1924; original 3-span wooden truss in 1853; 5-span iron mostly truss in 1870; 6-span steel, partly truss, in 1894

**Designer:**
Rock Island Railroad Bridge Engineer

**Bridge:**
#1816

**Owner:**
U.S.Government

_____
* center to center

Sylvan Slough Railroad Bridge

Mary C. Costello

121

# Sylvan Island (Wagon) Footbridge, Moline, Illinois

*T*he Sylvan Island Bridge is now used only by walkers "determined for adventure" or by fisher men or women. Closed to cars since March 1969, the former single-lane wagon bridge has pipes at the entrance so placed as to prevent all persons over 13 inches wide from passing through the opening. After a quick inspection of the two-span through-truss, I decided to take a picture of it. As I stood back to snap the photo, a 79-year-old man, looking 50, came up behind me and waited. He had no fishing gear so I wasn't sure what he wanted. He opened the conversation by saying, "Do you plan to buy it?"

This was Emmett Duvendistel from Rock Island. He encouraged me to go over to the "jungle island" opposite (really Sylvan Island), where it appeared Tarzan would feel at home. I was hesitant, even though it was a beautiful sunny morning. Emmett assured me, however, that there was nothing to worry about. In fact, he offered to go with me. We crossed the bridge's greyed blacktop deck that had no curbings. I noted the interesting parapet. It was like a long 24-inch-wide ladder hung horizontally along the bridge sides, approximately four feet above the bridge floor with X's instead of rungs.

Emmett led the way along the paths of Sylvan Island, next to tall dead sweet clover, goldenrod, sunflowers and other wildflowers. Emmett was a fountain of information. He pointed out a huge beaver dam next to the shore. Two trees lay across our path, and Emmett's comment was, "The beaver made a big mistake here. It intended them to fall toward the slough." Along the shore were lots of dead trees standing, stripped of bark. Light green seeds that fell and collected between my sketchpad and arm are called "beggar's lice," according to my guide. Emmett cleared the way as he walked, breaking and bending tall growth and pushing aside branches for me. On our two-hour trip around the island we saw Moline's Generating Station and, at the opposite end, the Arsenal Power Station—beautiful with its long line of arched openings. Emmett pointed out large concrete blocks in the middle of Sylvan Island, where Republic Steel had been located from 1894 to 1957, employing as many as 1500 people. The river was quite high with weed-tops bobbing back and forth. Emmett remarked, "We are taking the high road. Normally, if the water were down, I would take a lower path."

Finally we arrived back at the bridge with its cut-stone single pier. The Sylvan Island Wagon Bridge was constructed in the fall of 1872. After the Civil War, the government needed more power to operate its shops—power a dam could provide. In order to build such a dam, though, the government required land opposite Arsenal Island owned by the Moline Water Power Company. In negotiations for that land, the U.S.Government agreed to give the Power Company 25% of the water power produced, and "to construct and maintain a wagon bridge for the use of said company." (Hallberg 1980, 2) All were completed in 1872—the power dam, a canal (tailrace) and the wagon bridge over the new canal. In the 1890's a steel mill moved onto Sylvan Island and became the user and technical owner of the bridge. The greater utilization and heavier loads required a stronger and safer bridge, so in 1901 the government contracted the Clinton Bridge and Iron Works to "remodel"[4] the bridge, using the American Bridge Company's plans.

The present Pratt truss Sylvan Island Footbridge looked attractive "in profile" that Tuesday morning after Labor Day, mostly because of its repetitive railing design and frail diagonal tension rods. Emmett, like a guardian angel, had seen me safely around Moline's island wilderness and introduced me to the Sylvan Island Footbridge and tailrace. My work completed, we said,"Adieu!"

**Use:**
Recreation—walking and fishing; former access to Republic Steel

**Location:**
From 2nd Street Moline to Sylvan Island

**Style:**
2-span through-truss

**Length:**
Total length - 199 feet, has no approaches

**Width:**
14 feet

**Clearance:**
16 feet MLW

**Date completed:**
1901; original span September 1872; replaced wooden deck for corrugated steel with asphaltic cement cover in 1953

**Designer:**
American Bridge Company; original span by Baltimore Bridge Company

**Bridge:**
#A5443

**Owner:**
City of Moline; received bridge as gift from the army, 7 May 1975

*Sylvan Island Wagon Bridge*

*Mary C. Costello*

123

# Sylvan Island Railroad Bridge, Moline, Illinois

*W*ith Emmett Duvendistel as my guide, I followed the narrow path from the Sylvan Island Wagon Bridge for about two city blocks. The pathway went through the island wilds opposite the Iowa-Illinois Gas and Electric's Generating Station (formerly People's Power, originally called the Moline Water Power Company). The Sylvan Island Railroad Bridge crosses the tailrace here in a single span. Water bubbling in spots near the large brick power dam three-quarters of a block away told Emmett that some turbines were still working. Later I found he was right. The plant still produces a very small percentage of the local power (3,200 kilowatts of the total 1,392,788 kilowatts).

The railroad tracks have been removed on the Sylvan Island Railroad Bridge itself but remain on the island at least for a short distance. In place of the bridge train tracks there are heavy timbers, and outside of the timbers are sturdy planks securely fastened with countersunk bolts. This railroad bridge was built to supply the island's old Republic Steel Mill with raw materials and to distribute the finished product. Emmett said that since the tracks have been removed, heavy loads have been transported across the bridge on these planks. I later read that "two carloads of coal per year were utilized by the Arsenal power plant...access by truck over the present railroad bridge is needed and necessary." (Langworthy 1968, 1) The bridge is certainly strong enough and a convenient way to transport goods to the government power dam on the opposite end of Moline's island-park.

With the help of William Riebe, Chief of Survey, Rock Island Corps of Engineers, I discovered that the Sylvan Island Railroad Bridge had an interesting beginning. The old truss bridge actually came from Burlington, Iowa. The CB&Q Railroad in 1891 replaced the original 1868 Burlington Bridge with a newer, wider superstructure and double-tracks (a George Morison design), and sent one 247-foot old span to Moline. How convenient that when one bridge was being dismantled another could use some of its parts!* However, the span was 52 feet too long for the small Sylvan Island canal. Therefore, the engineers took out panels number 8 through 11 in the center of the single "hand-me-down" truss and still kept the attractive 1868 Whipple design intact.

One of the Rock Island Arsenal historians thinks that these two old Sylvan Island Bridges are the most attractive bridges in the Quad-City area. The 1868 truss railroad bridge, made to accommodate steam engines, is taller, narrower and heavier than the footbridge two blocks away. Its single span is divided into fifteen segments, each 13 feet wide, with Phoenix rolled posts and double rods for diagonals. There is no parapet on the Sylvan Island Railroad Bridge.

From 1894 until 1956 the Republic Steel Mill had a plant on Sylvan Island, at one time hiring 1500 people. The railroad bridge provided a means for bringing in raw materials and distributing the finished products, but the rail service was not always dependable, so heavy teams of horses carried produce on the wagon bridge. There was a shortage of railroad cars in 1946 (WWII), so the mill had to use the wagon bridge more often.

Today the man-made Sylvan Island** and Sylvan Island Railroad Bridge are deserted except for fishing enthusiasts and, of course, Emmett Duvendistel.

---

\* Reusing bridge parts was a standard practice of railroads.

\*\* In 1871 when the canal (tailrace for the dam) was dug from Sylvan Slough on one side of the Moline peninsula to the other, Sylvan Island was created.

---

**Use:**
Recreation, mostly fishing; abandoned spur of Rock Island Lines

**Location:**
Sylvan Island to Moline's Second Street

**Style:**
Single span through-truss with Phoenix columns

**Length:**
202 feet total

**Width:**
Single track, 15.65 feet originally with a two-foot walk

**Clearance:**
17 feet MLW

**Date completed:**
1891; span is 1868 construction from the original Burlington Bridge

**Designer:**
Max Hjortsberg; constructed by Detroit Iron and Bridge Works

**Bridge:**
#251.05C

**Owner:**
Iowa-Illinois Gas and Electric Company of Davenport, Iowa

**Unique feat:**
Bridge span came from Burlington, Iowa, when the CB&Q rebuilt that bridge

Sylvan Island Railroad Bridge

Mary C. Costello

125

# Moline-Arsenal Bridge, Moline, Illinois

*T*raveling onto Arsenal Island from Moline, I never expected a problem. However, as in Baton Rouge, security people are afraid of saboteurs, and the guard denied my walking under the bridge at the east end. Perhaps there is just cause for such safeguards at this important installation, but for me this was by far my best view, so I waited. The guard checked with another person and eventually agreed to allow me to go below to the river's edge.

Three things make the newest Moline-Arsenal Bridge out-of-the-ordinary: the overhang of the concrete deck, which produced a dramatic horizontal shadow in the morning sun; the gentle arch of the weathering-steel girder between the four piers; and the unusual terminal flanges on the double-columned concrete piers. These are designer touches that the engineers created for the sensitive viewer's eye.

The bridge's history is fascinating as told to me by both Dr. Robert Bouilly, former Arsenal Historian, and my cousin, Grace Aubry, now deceased, author of St. Mary's Church, Moline, Illinois, 1875 to 1975. From 1837 to 1868, there was a "brush-and-stone dam,"⁵ from today's 15th Street, Moline to the island, later to become the Rock Island Arsenal. People walked on top of this dam wide enough for teams of horses to pass. There were different reasons for crossing Sylvan Slough. Millwrights living across the slough went to work in the mills on the east end of the island. In the early 1840's Irish Catholics living where Moline would later be laid out (1848), had no Catholic Church—the nearest being in Davenport. Therefore, Moline church members walked across "Sears' Brush Dam," the length of the present Rock Island Arsenal, and took a rowboat across the Mississippi River to St. Anthony's Church. Squatters, who poured onto the island after Fort Armstrong closed, used the dam to cross to Moline for supplies.

In the 1860's a wooden bridge was built by the city of Moline. The Arsenal gained possession of it in 1867, but an ice gorge in April 1868 severely damaged the bridge and dam. The government removed both in 1869. Moline was without a bridgeway until 1873, when a flat-top wrought-iron Pratt-truss bridge was built. This structure survived until the third bridge was completed in October 1932.

Here there is another story. The iron bridge (the second) was old and rickety, so the city was informed that a new structure would be approved if they had a bridge design. Since it was 1929, the Depression era, the Arsenal could not afford to hire anyone to do it. William Butterworth, a Moline resident and head of the Chamber of Commerce of the U.S., convinced a former college classmate and prominent bridge engineer, C.A.P. Turner, to design the new bridge, gratis!

The third Moline-Arsenal Bridge had five concrete deck-arches and spandrel columns to support the road. I thought it to be the most attractive and unique of all Quad-City bridges. When pieces began to fall from its piers and main structure, engineers looked for the cause. Usually in cement mixtures, crushed rock is used because of its rough edges. Instead, river shells and smooth river rock had been substituted. When the "mix" was discovered, the bridge was watched closely.

One day in the summer of 1981, Moline Arsenal employees crossed the bridge when they went to work, but when they left at the end of the day, the bridge was closed—too dangerous to use. It was a sad day for many when the third Moline-Arsenal Bridge, with its concrete deck-arches, was later destroyed.

**Use:**
Arsenal Employees from Moline

**Location:**
Between Moline and the Rock Island Arsenal

**Style:**
Corten steel plate-girder

**Length:**
Channel span -  220 feet clear
230 feet total
Total length -   3,300 feet

**Width:**
2 lanes plus shoulder, no walk

**Clearance:**
28 feet MLW

**Date completed:**
April 1982, preceded by 1932 concrete span, 1873 iron truss, and original wooden bridge of 1860

**Designer:**
Corps of Engineers, Omaha District; H.W. Lockner, Chicago engineer, did the three Moline ramps

**Bridge:**
#48

**Owner:**
U.S.Government

Moline-Arsenal Bridge

Mary C. Costello

127

# Iowa-Illinois Memorial Bridges, Bettendorf, Iowa I-74

*T*he river was high and raging under a very strong wind. I had trouble holding my balance and the pages of my sketchbook even with the protection of the Iowa-Illinois Memorial Bridges.

Although I knew they were not twinborn (really built almost 25 years apart), I always thought of the two suspension bridges as identical, except that one carries traffic north and the other south. When I started to sketch them, however, I found that there are differences, mostly in the bridge railings; the older northbound bridge has a round handrail and posts with many steel verticals between, and the newer southbound bridge has short widely-spaced angular posts connected midway and on top with angled rails. This is not a major feature of the bridges but one I would not have noticed if I hadn't sketched them.

The Moline-Bettendorf Bridges are a combination of styles—suspension over the main channel, pony trusses over the Moline Pool, and girders at the ends.

How do suspension bridges operate? I will explain in relation to the I-74 Twin Bridges. Cables are a unique and important part of the suspension bridge—here 37 steel strands, each 1 to 1 1/2 inches in diameter wound together and wrapped with wire. The 10-inch cables thus formed are anchored in giant blocks of concrete near the end where I stood. From here they travel to short "cable bents, which sit on pins and can actually lean back and forth in response to the expansion and contraction of the bridge." (Theobald 1985, 1)  The cables rise to the tops of the 160-foot towers, travel to the next tower, a distance of 740 feet, and finally descend to the cable bent and anchorage on the opposite side. Hanging from these main 10-inch wire ropes are compressed wire "suspenders." Like the straps that hold up trousers, the bridge suspenders attached to steel beams hold up the deck.

A suspension bridge is made to move. However, too much movement can cause twisting, as occurred on the Tacoma Narrows Bridge at Puget Sound, Washington, in 1940, when a 35 to 42-mile-an-hour wind made the bridge wrench, tear apart and fall. To prevent such an accident, a number of safeguards are installed in suspension bridges today, like the truss stiffeners or steel beams seen on the I-74 Bridges next to the roadway. Other safety features include two mechanisms at the towers—a rocker-link and a wind-tongue assembly. These added parts control the movement of the suspension and keep the bridges in line during a strong wind.

The tower designs on suspension bridges distinguish them one from another. These green-colored towers on the I-74 have steel bands of zigzags at the top and bottom, along with two large X's above the decks and one below.

Since the Moline-Bettendorf Suspension Bridges can't tell their stories, I will share a couple involving animals. In 1942 an accident involved a bus and a semi-truck of steers. Eight steers broke loose, and the toll people in their bridge-car herded them into Bettendorf. Again in the '40's, a semi-trailer hauling an elephant stalled on the I-74 Bridge. The desperate toll-taker suggested that the elephant push the trailer off the bridge, which the trainer had him do, relieving the traffic jam and solving the problem. (Finch 1969, 12)

Now with toll-days past, it is mostly weather-related events we hear about on the I-74. However, no matter how much the river rages and the wind whips, it is comforting to know that these tall slender Bettendorf Twin Bridges can withstand the turbulence.

**Use:**
Highway I-74 & local traffic

**Location:**
Between Bettendorf, Iowa, and Moline, Illinois

**Style:**
Twin suspension, pony truss and girder combination

**Length:**
Channel span - 710 feet clear
            - 740 feet total
Total length -   5552 feet

**Width:**
2-lanes each bridge

**Clearance:**
66 feet MLW

**Date completed:**
Northbound - November 1935
Southbound - December 1959

**Designer:**
Modjeski, Masters & Case

**Toll:**
15 cents, removed in 1970

**Bridge:**
#8205,0L074 & 8205.0R074 in Iowa,
0819902 & 0819901 in Illinois

**Owners:**
Iowa & Illinois Departments of Transportation

**Unique Feat:**
Only twin suspension on Mississippi River.

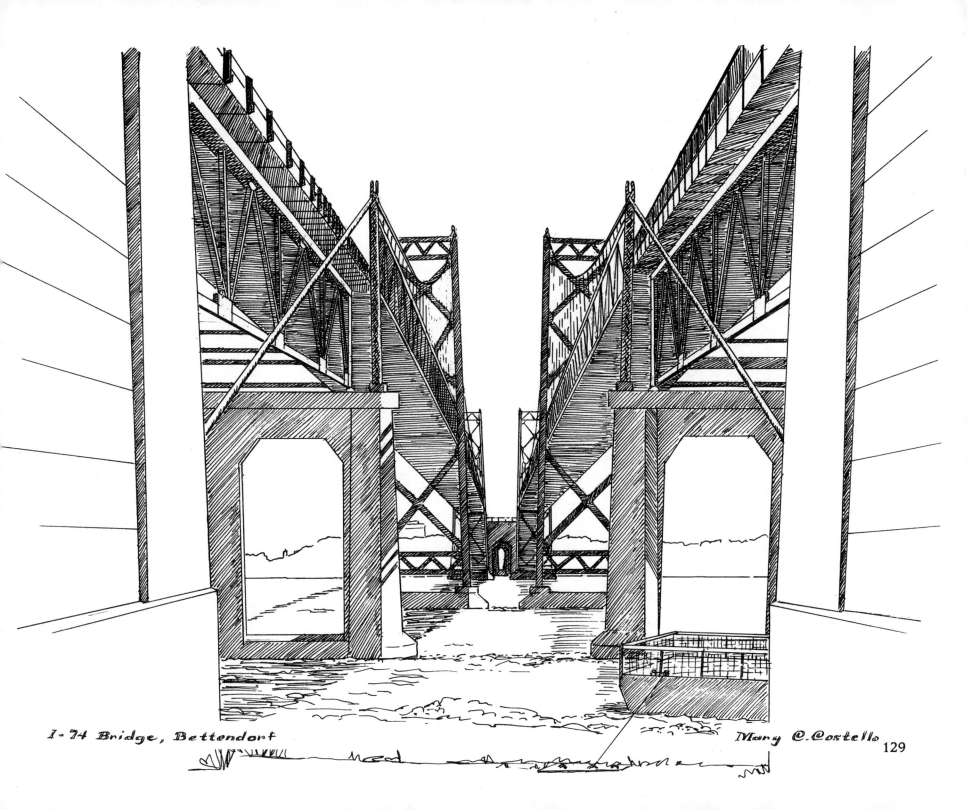

I-74 Bridge, Bettendorf

Mary C. Costello

129

# Campbell's Island Bridge, East Moline, Illinois

"*H*ave you included the bridge at Campbell's Island in your book?" asked a friend three years after I had begun my bridge research. I was surprised that I had missed this three-span steel-beam structure. Correcting my oversight, I found the bridge to be of great historical as well as personal interest.

Campbell's Island Bridge is a short bridge (only 235 feet long) going from East Moline to "a rather small bushy island near the mainland." (The Past... 1877, 115) The balustraded concrete railing on either side of the bridge is attractive, but the two-foot wide concrete walks and deck are fast deteriorating. Margaret Bolich, a teacher-friend accompanied me. We both felt, as we inspected the bridge, that our safety was not on the minds of the inhabitants who sailed by us in their cars. We collected data from the metal bridge plaque, dropped a cord to measure the boat clearance below, and stretched a line to measure the roadway width. It was a cold September day and I was dressed in a borrowed winter coat as I stood to sketch the bridge. Margaret retreated to the car.

Before today's Campbell's Island span was constructed in 1938, a timber-trestle bridge, about 800 feet in length, stood just east of the present bridge and carried both street cars and automobiles. Planking was placed on the timber ties for the cars but driving was risky because, according to Jerry Virtue, district maintenance engineer for the Illinois DOT, autos had to straddle the tracks and there were no railings. My cousin Virginia remembers, as a child of seven or eight, going across the bridge to a birthday party and being "scared to death." To add to her worries, the driver of the car was young and had never driven the route before. Then there was the thought of having to make the return trip after the party. Virginia still "shivers in her boots" thinking about that trestle bridge!

The known history of Campbell's Island began during the War of 1812. It was 1814, ten years after the Indians signed away their right to a large tract of land which included Saukenauk Village, now Moline, Rock Island and the Rock Island Arsenal (all a part of the Sac and Fox playground). Black Hawk claimed the treaty was signed by some of his tribe while under the influence of firewater but could not contest it. Whatever was on his mind this 19 July, Black Hawk and his war party savagely attacked one of three boats on the small island now a part of East Moline.

The boat commanded by Lieutenant Campbell was forced to shore by wind and waves, and after the attack ten regular soldiers, a woman, and a child were dead and most of the others seriously wounded. The other two boats fought their way back, loaded the wounded, and retreated downstream. (Pierce 1981, 12)[6]

This tragic incident gave Campbell's Island its name, and due to the hostile Indian action described above, machinery was set in motion in 1815 for Fort Armstrong to be erected a few miles downstream.

The Campbell's Island Bridge over Mississippi backwater is an interesting structure, surrounded by history I am glad I didn't miss.

---

**Use:**
Vehicular traffic to the island

**Location:**
East Moline, Illinois to Campbell's Island

**Style:**
Three-span continuous wide-flange beam

**Length:**
Channel span - 103 feet
Total length - 235 feet

**Width:**
2 lanes, 26 feet wide including two 2-foot curb/walks

**Clearance:**
11 feet approximately

**Date completed:**
1938, previous timber-trestle bridge built late 1800's or early 1900's

**Designer:**
Illinois Department of Public Works and Buildings, Division of Highways

**Bridge:**
#081-0089

**Owner:**
Illinois Department of Transportation

*Campbell's Island Bridge.*

*Mary C. Costello*

131

# I-80 Bridge, LeClaire, Iowa

*F*rom LeClaire, Iowa, to Rapid City, Illinois, there is "a graceful ribbon of steel and concrete"[7] known as the I-80 Bridge. It is part of a cross-country highway system that connects Iowa and Illinois.

It was misty and cold when I drove over the long span. On the Illinois side, just south of the bridge, I stopped and walked for a closer view. When I had gone a car's distance with camera and sketching supplies in hand, a van stopped and asked if I needed help. Even before I started to draw, I had two more offers of assistance. It was reassuring to find people as friendly and helpful in Rapid City as they were in Cairo and Burlington.

Standing close to the concrete approach piers, I found a number of things noteworthy about this I-80 Bridge. The land piers are three columns with a long concrete top to secure them together. The heavier, in-water piers are two columns with a base that is stone faced, unusual for a modern bridge. Stone facing is used to resist abrasion from ice and water and to reduce maintenance. The arch in the piers is repeated in the main channel girder, the only curve in the long teal-blue "ribbon."

The road is bracketed-out beyond the piers and girder underneath. It gives the bridge a "small base, broad top" appearance. In building the span, engineers brought in materials by rail, since there are train tracks on each side of the river. However, the heavier girders including the center span, which was floated in during the summer of 1966, came by river barges.

The last and probably the most noticeable feature of the I-80 is the great number of piers (16 in the river alone). The river is 2,636 feet wide here at the I-80 Bridge, and turns from its east-west direction north again for our trip upstream. The main channel span is 370 feet long and the five on each side are 162 feet. The shorter spans are not small; the last five on the Illinois end are 141 feet long. Bob Milano, Illinois DOT maintenance engineer/technician, said that the bridge is built across the horizontal curve of the river, with the location and width of the channel span designed "to allow navigation to meet and pass on the curve."

In planning the I-80 span there was a controversy as to how high a clearance there should be...45, 55 or 68 feet above normal water. Henry Pfiester, retired Chief of Operations with the Corps of Engineers, Rock Island District, as well as a riverboat pilot, informed me, "Engineers just changed bridge height criteria as they saw fit. It had never been fixed. This I-80 Bridge established the modern precedence—60 feet above norm."

Because the bridge is so sleek and modern, it is difficult to imagine the rugged days of 1846 when "Buffalo Bill" Cody was born in the area. In his early boyhood he played along these shores just three miles upstream from where the bridge is located. No doubt, this is where he got his spirit of adventure, his desire to scout and hunt, and, from the many rivermen and immigrants, his interest in the West.

On a granite slab on the riverbank in LeClaire is a memorial to Colonel Wm. F. Cody from his friend and boyhood playmate, Joe Barnes, 1924. The plaque is dedicated to "Buffalo Bill"—the scout and guide, rider for the Pony Express, buffalo hunter, and Congressional Medal of Honor winner. Perhaps "William F. Cody Bridge" would be a good name for the I-80 Bridge.

---

**Use:**
Interstate 80 traffic

**Location:**
LeClaire, Iowa to Rapid City, Illinois

**Style:**
Continuous welded plate-girder

**Length:**
Channel span - 350 feet clear
                      370 feet total
Total length -    3,487 feet

**Width:**
4-lanes, 4-foot median, 58-foot total

**Clearance:**
60 feet MLW

**Date completed:**
September 1967

**Designer:**
Modjeski & Masters

**Bridge:**
#8206.8S080 in Iowa, 0810011 in Illinois

**Owners:**
Iowa & Illinois Departments of Transportation

**Unique Feat:**
Set precedence for 60-foot clearance above normal water

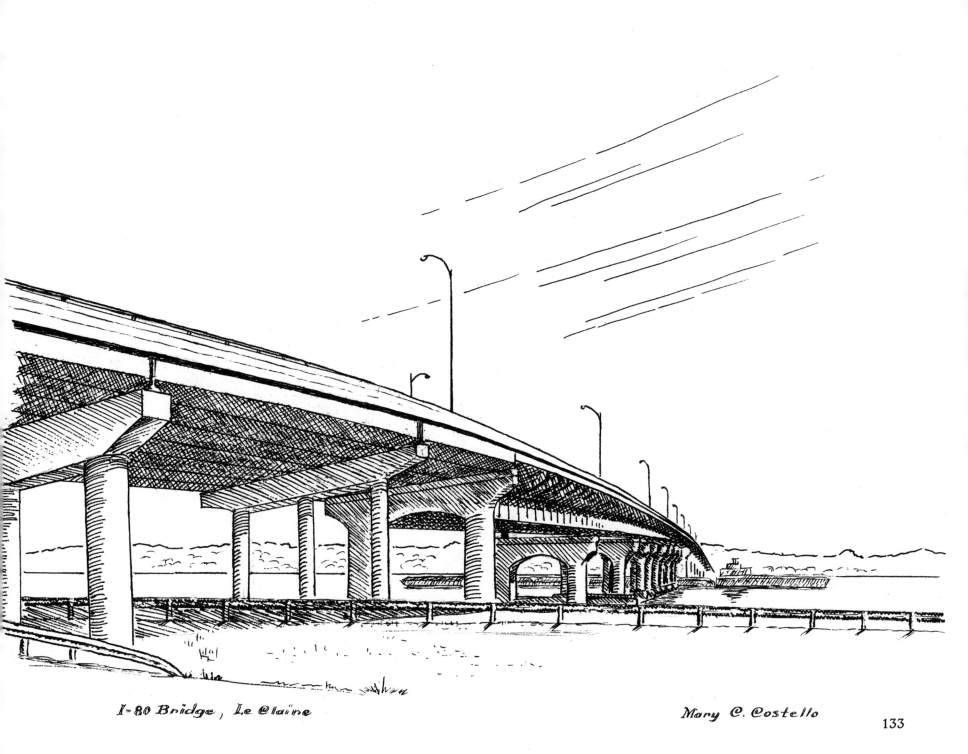

I=80 Bridge, Le Claire

Mary C. Costello

133

# C&NW Railroad Bridge, Main Channel, Clinton, Iowa

The Chicago and North Western Railroad Bridge spans the Mississippi River from Little Rock Island, Illinois, to the Iowa shore, crossing the state line in the center of the swing-span. This swing-span double-track railroad bridge at Clinton was constructed in 1909 by the Pennsylvania Steel Company. Each span is different. Starting at the east end there is a lattice flat-top, then a Parker camelback, a swingspan of Fink design and, finally, a short plate-girder span.

Standing on the attractive levee in downtown Clinton, I was enchanted by the blackness of the through-truss bridge off to my right, in contrast to the white riprap below me, the blue sky above with its soft white cirrus clouds, and the mixed greens of the trees seen through the bridge. As I sketched, a freight train crossed the bridge, and later when the swingspan opened, a barge went through with unusual cargo—large hollow cylinders of steel.

Interesting as this varied C&NW Bridge is in appearance, the story of its predecessor is much more so. Before any bridge existed in Clinton, up to 1860, freight and passengers were transported across the Mississippi River between Fulton, Illinois, and Clinton by the steamer "Commodore." When the Mississippi was frozen, loads were hauled across the ice by teams of horses. However, when the bridge from the Illinois shore to Little Rock Island (center of the river) was completed on 19 January 1860, the west channel crossing was handled by the steamer "Union" using ramps. Several loaded railroad cars could be simultaneously transferred this way, and since the current was swift between the island and mainland, ice rarely impeded the "Union's" passage.

By 1864 the Albany Bridge Company, employing mostly men from Clinton, started the main channel drawbridge. In 1865, the first train crossed. That was a big year for Clintonians, with the ending of the Civil War and the completion of total bridging of the Mississippi River to their town.

It was after the Main Channel Clinton Railroad Bridge's completion that Congress, realizing the need for controlling this great waterway, directed Brevet Major General G. K. Warren, (23 June 1866), to do a survey of all the Mississippi River bridges. The government also increased the mission of the Corps of Engineers to include bridge supervision.[8] In his book Warren described this first Main Channel Clinton Bridge as having three wooden spans of Howe truss in addition to the iron draw. His concluding suggestion proposed replacing the narrow drawspan, which had only 119 feet of horizontal clearance, with one that would allow 160 feet. (Today's 1909 swingspan has 177 feet of clearance.) The curve in the channel at the bridge's location, an eddy which affected the intensity and direction of the current, plus the narrow bridge opening, caused boat delays and accidents, especially during high winds and dark nights. A lawsuit in 1867, "Hurd versus the Burlington Railroad," the third litigation concerning bridge obstruction of the river, was settled in favor of bridging and ended all further bridge contention.[9]

For a long time after the building of the bridge, to prevent dangerous characters from entering the Iowa town, people were not permitted to walk across the bridge unless provided with a pass. However, when the sawmills hired people from the other side of the river, the rule became impractical.

"Is a railroad from the Atlantic to the Pacific Ocean practicable?" was the Lyons' 1855 Debating Club's subject. When a transcontinental railroad was completed in 1869, it would have been interesting to know those debaters' reactions.

Clinton's C&NW Bridge is still going strong today. One sees freight trains using the main channel bridge daily.

**Use:**
Chicago North Western Railroad

**Location:**
Clinton, Iowa to Little Rock Island

**Style:**
A through-truss swingspan, plus one camelback, one flattop span of riveted trusses and one small deck plate-girder span

**Length:**
Channel span - 177 feet clear
460 feet total
Total length - 890 feet

**Width:**
Two tracks

**Clearance:**
18 feet MLW

**Date completed:**
February 1909; replaced the original 1865 bridge

**Designer:**
Pennsylvania Steel Company to C&NW's specifications

**Bridge:**
#0 3/4

**Owner:**
Chicago and North Western Railroad

**Unique feats:**
The 1865 span was one of first fifteen bridges across the river; first drawspan turned by steam-power on the Mississippi; made a "post-route," July 1867

C & NW Railroad Bridge, Main Channel, Clinton      Mary C. Costello

# C&NW Railroad Bridge, Illinois Channel, Opposite Clinton

*S*tanding on Clinton Gateway Bridge's narrow sidewalk, I sketched the neighboring center-channel bridge of the Chicago and North Western Railroad, but felt a bounce for every truck that went over. It was like a carnival ride! The passing traffic was so close that the spiral sketchpad page I was working on wanted to blow away. If I had dropped anything, it would have gone 63 feet straight down into the river.

There are three different railroad bridges that cross the Mississippi opposite Clinton, Iowa. The first bridge position is over the main channel from the Iowa shore to the stratified limestone island called Little Rock Island in the middle of the river channel. The second bridge spans from the east side of Little Rock Island across what was formerly known as Willow Island,[10] and the main Illinois channel to the Illinois shoreline. A short distance inside the shore is the Mississippi backwater known as Sunfish Slough and the location of the third bridge.

The first bridge at Clinton was built by the C&NW Railroad over the Illinois channel—not the main channel as one might think—because the railroad was moving east to west. The first pile for the piers was driven in January and the last span was dropped on its bearings in December of the same year, 1859. The first train passed over the bridge 19 January 1860 from the Illinois shore to Little Rock Island and received a salute of twelve guns. In order to get to Clinton, however, from the end of the C&NW tracks on the island, one needed to cross the main channel of the Mississippi River by ferryboat. From 1860 until 1865 ramps with tracks were used to take trains to the ferry and across—several loaded cars at a time.

The original 1860 C&NW Railroad Bridge had seven spans of wooden trusses, each 200 feet long, (McCallum Patent Inflexible Arch design) supported by stone piers. However, by 1868 the wood had decayed, so the next year the bridge was entirely rebuilt using iron trusses. The first span near the Illinois shoreline remained the same length (200 feet), but the others were replaced by eight iron spans of 150 feet each. Here railroad officials did something that sounds bizarre. They hired four different bridge companies using different designs to build the trusses. This "spreading the work" no doubt sped the results. The first three spans were of the Post pattern truss, built by the American Bridge Company of Chicago; "the next two spans were built by the Detroit Bridge Company, Detroit, Michigan; the next two, by the Phoenixville Bridge Company, of Phoenixville, Pennsylvania; the next two, by Keystone Bridge Company of Pittsburgh, Pennsylvania. The last six were of the Pratt truss pattern." (Warren 1878, 95)

Today's 1909 bridge has ten spans. The first one, a small plate-girder 74 feet in length, and the next, the longest or channel span, (formerly used as the "raft" span), is a fixed 205-foot Parker truss design. The remaining eight spans are flattop and shorter both in height and length (146 feet). The first is 30 feet shorter than the rest. All eight truss spans are of the Lattice truss design; most are hidden by trees.

A C&NW train crossed the bridge as I watched. Then a young couple, having picnicked on an island below and behind me, got into their outboard-motor boat and went under both the Gateway and C&NW Bridges. A flock of birds flew overhead, making a prolonged twiti-i-i-i-i-i-i sound, but because of the strong sunlight I couldn't see them. Nature and humans alike made sketching at Clinton's Illinois Channel Railroad Bridge interesting.

**Use:**
Chicago North Western Railroad

**Location:**
Between the Illinois shoreline and Little Rock Island

**Style:**
Ten spans—one plate-girder, one humpback truss, and eight flattop trusses

**Length:**
Channel span - 185 feet clear
               205 feet total
Total length -    1437 feet

**Width:**
Two tracks

**Clearance:**
18 feet MLW

**Date completed:**
February 1909; replaced the 1869 iron bridge and original 1860 wooden bridge

**Designer:**
Wisconsin Bridge & Iron Company to C&NW's specifications

**Bridge:**
#0 1/2 East Channel

**Owner:**
Chicago North Western Railroad

**Unique feat:**
The 1869 bridge was one of the first fifteen spans across the Mississippi

Chicago & North Western Railroad Bridge, Back Channel, Clinton          Mary C. Costello

# Sunfish Slough C&NW Railroad Bridge, Rural Illinois

*B*ridge Number 0 1/4, as the Chicago and North Western Transportation Company identifies the Sunfish Slough Railroad Bridge, spans the back channel of the Mississippi River, not far inside the Illinois shoreline. It is the last of three distinct railroad bridges between rural Illinois and Clinton, Iowa. In order to reach the Sunfish Slough Bridge, I drove across Clinton's Gateway and Slough Bridges. Since it was late September, I saw only the stubble of corn stalks in fields close by, a handful of neat middle-class homes, and scores of leafless willow trees. I parked a short distance from the water on barren ground beside the slightly raised railroad tracks. As I looked at the plate-girder bridge from the Sunfish Slough bank, I was surprised at its length. Of the twelve piers only three were in water at the time (probably because the water was low at the end of three years of drought). Each pier consists of two concrete cylinders approximately three feet in diameter joined by a steel band of X's.

As I started walking across the bridge on the board walk to the right, I heard a not-so-distant train whistle and the sound of an approaching train. I left the tracks and watched from the side as two yellow and black C&NW diesels pulled a long freight across the bridge at what seemed to me great speed (actually just 30 miles per hour, I was informed later). The train was on the far track, so I needn't have moved. The engineer waved.

In 1878 Brevet Major G. K. Warren mentioned that what is today's Sunfish Slough Bridge was "trestling" attached to the first railroad bridge. Warren surveyed the Clinton span in 1866, when this 1390-foot-long wooden trestle was the approach to the seven-span truss bridge that crossed the Illinois channel. In 1877-78, because of its deteriorated condition, this backwater pile-way approach was rebuilt.

Today's bridge, constructed in 1909, is composed of a set of eleven deck plate-girder spans each 50 feet long. Even workers with whom I spoke, who travel the bridges daily, had not realized that the slough bridge is a distinctly separate span. The Sunfish Slough Railroad Bridge is deceptive because the tracks are level with those of the land approaching it, and there is no superstructure overhead—only an angled-out steel railing on the sides. It is a shame that the beauty of the Sunfish Slough Bridge's cylindrical piers, especially when seen in the fall sunlight, is lost to those that travel over them.

---

**Use:**
Chicago Northwestern Railroad

**Location:**
Rural Illinois over Sunfish Slough opposite Clinton, Iowa

**Style:**
11-span plate-girder bridge

**Length:**
Channel span - 50 feet total
Total length - 550 feet*

**Width:**
Two tracks

**Clearance:**
12 feet MLW

**Date completed:**
February 1909; original timber trestle 1860; rebuilt in 1877-78

**Designer:**
Wisconsin Bridge & Iron Company to C&NW's specifications

**Bridge:**
#0 1/4

**Owner:**
Chicago and North Western Railroad

---

* Approaches not included

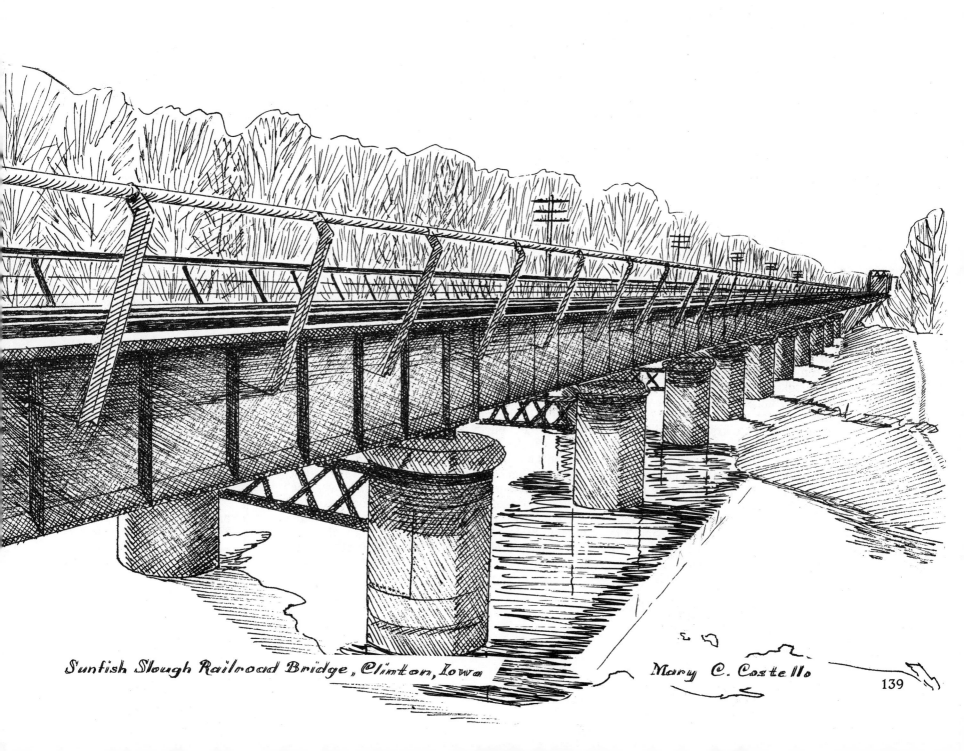

*Sunfish Slough Railroad Bridge, Clinton, Iowa*

Mary C. Costello

139

The Clinton "Gateway" Bridge is one of three suspension bridges (really four, since Bettendorf's is a twin) on the 2552-mile-long Mississippi. Older and fancier than its Quad-City counterparts, the Clinton Bridge was designed by the same consulting firm, Modjeski and Masters, in 1956.

For the first time I sat while I sketched. I was on the grassy levee, with park benches and a runners' track at my feet. On the river side of the levee, white rock lent a clean fresh look and texture, at the same time preventing ground erosion. It was 6:00 p.m., and the riverfront was serene, with cotton clouds in a blue sky. There was an 82-degree temperature, a gentle river breeze and peaceful solitude, because most people were home at supper. Only a few motorboats were out. A train crossed on the railroad bridge and a barge with an ominous-looking load floated down the river. I was enamored with the spot.

In front, to my right, was the Gateway Bridge with its two green-colored towers and huge cables draped between, looking deceivingly delicate. The important road-supporting suspenders or hangers (1 5/8-inch galvanized wire rope) coming from the cables were almost invisible from this distance. However, I counted 25 of these "fine threads" that support the deck before they stop abruptly at the towers. There is a deep stiffening truss between the towers—designed to prevent twisting during severe storms. It surprised me to find that on both ends, from the outside of the towers to the end of the long approaches, the bridge is really a girder span. The cables continue from the high tower down to the reinforced concrete anchorages but without hangers, unlike the traditional suspension bridge. The Clinton Gateway is called an "unloaded backstay." Only the central span is carried on the main cables.

Even from a distance the slender towers looked ornate. Instead of simple angular tubes, the tower columns have built-up layers of steel, each layer smaller than the previous one. The pinnacle is like a candle holder supporting aerial beacons which are no longer maintained. Up here the tower is six feet narrower than at the bottom and is connected with a band of two triangles. A single "X" that appears to be stretched vertically braces the tall tower columns. Below the deck is another flattened "X". The concrete base of the bridge towers extends high out of the water.

The piers of the western approach of the "Gateway" Bridge, set well back on shore, are double concrete columns connected top and bottom forming a slightly pointed opening. The towers of the suspension bridge are in the main river channel; but the Gateway's long girder crosses Little Rock Island (formerly called Willow Island) and the Illinois channel in 13 additional spans. In this eastern channel the piers are entirely different— deep concrete bases and two square "chimneys" that become shorter as the bridge nears the bank.

For the first 35 years of Clinton's history people had no bridges and crossed the river by ferry in the summer. In the winter, ice made the best roads for the horse and buggy and pedestrian. It wasn't until 1892 that the first "wagon bridge" was built from Clinton's business district, tall enough for the tallest riverboat smokestacks to go under. That first highway bridge crossed at a diagonal over the railroad bridge. There was also another bridge operating two miles to the north, but in 1954 the Clinton Bridge Commission bought both of these independent bridges and removed the southern one to make way for the Gateway Suspension Bridge.

**Use:**
Local traffic & U.S.30

**Location:**
Between Clinton, Iowa, and rural Illinois

**Style:**
A combination of "unloaded backstay" suspension and a long girder Illinois approach

**Length:**
Channel span - 568 feet clear
- 644 feet total
Total length - 5,216 feet

**Width:**
2 lanes, each 12 feet, plus 10 and 6-foot shoulders; 40 feet total with no sidewalk

**Clearance:**
63 feet MLW

**Date completed:**
October 1999 major renovations including a new concrete deck; built June 1956;1892 "Clinton Highway Bridge," continuous steel cantilever truss and 9 other through-trusses that jogged over the railroad bridge; originally a ferry crossed

**Designer:**
Modjeski & Masters

**Toll:**
20 cents; removed in 1978

**Bridge:**
#2332.4S030 in Iowa, 0986003 in Illinois

**Owners:**
Iowa and Illinois Departments of Transportation

Gateway Bridge, Clinton, Iowa

Mary C. Costello

141

# Sunfish Slough Highway Bridge, Rural Illinois Opposite Clinton

*S*unfish Slough is a backwater of the Mississippi located close to Clinton Gateway Bridge's long-gone toll-plaza. The highway bridge that crosses this backwater arm is a "440-foot continuous wide-flange beam bridge" according to Mahmoud Etemadi from the Illinois DOT in Dixon, Illinois, who maintains the bridge.

Standing on the Union Pacific Railroad Bridge which is over the same body of water (the Sunfish Slough), I could see the highway span about 200 feet away. Since it was summer, the fully-leafed trees blocked much of the bridge and years of growth had filled in the foreground as well.

A dear friend, Suzi, had given me a ride to Clinton and helped me locate a view of the Sunfish Slough Highway Bridge. We drove around for an hour to where train tracks blocked the road, as well as up an embankment overlooking a park, house and the slough. We drove on top of the narrow slough embankment to its end and then had to backup for what seemed a city block. All of this with no result. Where can I find a view of this slough bridge? A lifetime-resident of the area, who lived nearby, helped us by leading the way through a person's yard and along the train tracks to the spot on the railroad bridge to finally see the bridge and take pictures. When returning to the car, I let our guide look at my first volume and the account of the former Sunfish Slough Bridge. Humorously he read aloud how I had stated from where I had drawn and photographed that span. We could have saved ourselves much time and frustration by simply reading my own story of sixteen years ago. We had a good laugh.

This new backwater bridge has half (6) the number of the previous spans and heavier piers, tubular on the ends but solidly connected in the middle with a concrete wall. Like the renovated main span this bridge has two twelve-foot lanes with a ten-foot shoulder on the right and six-foot one on the left of the bridge. The walk has been eliminated so that bikers and joggers must go to the North Bridge to cross.

**Use:**
Highway 30, Illinois approach to the Gateway Bridge

**Location:**
In Illinois east of the former toll-plaza for Clinton's Gateway Bridge

**Style:**
6-span steel girder with a concrete deck

**Length:**
Main span - 85 feet
Total length - 440 feet without approach

**Width:**
2 lanes and 2 shoulders, 40 feet total

**Clearance:**
12.4 feet MLW

**Date completed:**
October 1999; replaced 1956 girder span; original was an 1892 timber trestle

**Designer:**
Steinman Consultants, Chicago

**Bridge:**
#0980106

**Owners:**
Illinois Department of Transportation

Sunfish Slough Highway Bridge, Clinton, Iowa

Mary C. Costello

143

# (Lyons/Fulton) North Bridge, Clinton, Iowa, SR 136

*F*or years I have shown my fifth-grade art classes the aerial view of the pier line-up for the North Clinton Bridge. This substructure portion was nearing completion in the 1971 newspaper photo. It is amazing what this part of the bridge tells about the finished span. Acting like Sherlock Holmes, one can deduct, besides the obvious number of piers and lengths of spans, the approximate width and clearance of the bridge, the location of the main span, and the deepest part of the river along the line of the bridge. Someone asked me, "How can you make these deductions?" "It is simple, my dear Watson." The width of the widest pier is usually the bridge width when completed, though roads are sometimes bracketed out, making the deck wider. The bridge clearance is the height of the main pier above normal pool water level, plus, at times, a foot or more for cushions or "feet" that rest on the piers. The main span is located where the widest spaced piers are situated. This channel span is also where the river is the deepest.

When I saw the North Bridge for the first time, I was disappointed—not because of the structure but rather because of its setting. I was on the ground behind the levee, where I could see none of the Mississippi. The sky was spectacular with clouds and their shadows, but in the area where the bridge is located there were no big trees, buildings or notable variations in terrain. In other words, the North Clinton Bridge just emerged out of nowhere. I was on a street with some houses, but there were only fields between me and the bridge.

Traveling over the green Pratt truss bridge I found to be the saving grace. The low overhead arch of steel in the through-truss lent a rhythm and feeling of strength to an otherwise cold bridge structure. This is the touch of the artist's pen, so to speak. A walk provided on one side only was protected by an inner and outer silver pipe railing.

The bridge located here has had a number of names. The 1891 bridge was called the "Lyons-Fulton Bridge," "Lincoln Highway Bridge,"[11] or "US 30." "North Bridge" is the popular title of the span today, now that Lyons has been incorporated into Clinton. However, the official name for the present 3-span cantilever is the "Mark Morris Memorial Bridge." Mark Morris was chairman of the Bridge Commission from 1944 until his death in 1972 and instrumental in seeing that the bridge was built.

Interesting to me was the fact that my cousin by marriage was "Project Manager" for the construction company for this 1974 North Bridge, no doubt the reason I saved the pier photo. My cousin's name is a homonym with the former town at the Iowa end of the bridge, but is spelled "Leins."

The first bridge, the previous 1891 4-span camelback truss bridge, like today's span located two miles north of Clinton's business district, had a sharp right angle at the point where the bridge reached the Iowa shore. This 90-degree angle must have been difficult to manage in a car in the 1970's, before the Lyons-Fulton Bridge was torn down. In the late 1800's, of course, with autos not yet on the scene and not so speedy when they did appear, the sharp turn was not a problem.

**Use:**
Local traffic & Iowa SR 136

**Location:**
Between North Clinton, Iowa and Fulton, Illinois

**Style:**
3-span through cantilever truss

**Length:**
Channel span - 450 feet clear
500 feet total
Total length - 3011 feet

**Width:**
2 lanes plus a 3-foot sidewalk, 34 feet total

**Clearance:**
65 feet MLW

**Date completed:**
January 1975 opened; predecessor was the original 1891 truss span

**Designer:**
Modjeski & Masters

**Bridge:**
#2300.0Sl36 in Iowa, 0989908 in Illinois

**Owners:**
Iowa and Illinois Departments of Transportation

*North Bridge, Clinton, Iowa*

*Mary C. Costello*

# Sabula Railroad Bridge, Iowa

*I*t was July in Sabula, Iowa. Along the riverbank I watched a log move swiftly in the Mississippi River current. Three motor boats roared past and left a wake that struck the bank with repeated swashes. The Great River was demonstrating its power.

The Soo Lines Railroad Bridge looked black under the overcast sky when I started my sketch. However, I could pick out the Pratt truss design in the four flat-top spans and one camelback. The closed swingspan had a variation, but before I took a picture of it, the span opened to allow the "Mississippi Belle II" to pass. The bridge-tender situated in the center of the draw must have received radio communication from the Belle II captain, because the span was ready and waiting for some time before the four-tiered excursion boat appeared.

I realized that there was something I liked about the Sabula turnspan but it wasn't until later, after analyzing my photos and the Corps of Engineer's sketch, that I knew why it was unusual. The supports on the four corners of the Warren swingspan's center section are trussed and are connected with X's both high and low, giving a fine, light-weight appearance. Even the tender's house at deck level doesn't interfere with this effect.

Just after the operator closed the bridge, a yellow and black railroad trouble-car crossed the tracks, but I saw no train. Built for the Chicago, Milwaukee, St. Paul and Pacific Railroad in 1881, the bridge now belongs to the Soo Line.

The sun appeared before I left and brightened the grass and trees in the riverside park where I stood. It also revealed that the bridge which had seemed so black was really quite rusty.

**Use:**
Soo Line Railroad

**Location:**
South of highway bridge between Sabula and Savanna, Illinois.

**Style:**
Swingspan plus five through-truss spans

**Length:**
Channel span - 154 feet clear
182 feet total*
Total length - 1,910 feet

**Width:**
One track

**Clearance:**
18 feet MLW

**Date completed:**
1881, modified in 1906

**Designer:**
American Bridge Company

**Bridge:**
# Z496

**Owner:**
Soo Railroad Lines

*Half estimated swingspan length

Railroad Bridge, Sabula, Iowa                    Mary C. Costello

# "Running Slough" Highway Bridge, Sabula, Iowa, US 52

*A*s soon as I arrived in Sabula, I found the "Running Slough" Bridge in an area with lovely small homes and very friendly people. Iola Roenfeldt and her friend were having a yard sale that I couldn't resist. Her property bordered the river and the small, back-channel bridge.

We helped each other. I bought a few items and Iola gave me some information. She said that her husband had built the dock and the steps down to it. Luckily the riverbank is high, so they have no worry about floods. She related, "Sometimes in the summer, boys jump from the top of the bridge here. It is dangerous, so we try to stop them."

I got busy with my sketch. It was a combination bridge with a single through-truss span and deck-girders. Over the portal on the west end was a sign painted yellow that said, "Low Clearance 13 feet 9 inches." Immediately I thought that there must be many a truck that has gotten this far and had to turn around and look for another crossing, until I was told that the maximum truck height is 13 feet 6 inches.

The silver Pratt truss span was built during President Franklin Delano Roosevelt's term of office. It has medium-blue colored plate-girders and a 3-foot high concrete parapet beside the deck. The piers for this Mississippi River backwater bridge are round columns of riveted metal filled with cast-in-place concrete. Kevin Mahoney, Iowa DOT resident maintenance engineer, said that the metal covering is to help break up the ice. These individual pier cylinders are joined together with concrete slabs in different ways, depending on the need for strength and the size of the pier—either totally, in the middle, or at the top.

John Risch, Iowa DOT's Bridge Maintenance Supervisor at Ames, now retired, told me that in the 1952 flood a 40 or 50-foot hole developed from a whirlpool in the riverbed. "We were afraid we would lose the bridge," he stated. In the flood of '93 the bridge was closed for two weeks out of concern for scour undermining and the water level being at the bottom chord. Though engineers found the deep scour hole still exists, no problem developed.

While I drew, unbeknown to me, Iola called the main channel bridge toll-taker to ask if he knew of a spot from which I could sketch the main bridge. He answered, "Send her right out!" What a thoughtful thing for her to do! So I finished the back channel span and headed across the long causeway to the main channel Savanna/Sabula Bridge.

**Use:**
Highway 52 back channel

**Location:**
At the end of Broad Street in Sabula

**Style:**
Single span through-truss with deck plate-girder approaches

**Length:**
Main span - 121 feet
Total length - 354 feet

**Width:**
2 lanes, no walk

**Clearance:**
11 feet 8 inches MLW

**Date completed:**
1932, August 1933 dedicated

**Designer:**
G. A. Maney, Minneapolis

**Bridge:**
#4902.0S052 in Iowa

**Owner:**
Iowa DOT

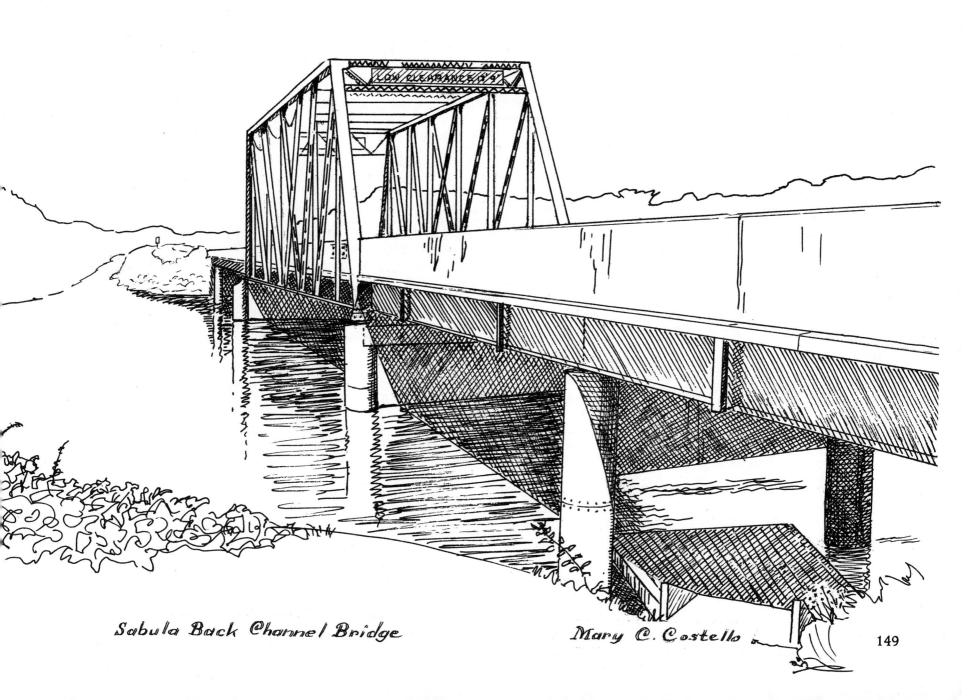

*Sabula Back Channel Bridge*                    Mary C. Costello

149

# Sabula/Savanna Highway Bridge, US 52

*R*eaching the Sabula Bridge tollhouse at the end of the two-mile rock-filled causeway,[12] I parked on the wide paved area to the right. The toll-takers were expecting me. "Over there," was one's short direction. The spot he pointed to was on the edge of the plaza, a little ahead and to the right. Not much of the bridge was visible, but there was no choice of views on this paved way high above island and slough. From here I saw sixteen approach spans and a big dip in the roadway before the main bridge began. The Sabula/Savanna Bridge looked tall and airy, almost ethereal, with the sun and cloud-shadows playing on it.

I found later that US 52 is a Pratt truss bridge. The truss pattern changes, however, at the kingposts to a K-truss. The center of each kingpost is a large diamond with diminishing half diamonds on either side. Although mostly cantilever, the bridge has an extra simple through-truss and continuous I-beam (girder) spans on the western end.

The piers are composed of two round concrete columns. Under the main channel bridge they are tall, heavy supports connected at the top, middle and bottom. The thinner upper connections are arched underneath but the lowest one acts as a pier base and encases the cylinders. The piers under the Iowa approach are more slender columns and have only a top connection visible, with those piers stouter in key places.

When I showed the busy toll-men my sketch, they seemed impressed and invited me inside to look at an article that hung on the wall of the small tollbooth. I had to stand on a box to read the story of the new bridge from the 1932 end-of-the-year newspaper. It was yellowed and brittle, with a photo of the bridge—a real treasure.

Because the Sabula/Savanna Bridge has no sidewalks, bikers were advised to walk their bikes on their Tour of the Mississippi River Valley (summer 1988). "Since it has a metal grid roadway, they might fall," explained Kevin Mahoney, DOT maintenance engineer. "The railings are built for cars, not bikes, and they might end up in the river."

The silver chords and trusses of the Sabula/Savanna Bridge gleamed in the sun. Though the bridge has two narrow lanes, on my sketchpad I had jotted, "a feeling of airiness...frail... lacy...refined and well-kept." The "lacy" description referred to the effect of light through the old trusses. These were long angle-irons laced together with steel and used throughout the bridge for the diagonal and vertical trusses as well as overhead crossed-struts. The only solid beams on the structure are the top chords. All of these steel parts are kept well painted, thanks to the Illinois DOT now in charge of the Sabula/Savanna Bridge maintenance.

When I reached the Illinois approach, the low concrete wall curved out as if to give a gracious invitation to those who enter or exit the bridge. The wall has wide posts with 17 arched "windows" in each section for light and shadow.

Being in the lane of traffic as I recrossed the Sabula/Savanna Bridge, I paid the 60-cent toll and just said goodbye to those friendly bridge people on my way to the next Mississippi River crossing.

**Use:**
Local and US 52 traffic

**Location:**
South of Dubuque between Savanna, Illinois and Sabula, Iowa

**Style:**
3-span cantilever through-truss plus a simple through-truss span; 17-steel beams span Iowa approach and 3 concrete girders the Illinois approach

**Length:**
Channel span - 508 feet clear
                        520 feet total
Total length -   2481 feet

**Width:**
2 lanes, no walk, 21 feet total

**Clearance:**
64 feet MLW

**Date completed:**
31 December 1932; formally dedicated 12 October 1933; deck replaced 1986

**Designer:**
G. A. Maney, Minneapolis

**Toll:**
60 cents, removed July 1987

**Bridge:**
#4900.0S052 in Iowa, 0086000 in Illinois

**Owners:**
Iowa and Illinois Departments of Transportation since 1972; previously owned by Sabula/Savanna Bridge Company

Savanna - Sabula Highway Bridge

Mary C. Costello

151

# Julien Dubuque Bridge, US 61 & 20, Dubuque, Iowa

*F*or the first time I had company on my sketching trips. My brother and his wife allowed me to stay with them and then kindly drove me to the Julien Dubuque Bridge on a bright July morning. Being young of spirit at 72, Joe brought along a sling shot for some pebble shooting into the Mississippi, while I drew from atop a 5-foot-high protective cover near the river.

Historically there has been a bridge close to this spot since 1887. The original span was called the "High Wagon Bridge," a descriptive title often used because the bridge was lofty enough for steamboats and their tall smokestacks to go under. Old photos show that the Wagon Bridge was next to the old railroad bridge, appearing very frail in contrast. Smoke from steam engines on the railroad bridge rose to the High Bridge, making driving across it less than pleasant. When the new span was complete in 1943, the old Wagon Bridge was demolished.

The Julien Dubuque Bridge is a tied arch. "In this 'hybrid form,' the arch is flatter than in a 'true' arch, so the drama of the arch is often diminished." (Plowden 1974, 260) In the Dubuque Bridge the tied arch is used in a continuous truss. Being continuous (with the deepest trusses over the intermediate supports), it is stronger than if it were three separate truss spans. Continuous truss bridges were not used much until the turn of the century because engineers lacked the mathematics to calculate the loads and stresses, according to D.B.Steinman, author and engineer. In 1917, the Sciotoville, Ohio, railroad bridge established the continuous truss as an important American bridge design with two such spans 775 feet each. In 1943, the Julien Dubuque Bridge was built and set a record for continuous truss main-span length at 845 feet—the fourth longest[13] in the United States and eighth in the world. (Colliers 1992, 545)

Judged "The Most Beautiful Bridge of 1943" by the American Institute of Steel Construction, the US 20 Bridge between Dubuque, Iowa, and East Dubuque, Illinois, has a tied arch center span that is refined and elegant appearing. Ned Ashton, the Julien Dubuque Bridge designer, when speaking to the Tri-Cities Civil Engineers in 1944, said, "The effect of the arch tie is similar to that of having another pier in the middle of the long 845-foot span...The Warren truss is adopted because this type has fewer main members, fewer main joints, and therefore the smallest percentage of details as compared with any other type truss. Ashton always had aesthetics and economy in mind with his designs. The end truss spans were erected simultaneously on both sides of the river with falsework. However, the bridge was cantilevered out from the intermediate piers until the two sides met in the middle. The approach spans are continuous variable-depth girders.

The bridge is named the Julien Dubuque after the French fur trader who received permission in 1788 from the Fox Indians to mine the lead in the area around present-day Dubuque. His friendship was so great with the Indians that when he was buried in 1810, his funeral was equal to that of an Indian chief. His huge limestone marker overlooks the Mississippi River today. First remembered in 1832, when the young lead-mining and saw-milling village was named after him, Julien Dubuque was honored by the citizens a second time in 1943 when they named this attractive bridge in his memory.

**Use:**
Local and US 20 traffic

**Location:**
Between Dubuque, Iowa and East Dubuque, Illinois

**Style:**
3-span continuous tied-arch truss with girder approaches

**Length:**
Channel span - 803 feet clear
845 feet total
Total length - 5,760 feet

**Width:**
2 lanes, 28-foot road plus 4.5-foot walk bracketed on south side

**Clearance:**
65 feet MLW

**Date completed:**
August 1943; replaced the 1887 High Wagon Bridge; new deck and major rehabilitation 1991.

**Designer:**
Ned Ashton, chief designer with Howard Needles Tammen & Bergendoff

**Toll:**
From the opening until 26 December 1954

**Bridge:**
#3120.1S020 in Iowa, 0430001 in Illinois

**Owners:**
Iowa and Illinois Departments of Transportation

**Unique feats:**
American Steel Award For Beauty in 1943; fourth longest continuous truss bridge in U.S. and eighth in the world

Julien Dubuque Bridge

Mary C. Costello

153

# Chicago, Central & Pacific Railroad Bridge, Dubuque, Iowa

*D*uring a telephone interview Richard Roth, bridge tender for Dubuque's CC&P Railroad Bridge, reported:

In 1982, an Illinois Central freight train lost some wheels and jumped the track while it was crossing the bridge. Neither the engineer nor the crew members knew what had happened, but I could see from my office on the bridge. By radio I immediately told the engineer, who stopped the train on the bridge. It was ten cars from the caboose and could have piled up or gone off the bridge. The 'guard rail', the narrow track inside the main track, helped to give stability to the car when it jumped. That inner rail has helped more than once.

The railroad bridge in Dubuque was part of the Illinois Central Railroad until 1985, when it was sold to the Chicago, Central and Pacific. It is the second swingspan bridge on the Mississippi River that has a tunnel near its entrance. I made a special trip to Dubuque to see the tunnel up close and to accept an invitation onto the swingspan. For that experience I asked my brother from Dubuque to come along.

Just getting to the bridge was a problem. With permits from the Dubuque Freight Depot in hand, we drove across the Julien Dubuque Bridge to East Dubuque, Illinois. Here we consulted the Burlington Northern Dispatcher to be sure no trains were due on the "cross-track" we'd be using to get to the bridge. "There are no trains for half an hour, but then there will be three close together," he informed us. Also from the dispatcher's office we telephoned the bridge operator to say we were on our way.

While the bridge tender closed the swingspan, my brother Joe parked the car, and we walked the BN track for a block. Taconite balls[14] between the ties rolled when I stepped on them. We arrived at the spot where the tunnel was on our right and the bridge on our left. Between the two were 150 feet of CC&P track crossing over the BN rails. It was a dangerous and busy area. From the end of the first bridge span we could see Mr. Roth in the middle of the next span as he waved, indicating it was safe to come out. We walked on an 8-inch-wide board beside the single track discussing what we would do if a train came; there were no guard railings. Perhaps the heavy trusses on the side of the bridge would be a good retreat support.

Mr. Roth's office was small and full. There was a wooden bench on which we sat, a large desk covered with radio, receivers, other communication equipment, and paper work, a rack of water samples, a refrigerator, a closet, and four long levers on the floor. Roth told us that the latter control the bridge—its turning, the brake, the control panel above, and a latch for securing the bridge when it is windy.

Roth opened the bridge for "Tigre," a tug, and later for the "Spirit of Dubuque." He communicated by radio with the bigger boat; the smaller one blew her horn for the bridge to open. When the bridge closed, the operator walked to the end of the turnspan to see that it lined up properly for the train that was coming. Train #8063, a Chicago, Central & Pacific diesel pulling freight, came out of the tunnel and onto the bridge, going 10 mph. The train with its eighty-four cars shook the closet as it passed Roth's office.

The operator explained that a 30-horsepower motor supplies the energy to turn the 495-ton drawspan. It rotates on 40 cast-iron rollers underneath, each weighing 500 pounds. A 20-mph wind could blow the swingspan, it is so perfectly balanced.

On our way back to the car, Joe and I stopped to look at the huge railroad tunnel opening—18 feet high, 22 feet wide and 851 feet long—built into a limestone cliff. We were impressed!

**Use:**
Chicago, Central & Pacific Railroad

**Location:**
Between Dubuque, Iowa and East Dubuque, Illinois

**Style:**
A swingspan bridge with five humpback truss spans

**Length:**
Channel span - 146 feet clear
                      360 feet total
Total length -    1260 feet

**Width:**
Single track

**Clearance:**
19 feet MLW

**Date completed:**
1899; original bridge 1868

**Designer:**
Keystone Bridge Company

**Bridge:**
#182 West

**Owner:**
Chicago, Central & Pacific Railroad

**Unique feat:**
Location of one of the first fifteen bridges on the Mississippi

Dubuque  Railroad  Bridge                    Mary C. Costello

# 16th Street Bridge, Dubuque, Iowa

*O*ver the back channel of the Mississippi River, the 16th Street or "Old Peosta Channel Bridge" stands only five spans long with all four piers in the water. Painted the same color as the main channel Iowa-Wisconsin Bridge, the "Old Peosta" was the only approach from Iowa until the new span was completed (see Bridge #74). The steel girder, called a composite rolled beam, is designed to match the mother-bridge but is narrower.

The piers of the "Old Peosta Channel Bridge" are different from those of the main channel span. Here they are composed of two concrete cylinders encased at the top with a wide, round-ended band.

The two-lane roadway of the 16th Street Bridge has a pedestrian walkway on the south side only. The outside concrete parapet has an additional chain link fence for the walker's protection, and inside there is a low concrete wall acting as a barricade against cars.

There was a little breeze as I studied this Dubuque bridge. It ruffled the water, made reflections fuzzy, and caused the daisies along the grassy embankment to nod in unison.

**Use:**
Access to the marina and other island-park facilities as well as the Iowa-Wisconsin Bridge

**Location:**
16th Street to Chaplain Schmitt Memorial Island, Dubuque, Iowa; crosses the Peosta Channel

**Style:**
5-span composite rolled beam

**Length:**
Main span - 70 feet
Total length - 340 feet

**Width:**
2 lanes plus a sidewalk

**Clearance:**
23 feet MLW

**Date completed:**
1982

**Designer:**
Sverdrup and Parcel and Associates

**Bridge:**
#3190.8S06 in Iowa

**Owner:**
Iowa Department of Transportation

Peosta Channel Bridge, Dubuque

Mary C. Costello

*T*he second phase of the Iowa/Wisconsin Bridge at Dubuque is this span which connects Dubuque to the US 61 Bridge, replacing the smaller Peosta Channel, or 16th Street Bridge, as the main approach.

The new bridge extends 4,023 feet over the Peosta Slough, a part of the Mississippi that is only 700 feet wide. However, most of the long elevated structure is over city streets and industrial property. Only 4 of the 20 spans cross water.

Alfred Benesch & Company designed the four-lane steel girder bridge with eight composite plate-girders and 20 spans ranging from 170 to 260 feet in length. On land the bridge is supported by three-column piers topped with cantilever cap beams. The columns are not connected at the bottom, so each column has an H-pile footing. In the water the piers have triple columns also connected at the top, but at the bottom a solid wall of concrete binds them.

Construction of the bridge was delayed for one year (1987) while the solution to the problem of lead from a nearby foundry was found. As a solution the bridge was shortened 77 feet and a clay embankment built to capsulate the lead contaminate where it will hopefully remain forever. The anticipated danger was that when putting in the piers, lead would be pushed down and pollute the underground water.

The island around which the Peosta Slough flows and over which the new bridge crosses was formerly called "City Island," a name given it when it was a city dump. It was renamed "Chaplain Schmitt Memorial Island" on the 25 March 1969 in honor of Father Aloysius Schmitt, a priest who taught at Loras College before becoming a naval chaplain. He was killed at Pearl Harbor along with 2,335 other servicemen, 1,177 of them aboard the "USS Arizona." Today, Schmitt Memorial Island is the location of the marina, a recreation center with baseball diamonds, soccer fields, and a children's park as well as the track and kennels for Dubuque's successful venture into dog racing.

The bottomland area that the new bridge crosses often floods in the spring so that it becomes one with the main body of the Mighty Mississippi. The river width swells from 2000 to 4000 feet during flood season. These are the times when this new bridge will be appreciated, for the spectacular view of the area as well as for the safety it provides.

**Use:**
Approach to the Iowa-Wisconsin US 61 Bridge and access to Chaplain Schmitt Memorial Island

**Location:**
Over the Peosta Channel Slough and industrial area in Dubuque, Iowa to main channel bridge

**Style:**
20-span steel composite plate-girder; split bridge

**Length:**
Main span -    258 feet
Total length -    4,023 feet

**Width:**
4 lanes

**Clearance**
40 feet MLW

**Date completed:**
Late summer or fall 1991

**Designer:**
Alfred Benesch & Company, Chicago

**Bridge:**
#3190.2S061

**Owner:**
Iowa Department of Transportation

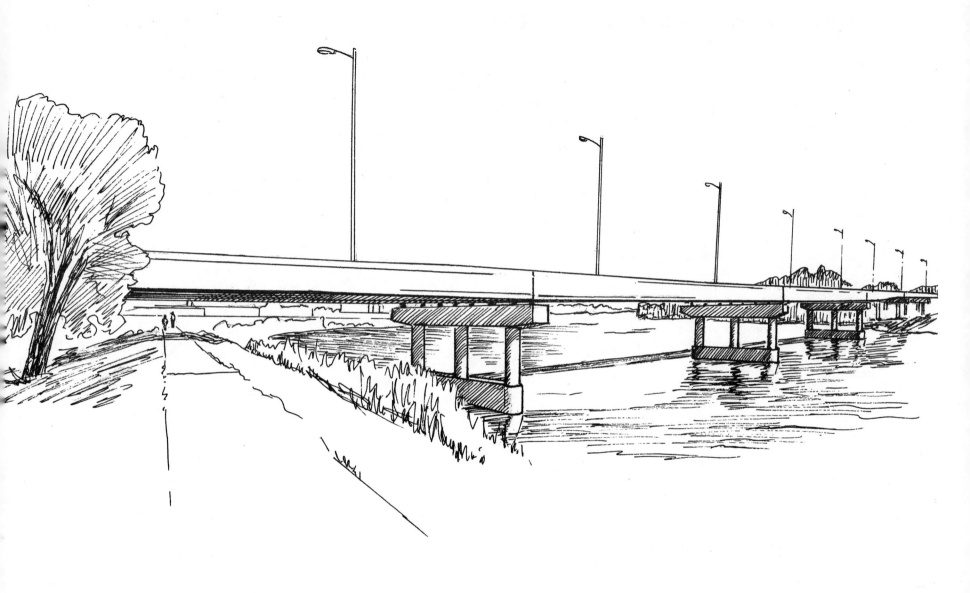

*Iowa-Wisconsin Approach Bridge*

*Mary C. Costello*

159

# Iowa/Wisconsin Bridge at Dubuque, Iowa, US 61

*C*hanging times means changing bridge styles. Dubuque's move from the rigid, narrow, multi-triangular truss bridge of 1902 to the wider, flowing, simple arch bridge of 1982 is indicative of the times. When the former span, the Eagle Point Bridge, was built, the American lifestyle was well-defined and family-oriented. By contrast, the Iowa/Wisconsin Bridge reflects the more open, casual life-style we have today. This newer Dubuque Bridge is a single tied-arch bridge, 670 feet long, with a continuous plate-girder carrying the rest of the 2,281 feet of the bridge.

The new green structure, the second largest tied-arch bridge on the Mississippi, (the longest being Jefferson Barracks at 910 feet), goes from Dubuque's City Park to the high cliffs of Wisconsin. Here the hills are partially sheared to make room for the bridge road. From the ground, the bridge does not appear to have a steep grade until it nears Wisconsin, where it has a 4% rise.

There are two kinds of piers plainly visible under the bridge, but it is the tied-arch that deserves our attention. The steel arch is braced overhead with wide-based isosceles triangles rising from both ends of the rib arch, one on top of the other—geometric shapes in an artistic yet functional arrangement. To me this bridge appears, both at a distance and close-up, to be gracefully light in weight. This effect must be the result of spacing and relatively fine parts, because the Iowa/Wisconsin Bridge is, in fact, larger than the I-280 (Davenport) or US 18 (Prairie du Chien).

To support the bridge roadway, 14 hanger cables are equally distributed along the arch. These seem more visible than on some arch bridges. The bottom of the arch is "tied" together with a steel girder, as the cord would be on an archer's bow.

People from Dubuque and Wisconsin must have experienced great joy traveling over this new four-lane bridge for the first time after being used to the old Eagle Point two-lane. With a dogleg turn almost halfway across, the earlier bridge must have been a great challenge to drivers. That old truss span was a combination of many styles: both a deep deck and through-trusses, flat as well as camel tops and three different truss patterns. The Eagle Point Bridge served its generation; now the Iowa/Wisconsin Bridge, straighter, tied-arch design, has a new age to serve.

---

**Use:**
Interstate traffic, US 61

**Location:**
Between City Island in Dubuque and Wisconsin

**Style:**
Single tied-arch with girder approaches

**Length:**
Channel span - 650 feet clear
670 feet total
Total length - 2,951 feet

**Width:**
4 lanes with a 2-foot median & 70-foot roadway

**Clearance:**
Varies from 52 to 62 feet MLW because of the bridge angle

**Date completed:**
1982; replaced the Eagle Point Bridge built in 1902

**Designer:**
Sverdrup and Parcel and Associates

**Bridges:**
#3191.8S061 in Iowa & B-22-0060 in Wisconsin

**Owners:**
Iowa and Wisconsin Departments of Transportation

Iowa - Wisconsin Bridge, Dubuque                    Mary C Costello

161

# Prairie du Chien Railroad Bridge, St. Feriole Slough

*I*n researching this bridge, I learned not to believe everything people tell me. First, I asked a person living across from the Prairie du Chien East Channel Bridge approach if the railroad bridge was used anymore. "No,...ohhh, maybe once in awhile they use it to switch engines," was his reply.

I continued down the street to a road that he told me went right near the bridge. When I arrived, I found a man who was just returning from fishing in the Marais de St. Feriole (official name for the slough). I asked him the same question, and he said that the bridge definitely was no longer used. "You can go right out on it," he stated. "Go up the path and turn to your right at the top. It'll take you right there."

I followed his directions up the rock-laden, sun-spattered incline along the picturesque, shaded tracks to the end of the curve, where the sun shone full-strength on the trestle bridge. However, something was wrong. The tracks were shiny!.

I started my sketch after taking a few pictures. The bridge was curved on trestle supports which stood in the narrow stream. A board walk with wooden-post-and-wire railing, sagging in part, outlined the left edge. The Mississippi backwater, mostly covered with scum, looked disturbed near the bridge, but behind the span the water was free of any such film.

I heard train sounds on St. Feriole Island ahead. "Switching," I thought, until a pretty blue diesel engine came through the trees...followed by a second engine. Slowly the locomotives crossed the wooden structure, pulling car after car of freight. I moved down the embankment and clung to some shrubs, but I was still almost within arm's reach of the moving train. My heart was pounding as I watched the solid train wheels and thick springs on the side-frame[15] pass on the track. The wooden ties sank with each new truck of wheels and rose between. I was so close I could have talked to the engineer but instead only waved. It was an experience I'll remember!

Originally built in 1890 by the "Milwaukee and Mississippi Railroad Company," later called the "Chicago, Milwaukee, St. Paul and Pacific Lines," and today the "Soo Line," this Prairie du Chien span has gradually been reduced in length from its original 919 feet to its present 195 feet. (Despite its proximity, this railroad bridge was not related to the first bridge here in 1874, a pontoon bridge[16] built across both the Iowa and Wisconsin channels of the Mississippi River.)

The state purchased the land in 1980 after the Milwaukee Road had abandoned the bridge, and the Wisconsin River Rail Transit Commission, a public body composed of eight counties, bought the bridge and the track. Three times a week freight trains carry coal and grain to the University of Wisconsin at Madison; other trains go to Lake Geneva or Chicago with cargo almost daily. Though at one time the plan was to remove the tracks, now the Transit Commission is hoping to add a dinner train. Not everyone in Prairie du Chien is aware, but "Yes, the Prairie du Chien Bridge is being used...daily!"

**Use:**
Daily freight trains

**Location:**
Between Prairie du Chien and the south end of St. Feriole Island over Marais de St. Feriole Slough

**Style:**
11 spans: 7 steel-pin truss spans, one 35-foot trestle deck girder, plus 3 more trestle spans

**Length:**
Channel span - 31 feet clear
               35 feet total
Total length -  195 feet

**Width:**
One track

**Clearance:**
15 feet MLW

**Date completed:**
1927; replaced the 1898 346-foot span; original bridge finished in 1890; in 1962 added one 35-foot steel span

**Designer:**
Milwaukee & Mississippi Railroad Company

**Bridge:**
#B-376

**Owner:**
Wisconsin River Rail Transit

**Unique feat:**
One of three privately owned bridges on the Mississippi—this over backwaters

St. Feriole Slough Railroad Bridge, Prairie du Chien          Mary C. Costello

165

# Marquette/Prairie du Chien Highway Bridge, Main Channel, US 18

From the bluff road north of Marquette, Iowa, I saw the "Marquette-Jolliet* Bridge"—a single blue arch, alone and impressive. Perhaps because it was so isolated, or maybe because I was so close, the arch appeared as large to me as the St. Louis Jefferson Barracks Bridge, which is almost twice its size.

The Marquette/Prairie du Chien Bridge is a tied-arch. The large arch ribs and girder that tie the arch ends together are all tubular in shape. The term commonly used to describe this structure is "boxed" as opposed to "plate," which is two-dimensional. The rest of the bridge is a deep plate-girder—deeper than the box-girder below the arch.

The horizontal struts that unite the arches overhead are much smaller, almost like rods as seen from below. These form a pattern as follows: -X—XX—X-. At the end of each of the ten straight crossbeams is a strong wire suspender connected to the roadway below, supporting it, although these wire suspenders are almost invisible from any distance.

When I drove across the Marquette/Prairie du Chien Bridge, the parapet was low enough for car passengers to view the river and scenic shores—a lovely and unusual arrangement today. All of this natural beauty was impressive, but it was my subsequent experiences in Prairie du Chien—meeting the mayor, hearing what happened to the new bridge and how the cities coped with the situation—that are the most memorable.

The Wisconsin Tourist Information Center is located in the space between the exit and entrance ramps to the bridge. I stopped there to talk to the President of the Chamber of Commerce about the bridge file I had just been given to explore. He said that in January of 1981 an engineer noticed a bubble in the paint on the bridge and touched it, only to find a crack in the steel underneath. The

governor was informed and in turn tried to contact the mayor of the town, James Bittner. While we spoke, Mayor Bittner came along and continued telling the story. Bittner related that he had been out of town when he received the telephone call from the governor saying, "Sit down, Mayor!—I'm closing your bridge today!"

"I came flying home," the Mayor continued, "and along the way passed a sheriff's car. I pulled over to explain but he just waved me on saying, 'Go on, Mayor, we know you're in trouble!'"

From that time on things happened fast. The bridge was closed and found to include some steel made with too much carbon and low toughness. This steel had not been tested for strength. (Now testing is required.) The end result was that the bridge was jacked up and the box girders replaced. It was winter and the river was frozen. With boats not able to cross the river, people felt stranded. Many local people work on one side of the river and live on the other. It was finally arranged for a boat to ferry people from St. Feriole Island. When ice covered the river, ice-cutters broke the ice up and found a way to keep it from filling in again. "Everyone worked together without blaming anyone. The situation brought our communities together," said the Mayor.

A general sense of humor made interesting things happen. The city wrote for "foreign aid" to Japan and West Germany. This shocking act got media attention and eventually state funding. Red ribbons were flown representing the "red tape"! Two hundred ten days later at the bridge reopening, instead of cutting a ribbon, the officials burned all the symbolic red ribbon.

---

* A local historian said Jolliet spelled his name with two "l's" in France; therefore, the city uses that spelling in its bridge name.

| | |
|---|---|
| **Use:** | US Highway 18 and local traffic |
| **Location:** | Between Marquette, Iowa and Prairie du Chien, Wisconsin |
| **Style:** | Single tied-arch with girder approaches |
| **Length:** | Channel span - 451 feet clear / 462 feet total / Total length - 2,560 feet |
| **Width:** | 2 lanes with shoulder space for walkers & bikers, roadway varies from 40 to 50 feet |
| **Clearance:** | 60 feet MLW |
| **Date completed:** | June 1975; dedicated 14 November 1974; rebuilt for faulty steel August 1981; replaced a 1932 suspension; before that a car-ferry and original 1856 ferry |
| **Designer:** | Ronald Pluim led the design team, Wisconsin DOT, bridge section |
| **Bridge:** | #2205.8S018 in Iowa, B-12-0027 in Wisconsin |
| **Owners:** | Iowa and Wisconsin Departments of Transportation |
| **Unique feat:** | American Institute of Steel Construction judged it as 1976 Outstanding Aesthetic Design; Pontoon Railroad Bridge was one of Warren's first fifteen bridges across the Mississippi; use discontinued 1961; removed about 1963 |

Marquette - Prairie du Chien Highway Bridge    Mary C. Costello

# Prairie du Chien East Channel Bridge, US 18

A girder bridge crosses the Wisconsin channel of the Mississippi River from Prairie du Chien, the second oldest settlement in the state. It is part of the total Mississippi River crossing entitled the "Marquette-Jolliet Memorial Bridge."

Before this Memorial Bridge was built, there were twin suspension bridges slightly north, one for each of the two river channels between Marquette and Prairie du Chien, designed by J. Max Yingling of Little Rock, Arkansas. The earlier bridges were constructed in 1932, ten feet higher and twenty-one feet narrower than today's bridges. The newer bridge is more than twice as wide.

Going back further in history, I found that in 1856, before any bridges crossed the Mississippi at Prairie du Chien, Alexander McGregor had built a ferry to run from Prairie du Chien to North McGregor (called Marquette since 1920). Because of the three-mile-long island in the middle of the river, the ferryboat pilot had a 4-mile trip one way around the end to get from landing to landing. Had he been able to go "straight as an arrow," the distance would have been shortened to about 1 1/4 miles. (Warren 1878, 87)

This old town is built on sand terraces near the river, some as high as 40 to 50 feet, with rocky bluffs 2 1/2 miles behind, Warren explains. I understood this as I stood in the sand, drawing the East Channel span. "Prairie of Sand" seems an appropriate interpretation of the city's name and one I was given in error. Later I discovered that Prairie du Chien is French for "Prairie of the Dog" or "Dog Prairie," the name of a local Indian chief.

As I sketched, it appeared to me that this Wisconsin channel was wider than the main channel, and so it is—shore to shore about 1100 feet here as compared to 750 feet over the Iowa channel.

The US 18 East Channel Bridge is nothing unusual—medium blue steel girders with simple straight lines—but has a slight arch in the girder over the channel. The piers are of two designs. The two largest piers in this Wisconsin channel form a solid rectangle with a "U" frame and are, therefore, heavier than the others. The long line of other supports are single T's, which match the main or west channel piers.

This east bridge is designed with no walk, but it has extra road room for both bikers and joggers, a section well used. In addition to the many people who live on one side of the river and work on the other, the Prairie du Chien Bridge is used extensively by health enthusiasts as well as for recreation purposes.

The geographical area here is not glaciated or smoothed over by the continental glacier; therefore, in its natural state, it has extremely high hills and low valleys. It is a beautiful location for the beautiful Prairie du Chien Bridge.

**Use:**
US 18 and local traffic

**Location:**
Between Prairie du Chien and St. Feriole Island over the Wisconsin Channel

**Style:**
8-span steel plate-girder

**Length:**
Channel span - 340 feet clear
350 feet total
Total length - 1,916 feet

**Width:**
2 wide lanes, 40 feet

**Clearance:**
60 feet MLW

**Date completed:**
June 1975

**Designer:**
Wisconsin DOT at Madison

**Bridge:**
#B-12-0028 in Wisconsin

**Owner:**
Wisconsin Department of Transportation

East Channel Bridge, Prairie du Chien, Wisconsin    Mary C. Costello

# Prairie du Chien Twin Approach Bridges

*I*t was 8 a.m. on a bright, warm summer day when I arrived at the first of two matching bridges in Prairie du Chien. Although there is a 15-foot difference in length and a $29,000 difference in building costs, the Wisconsin and Iowa Street Bridges are the same design. The grayed-white of the concrete Iowa Street Bridge cut a wedge into the palette of yellows, yellow-greens and blues on that August day. Each of the four T-shaped piers, called "hammerhead" by the Wisconsin DOT, was caught for the moment by the sun at its outer extremity. In the water the piers reflected like boots with a bright toe. In contrast, the bridge underside reflected as a dark shadow in this Mississippi backwater called "Marais de St. Feriole."

The Wisconsin and Iowa precast concrete girder bridges are functional and free of any unnecessary ornamentation. The Iowa Street Bridge (the only one of the twins that I sketched) has a sloping parapet with an overhanging cap on the outside, which casts a striking shadow. Below it is the 45-inch-deep girder, divided directly above the pier by a downspout embedded in the concrete. There are no lightposts, inner railings, or median strips since each bridge handles traffic in only one direction.

On the grounds between the two bridges in Prairie du Chien is a statue of Father Jacques Marquette, a French missionary after whom the bridge is named. The monument recognizes that he, with Louis Jolliet, a fur trader, discovered the Mississippi River in 1673, where the Wisconsin River meets the Great Mississippi just south of Prairie du Chien. The statue was one of seven sculptures of famous Frenchmen throughout the United States, designed by the French artist Louis Hernant. It was erected in 1910 and stood until 1976 on the campus of the former St. Mary's College. Father Marquette's statue was donated to the city of Prairie du Chien at the time of the United States Bicentennial, two years following the completion of the Marquette-Jolliet Bridge.

---

**Use:**
Approaches between Prairie du Chien and Marquette, Iowa (to and from the Wisconsin Channel Bridge)

**Location:**
Over the Marais de St. Feriole slough at the east end of the Marquette/Jolliet Bridge in Prairie du Chien

**Style:**
Twin 5-span continuous prestressed concrete girder bridge

**Length:**

|  | Iowa St. | Wisconsin St. |
|---|---|---|
| Channel span - | 85 feet | 88 feet |
| Total length - | 423 feet | 438 feet |

**Width:**

| 2 lanes - | 38 feet | 38 feet |
|---|---|---|

**Clearance:**

| MLW average - | 23 feet | 21 feet* |
|---|---|---|

**Date completed:**
1974

**Designer:**
Wisconsin DOT bridge section

**Bridge:**
#B-12-0029 (Iowa St.), B-12-0030 (Wisconsin St.)

**Owner:**
Wisconsin Department of Transportation

---

* Because of the incline of the bridges, the vertical clearances vary. These are the average of those heights.

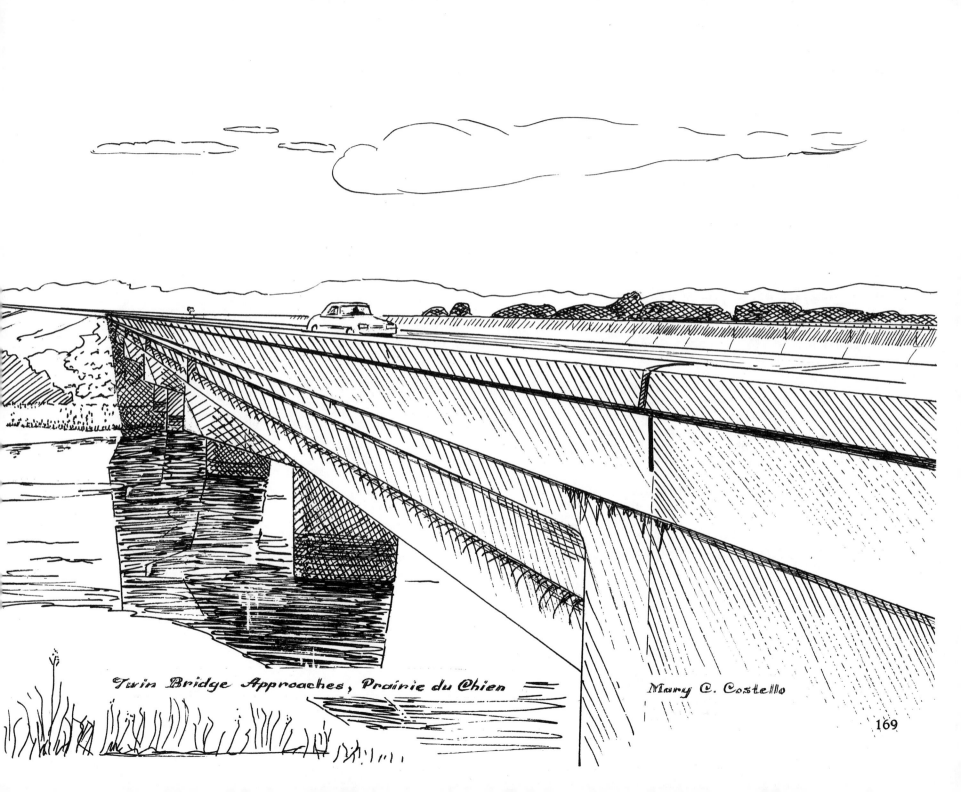

Twin Bridge Approaches, Prairie du Chien

Mary C. Costello

169

# Blackhawk Avenue Bridge, Prairie du Chien, Wisconsin

*I*t is hard to escape history in Prairie du Chien. Even this small, in-town bridge over the Mississippi Slough has a name based on an incident from the city's past. The town's main street has been named Blackhawk Avenue after the Sauk Indian Chieftain. Legend has it that in 1832, while trying to evade the militia and armed settlers, Chief Blackhawk hid all day in a tree located on this street. The Blackhawk tree is gone now, but Mayor Bittner of Prairie du Chien has a piece of it framed in his office, a piece that was saved by a boy at the time the tree was cut down.

According to Mary Antoine de Julio, researcher for the Historical Society located at Villa Louis, Prairie du Chien, the Blackhawk Avenue Bridge was originally built in 1857 to connect Bluff Street with the Main Village, an island across St. Feriole Slough. The bridge gave greater access to the Milwaukee and Prairie du Chien Railroad, which came to town that same year, and to a new commercial and residential area that was developing around Bluff Street and South Main. The Blackhawk Avenue Bridge has been rebuilt several times since then, with the most recent reconstruction in 1955.

The three-span Blackhawk Avenue Bridge has two striking features not commonly seen—fluted piers and ornamental railings. The piers are composed of concrete multi-legs 16 inches in diameter, cast-in-place, with classical grooved columns. The attractive green steel railing dominates the upper-bridge scene.

It was August and high noon. Quite a few people were drawn to the water. First, a man and his young son drove up and started fly-fishing over the sturdy railing. As far as I could see, they caught nothing but enjoyed the time together. Two teenagers on bikes arrived to go swimming on the opposite side of the bridge. Though I couldn't see them swim from my vantage point, they came back my way looking cool and refreshed. Finally, a boy on a red Yamaha 80 arrived with his pole. I would like to have witnessed his success, but I had to leave for a meeting with the mayor.

**Use:**
Local travel between St. Feriole Island and the Prairie du Chien mainland

**Location:**
North of the main channel bridge over Marais de St.Feriole Slough on Blackhawk Avenue, Prairie du Chien

**Style:**
3-span continuous steel girder

**Length:**
Main span -      50 feet
Total length -   135 feet

**Width:**
2 lanes, 30-foot road, one 6-foot-wide sidewalk

**Clearance:**
15 feet MLW,

**Date completed:**
1955; original span 1857; rebuilt several times between

**Designer:**
J. S. Piltz

**Bridge:**
#B-12-0014 in Wisconsin

**Owner:**
City of Prairie du Chien

Blackhowk Avenue Bridge, Prairie du Chien                    Mary C. Costello

171

# Washington Street Bridge, Prairie du Chien

*T*his Prairie du Chien Bridge is interesting not for its size, nor for its beauty, but for its history and for the materials used in its construction. The abutments have flexible metal sheets on end, stacked one on top of the other. The metal sides "wing-out" to hold back the ground. In front of this retainer are 16-inch wooden pilings spaced about 3 feet apart. Large-sized riprap protects the embankment next to the narrow span.

Heavy lengthwise I-beams support the bridge. At their end, outside the metal sheets, are two concrete slabs forming a partial wall twice the depth of the girder. The substantial railing is made up of two bumper-width "flair" rails, the type often found on highway guardrails. The supporting 6-inch-deep I-beam posts are angled at the top.

St. Feriole Island is the location of the second earliest settlement in Wisconsin. Indians lived here in the 1600's. The French-Canadians established a settlement in 1781. By 1816 it was a fur-trading center. In 1825, Crawford County Commissioners appointed Jean Brunet supervisor of roads and gave him an order to levy a tax to erect a bridge over Marais de St. Feriole (the slough between the mainland and the island "Main Village"). In a letter, historical researcher Mary Antoine de Julio stated, that it was doubtful this bridge was ever built or the tax even levied, because in May, 1826, the highest flood remembered up to that time occurred. Again in 1837...(a bridge) was built and washed away...Then in 1839 another span was constructed across the Marais by Julien LaRiviere, who lived on the corner...next to the east terminus of the span. This seems to have been a more permanent structure and the position of the bridge remained the same.

Mrs. de Julio remembers that when she was a child, the bridge was called the "Little Bridge." Successive floodings, especially the 1960 inundation, caused the span to be replaced in 1961 by the present bridge. Because of the marina slightly to the northwest, lots of dredging was required for the bridge to accommodate large pleasure boats. This span was made higher and the western end was placed slightly south of the original location. (The early history of the Washington Street Bridge would make an interesting study of its own.)

Children frequented the site of the Washington Street Bridge while I was there, possibly because it is next to the city park. Three little girls, about eight years old, circled past on their bikes. A mother, pushing a stroller, had two other children, about four and ten, running ahead then waiting for her to catch up. Mother was hurrying; it was about suppertime. A couple of teenage boys, intent in their conversation, passed. I saw no boats go under the bridge, though the marina was within a stone's throw. The reason probably was low water with the recent drought. The "Little Bridge" appears to be one that is as much needed today as in the past and would be sorely missed by the average Prairie du Chiener if it were removed.

**Use:**
Local traffic and pedestrians

**Location:**
Over Marais de St. Feriole Slough between St. Feriole Island and the Prairie du Chien mainland on Washington Street

**Style:**
1-span steel deck-girder

**Length:**
Only span -     50 feet total
Total length -   52 feet

**Width:**
2 lanes, 30-foot roadway, plus a 3-foot and 4-foot sidewalk

**Clearance:**
10 feet MLW (approximate)

**Date completed:**
1961; original span 1837; another 1839 was kept in the same spot until the 1960 flood

**Designer:**
Bartels & McMahon of Dubuque

**Bridge:**
#P-12-0709 in Wisconsin

**Owner:**
City of Prairie du Chien

*Washington Street Bridge, Prairie du Chien*          *Mary C. Costello*

173

# "Black Hawk Bridge," Main Channel, Lansing, Iowa, SR 82

*I*owa's northeastern river city, Lansing, has five bridges that are considered one by most travelers because all are in line to Wisconsin. I will treat them individually because they do differ.

In the upper Mississippi River there are, "more than 500 islands large enough to have names or at least numbers and thousands of islets." (Price 1963, 86) A number of those islands are in the Lansing Bridge area and create stepping stones for the bridge spans.

From the Iowa shore to the first island is the main channel bridge, called the "Black Hawk Bridge," dedicated to Black Hawk, a great Indian chieftain.

The bridge has an interesting history. Groundwork was laid by concerned citizens who formed the Interstate Bridge Company in 1914 and in 1929 sold the charter to the Iowa Wisconsin Bridge Company, a private concern who built the bridge. It was a toll bridge, one of five being built on the Mississippi at the time. Constructing the bridge at the start of the Great Depression meant supplies were cheaper, bids were lower, and jobs were provided. Fortunately, no deaths or serious accidents occurred during construction. Almost 14 years later on 18 March 1945, an ice jam at an approach bridge splintered the timbers and forced the closing of the entire bridge. The long Black Hawk Bridge was left idle until Iowa and Wisconsin bought the bridge in 1952 and opened it again in 1956.

The Black Hawk cantilever truss structure is especially beautiful when seen from a 450-foot-high bluff in Lansing, called Mount Hosmer.[17] From there one sees the bridge, views of three states, and islands in the river for miles. This high vista shows the bridge's two kingposts and the curved middle suspended span.

Amazingly, the navigation channel of the Black Hawk Bridge is "660 feet wide, a distance greater than two city blocks," (Tousley 1931, 3)

which one would feel is adequate space for any width boat or barge. Despite this and maybe because of what has been called "the worst curve on the Mississippi" slightly to the north, boats have hit the center pier a number of glancing blows over the years. Because of its location, that center pier was the largest item in the bridge's construction. It rests on 143 piles, 40 feet deep in the riverbed and 55 feet below the water's surface. This pier alone required enough concrete "to fill a two-story building twenty feet wide by sixty feet long to the top." (Hagen 1990, 9)

The nationally known engineer who designed the Black Hawk Bridge planned three piers in the water, each different in appearance. When asked about this, John Risch, Bridge Maintenance Engineer with Iowa DOT in Ames, said, "Basically the piers are the same though one has a large opening, another two openings, and the other is solid. They could be more creative in those days (the 1930's)."

Driving across the bridge, I found the deck is a steel grid though the approaches are paved, a change made from a wooden floor when the two states took over. After crossing this main channel, I left the highway and parked. The way was blocked by a mountain of sand. Climbing it I found the shore area was mostly sand with a few blades of grass and one long-legged, white-breasted, tan-colored bird. The white ring around its neck identified it. I had never before seen nor heard the "cheep-cheep-cheep" of a sandpiper!

It was only a few miles below this bridge location that the Chief of the Sauk (Sac) and Fox Indians tried to surrender but was fired upon by opposing forces (1832, Battle of Bad Axe). One hundred years later the silvery Black Hawk Bridge was built and named to honor the heroic Indian who fought courageously for his people and homeland.

**Use:**
Local, SR 82 and SR 9 traffic

**Location:**
Between Lansing, Iowa and De Soto, Wisconsin

**Style:**
3-span cantilever through-truss plus deck-truss approach

**Length:**
Channel span - 640 feet clear
653 feet total
Total length - 1735 feet

**Width:**
2 lanes, 25 feet total

**Clearance:**
67 feet MLW

**Date completed:**
May 1931; closed March 1945; reopened October 1956 by the bordering states

**Designer:**
Melvin B. Stone, chief engineer and designer, from Minneapolis

**Toll:**
Until it closed in 1945

**Bridge:**
#0396.1S009 in Iowa; B-12-0009 in Wisconsin

**Owners:**
Iowa and Wisconsin Departments of Transportation

*Lansing, Iowa, Highway Bridge, Main Channel*　　　　　*Mary C. Costello*

175

# "Big Slough" Bridge, Lansing, Iowa, SR 82

*T*wo fishermen put their red and white outboard-motorboat into the water and headed under the second bridge from Lansing to Wisconsin to make their catch. Before long, a young couple and their two sons started down the nature trail behind me. This "Big Slough" area was an active place this July morning.

Number two span, in the Lansing line-up of bridges, is a steel plate-girder structure. It has three piers, each having two fat round concrete columns connected at the top with arched concrete.

The Big Slough Bridge has a 19-foot clearance at normal water level, high enough for any pleasure boat that might want to navigate it from the boat launching area adjacent to it. This is the highest of the four slough bridges on State Road 82. The islands on either side are built up to allow highway-level crossing and to prevent flooding. To protect the river bank under the bridge from erosion, riprap covers the ground.

Because of the deep water in "Big Slough" when it was reconstructed in 1956, special equipment had to be used to drive the pilings down. The concrete for one pier goes 30 feet below normal water level. The pilings range in depth from 35 to 75 feet below that into the river bed.

Here was a study in blues and whites. The rich blue water, deeper blue bridge girder, and pale blue sky were separated and enhanced by the white concrete bridge, vertical piers and the cemented boat landing. The lush green tree background, seen above and below the bridge, appeared to be drinking the water.

Thinking how lucky the Lansing residents were to have this attractive bridge and bit of nature so accessible, I continued across Big Slough Bridge to the next span.

**Use:**
Local and SR 82 and SR 9 traffic

**Location:**
Bridge #2 at Lansing over "Big Slough"

**Style:**
4-span steel plate-girder

**Length:**
Main span -     112 feet
Total length -   410 feet

**Width:**
2 lanes, 28 feet total

**Clearance:**
19 feet MLW

**Date completed:**
1956; replaces 1931 original wooden span

**Designer:**
Wisconsin DOT, bridge section

**Bridge:**
B-l2-0008 in Wisconsin

**Owner:**
Wisconsin Department of Transportation

Lansing Big Slough Bridge

Mary C. Costello

# Stevens & Henderson Slough Bridges, Lansing, Iowa, SR 82

*L*ooking more rustic than the other Lansing bridges, the third and fourth spans between Lansing, Iowa, and De Soto, Wisconsin, have I-beam girders. For all appearances and purposes the two bridges are twins end-to-end. The piers on both structures are multi-legged, each with a concrete band holding eight silver cylinders. "These cylinders are 16 inches in diameter, cast-in-place metal piles filled with concrete," said the Wisconsin DOT engineer, Jim Pautzke.

On each bridge attached to the edge of the concrete deck is a silver-painted steel parapet with heavy I-beam posts and a single opened-square steel rail, called by the Wisconsin DOT a single Z. Under the bridge, heavy rock protects the land from erosion and makes for an interesting textural effect.

Two sharp curves in the old 1931 road were eliminated in rebuilding the bridges in 1956. An embankment and three bays for fisherman parking were added beside the Stevens and Henderson Bridges. Trees were cleared, sand was pumped from the bottom of the river with a hydraulic dredge and then used with a crushed stone base to build the embankment, an average of five feet higher than the highest flood watermark.

Despite the fact that the sun was shining and the sky was blue, the Mississippi slough waters—Stevens and Henderson, in particular—appeared a very muddy brown. Was it because the water was not very deep and one could see the bottom? Does the water wash at the mud banks which color it? I don't know the answer.

It was close to mid-day and warm, though there was such a good breeze at times that the pages of my sketchbook were tearing off. On the riverbank, looking proud to be seen, were white and pink milkweed and blue verain. Both the Stevens and Henderson Sloughs were quiet except for fish jumping, a few birds singing, and two vacationers in an outboard-motor boat.

**Use:**
Local traffic & highway SR 9 and SR 82

**Location:**
Bridge #3 & #4 over Stevens and Henderson Sloughs between Lansing, Iowa and De Soto, Wisconsin

**Style:**
3-span continuous steel deck girder

**Length:**
Main span - 50 feet total
Total length - 134 feet

**Width:**
2 lanes, 2.5-foot curb, 26 foot roadway

**Clearance:**
15 feet MLW approximate

**Date completed:**
1956; replaced 1931 wooden span

**Designer:**
Wisconsin DOT

**Bridge:**
#B-12-0006 & B-12-0007 in Wisconsin

**Owner:**
Wisconsin Department of Transportation

Lansing, Iowa, Bridge #3 + #4

Mary C. Costello

# Winneshiek Slough Bridge, Lansing, Iowa, SR 82

*W*e're here...at the end of the line of bridges! With this inclined, deck truss span we have reached De Soto, Wisconsin. This last bridge crosses not only Winneshiek Slough, but also two sets of BN train tracks, before ending on Wisconsin mainland.

It was the 1931 wooden Winneshiek Slough Bridge that doomed the Iowa-Wisconsin Bridge Company, the former bridge owners who left the Lansing and De Soto area without a bridge for eleven years. On 18 March 1945, "ice jams splintered the soft timbers of the approach bridges and forced the closing of the route." ("Bridge Completed..." 1957, 1B) The Black Hawk Bridge went up for sale in 1949 at public auction but no one bought it. It was three more years before the Iowa and Wisconsin Departments of Transportation purchased the five Lansing Bridges, then rebuilt the four slough spans besides painting, strengthening and improving the main span.

Standing under a shade tree above the bridge, along Wisconsin Highway 35, I observed the Winneshiek Slough Bridge composed of a "combination" of styles. It is mostly a three-span continuous deck-truss but also has one I-beam, one reinforced-concrete and one plate-girder span. This variety may not be noticed by many because of the trees and the fact that the odd spans are at the ends.

Of the five piers under the Winneshiek Slough Bridge, three are in the water. The Corps of Engineers calls them "pedestal piers" on timber piles. Each consists of two round pillars with an arched connection, the same as on the Big Slough Bridge. The water looked high on the piers but really the piers are short, shorter than the truss below the deck (13 feet compared to 17 feet) giving it an inundated appearance.

On reaching the end of the Winneshiek Slough Bridge, the traveler is finally on mainland again. It is a long way from Second Street Lansing to the Wisconsin bluffs through the Winneshiek Bottoms. It takes five bridges and four islands to complete the crossing—a distance of 14,350 feet or 2.7 miles.

---

**Use:**
SR-9, SR-82 & local traffic

**Location:**
Over the Winneshiek Slough between Lansing, Iowa and De Soto, Wisconsin

**Style:**
3-span continuous deck truss plus 3 different girder spans

**Length:**
Main span -     164 feet clear
                170 feet total
Total length -  641 feet

**Width:**
2 lanes

**Clearance:**
13 feet MLW

**Date completed:**
1956; replaced original 1931 wooden span

**Designer:**
Wisconsin DOT

**Bridge:**
B-12-0005 in Wisconsin

**Owner:**
Wisconsin Department of Transportation

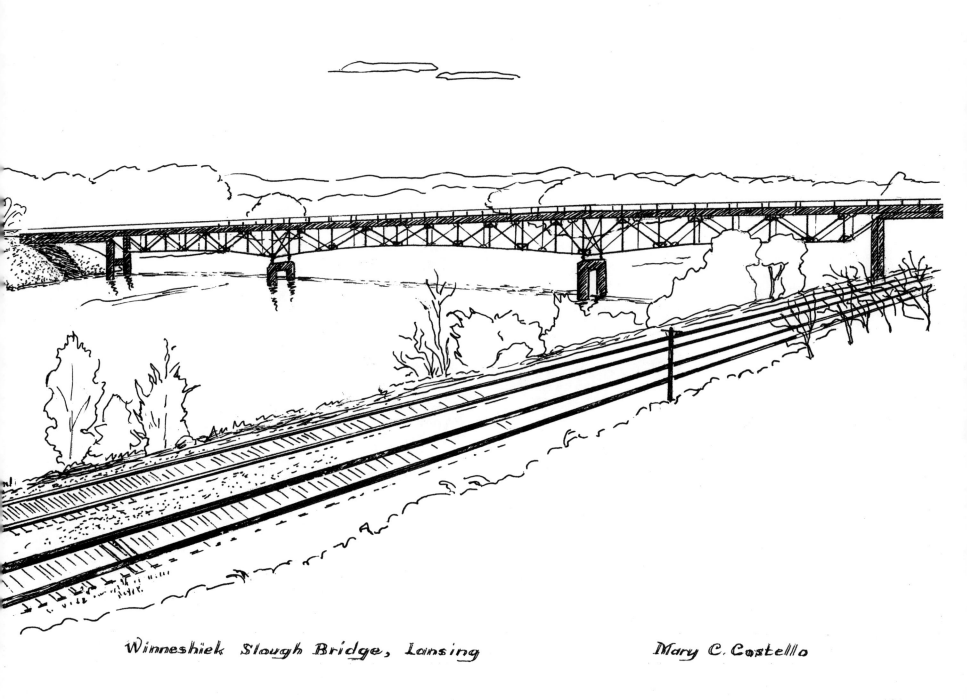

Winneshiek Slough Bridge, Lansing

Mary C. Costello

181

# NOTES

## PART ONE

1 The Louisiana Legislature on 1 July 1989 gave The Greater New Orleans Bridge a new title. School children had submitted names and "Crescent City Connection" was the name chosen.

2 The length of the river varies depending on the source of information:
2552 miles carved on a tree trunk at Itasca State Park
2450 miles recorded in the 1940 Corps of Engineers' book
2360 miles from Big Load Afloat by American Waterways Operators, Inc.
2340 miles according to the Minnesota Map

3 The Mississippi River below this US 190 Bridge reaches depths of 160 feet (at Burnside, Louisiana) to 200 feet (at the end of Canal Street, New Orleans) at mean low water. These depths are reached in "pools" formed in curves of the river when the moving water hits the opposite bank and erodes the river bottom. Above Baton Rouge's US 190 Bridge are depths of 83 feet in Vicksburg and 100 feet in Greenville. (Telephone interview with Civil Engineer, Steve Ellis, Mississippi River Commission, Vicksburg, Mississippi, 9 April 1990)

In contrast, an Act of Congress (3 July 1930) was needed to mandate that the river channel be kept at no less than a 9-foot depth to allow boats and barges to navigate on the Upper Mississippi. This level is maintained with the aid of the Lock and Dam System north of Saint Louis, sometimes by dredging.

4 Stories differ, but the daughter of Keith Montgomery, one of the lost crew members, verified that 13 died.

5 George S. Morison was a prolific designer who engineered five bridges across the Mississippi– Burlington, Memphis, St. Louis, Alton and Winona. The last two have been removed (ca.1990). Morison built bridges across other rivers, as well as being the principal engineer on the Erie Canal. Then in 1899, he was appointed by President McKinley to the Isthmus Canal Commission. He studied the political difficulties and technical factors of the giant project, and finally, in 1901, the commission recommended the Isthmus of Panama as the preferred site. The report was signed by George S. Morison. (Morison 1986, p.37,38)

6 Although the bridge is similar to the Frisco in span lengths, pier placement, and foundation–hard blue clay instead of bedrock–there are differences between the Harahan and the Frisco. To economize on materials and reduce difficulties in erecting the Harahan as well as stress on the suspended spans, pier IV is 17 feet closer to the navigation channel. Also, the anchor arm and suspended spans are shorter than the Frisco's. The Harahan has double train tracks, is much heavier and is riveted throughout. A 14-foot wide wagon roadway was added outside the trusses of the Harahan in 1916. D. F. Sorgenfrei, an engineer with Modjeski and Masters, on the telephone 3 May 1990, volunteered the following:

*As a child, I well remember the roadways with "cotton pickers" walking to Arkansas with their mule carts to work the cotton fields. Often these carts would break down on the bridge and cause traffic jams. After the adjacent Memphis-Arkansas highway bridge opened in 1950, the Harahan roadways were closed and later the deteriorated timber decks removed, leaving only the steel framework in place.*

## PART TWO

1 The Thebes Bridge elevated Ralph Modjeski to the front ranks of his profession. This bridge is similar in profile to the Frisco Bridge in Memphis (on which both Ralph Modjeski and Alfred Noble worked together.)

2 On the 31 August 1989, at 3 p.m., the city of St. Louis swapped bridges–the Eads for the MacArthur Bridge–with the Terminal Railroad. As previously planned, St. Louis owns the upper highway deck. The Bi-State Transit Authority owns the lower deck and refurbished the lower level for "light rail" to the St. Louis Airport (Lambert Field), with options to provide service to more destinations.

3 To make transporting goods by ship, train and truck safer and more efficient, standard-size containers with standard fasteners have been produced for international use. Example of the change: Kewpie Dolls from Hong Kong sent in the past in regular boxes would not all make their destination because workers handling quantities might take one or more home for their children. Now the Kewpie dolls (if they are still produced) would be sealed in containers at the factory, sent by ship across the ocean, by train across the country, and finally by truck to the destination in containers never needing to be opened, because all modes of transportation can handle them. These uniform containers are designed to be double-stacked, forcing railroad truss bridges to raise overhead bracing to accommodate the taller stacks. (Information related to the author on the telephone, 7 August 1990, by W.J. Gilbert, chief engineer of the Terminal Railroad Association, St. Louis.)

4 The lock and dam system has literally been a "life-saver" on the

Mississippi River. Before its installation the river sloped naturally from 750 feet above sea level in Minneapolis down to 375 feet here in Alton. Today, with the dams to contain the water in pools, like steps on the river, the water is controlled, and hazards, like the Rock Island Rapids before 1934, no longer endanger river traffic.

5 Howard Boren was a riveter on three Mississippi River bridges. I met him and his wife in Louisiana, Missouri, at their trailer-converted home in 1986. The Champ Clark Bridge at Alton was almost the setting for Boren's death when he fell as bridge falsework collapsed. The accident kept Boren from work for months but killed his partner.

6 Hannibal, Missouri's Norfolk Southern Railroad Bridge has had a bridge-tender's house on land since 1965. Prior to that it was high up in the center of the drawspan. This is one of few operator houses on ground on the Mississippi River. (Hastings, Minnesota, Vertical Lift Railroad Bridge also has an operator house on land.)

7 The Illinois DOT has stress sensors attached to the Quincy Bayview Highway Bridge to determine how the bridge is withstanding traffic, wind, rain, snow and powerful river action. These sensors are housed in one of the bridge's support towers and are checked periodically.

8 Lock and Dam 19, at Keokuk, was once the location of the first rocky barriers of the DesMoines Rapids. In 1913 the hydroelectric power station was built (largest low head generator station in the world at the time) with a 7/8 of a mile wide dam and 119 spillways. The lock was ceded to the United States Government for management after being built by the Mississippi River Power Company at its own expense. All of its original turbines are in use today, generating power for the Union Electric Company since 1925. Keokuk has the largest privately owned and operated dam on the Mississippi River.

9 Keokuk Junction Railway officials indicated to me by telephone that they make a daily round trip over the Keokuk Railroad Bridge with passengers. The Keokuk train then takes them to a junction in LaHarp, Illinois, where they can transfer to the BNSF going to Galesburg.

## PART THREE

1 The "Railroad Bridge Company" was formed and incorporated with Henry Farnam as president and chief engineer to see that the first railroad bridge was built across the Mississippi River between Rock Island and Davenport. "In 1853 the Bridge Company and the Mississippi and Missouri (M&M) Railroad Company executed an agreement to construct the bridge." In 1855, however, a tripartite agreement included (in addition to the above) the Chicago and Rock Island Railroad Company (C&RI), which agreement took precedence over the first. (Fowle 1940, 8) Bonds of the bridge firm were guaranteed by the two railroads. The Mississippi & MIssouri Railroad, in Iowa, owned the land up to the river (deeded by Antoine LeClaire) and had track already in progress to Iowa City. The Chicago and Rock Island Railroad in Illinois had track open to the Mississippi. By 1860 these two railroads had united under the title of the the Chicago, Rock Island and Pacific Railroad and then became sole owner of the original bridge.

2 The "Effie Afton" accident put the first railroad bridge out of commission for four months in 1856. In 1864 the swingspan of the bridge burned, forcing a closing for 40 days. It was ice damage that caused the shutdown of the second and fourth bridges in 1868 and again in 1896 respectively.

It is hard to imagine reconstruction work done to the total bridge without interrupting train service, but this was possible because new spans were always larger, so men could work outside the trusses. Falsework was used to build temporary track. At one point, track was laid down to the river for special "train-ferry service."

Probably least known is that one summer (1896) after ice damage to the swingspan, a lift span was put into operation. (Dr.Robert Bouilly, former Arsenal Historian, gave me most of this information in interviews.)

3 Sources differ as to who turned the first earth for the 1856 Rock Island Railroad Bridge.

George Wickstrom – Rock Island Argus, 26 April 1950 said: "John Warner turned the first shovelful of earth." Warner was contractor for the piers.

Jim Arpy – Quad-City Times 15 September 1978, reported: "Antoine LeClaire, founder of the city of Davenport,...turned the first shovelful of earth..."

Dr. Ira O. Nothstein, archivist at Augustana College, quoted the Rock Island Republican 1853: "...Mr. LeClaire personally shoveled some of the earth and the crowd went wild with enthusiasm to see him take off his coat and go to work."

Based on dates of events, I have concluded that it was John Warner, contractor for foundations and piers, who turned the first dirt for the first railroad bridge. According to the Rock Island Republican construction on the stone piers and abutments commenced across the Sylvan Slough on the 16 July 1853. It was from Rock Island that the bridge began and this Slough span was completed first. The article "Ho! for Council Bluffs" referred to

Antoine LeClaire's "breaking ground" for the Mississippi and Missouri Railroad in Davenport, which was started westward 1 September 1853, on the banks of the Mississippi. Not one mention was made in this article of the Mississippi River Bridge. The M&M Railroad was organized to connect with the Rock Island and Chicago line nearing completion on the Illinois side of the river—another separate event. On 28 September 1853, the Rock Island Republican said that the contract for building the piers of the Railroad Bridge across the Mississippi was let to John Warner and Company the week before. These piers on the main channel were to have been completed by 1 December 1854 but were not finished until late in the fall of 1855, at which time preparations for the superstructure were going on. It seems that John Warner turned the first earth for the main channel bridge also.

4 The "new bridge" of 1901 designed by the American Bridge Company (basically the bridge that is there today) has two different length spans, 110 feet and 89 feet, as opposed to two matching 87-foot spans on the first bridge, designed by the Baltimore Bridge Company. The style is a through-truss in contrast to the pony-truss span of 1872. (Hallberg 1980,2)

5 The "brush-and-stone" dam consisted of branches twisted together and forced down by layers of finely beaten stone. The first layer was 30 feet wide on the bottom of the river, which is solid rock. Then alternate layers of stone and brush were laid on top. It was called "Sears' Brush Dam" after David B. Sears, who was responsible for building the structure. Sometimes it was simply called the Moline Dam.

6 Accounts of the Campbell's Island incident vary. On the 16 July 1814, 120 regulars and militia led by Lieutenant John Campbell were headed to Prairie du Chien. When going through the swift Rock Island Rapids, they were grounded by the wind and waves and then attacked by Black Hawk and 500 warriors, who lay in waiting among the island willows. What happened after the attack has many versions. Some historians say that the wind floated the boat out of the Indians' range, others that the companion boats returned for Campbell and survivors on the beach. A third said that the American gunboat "General Clark" rescued the occupants of the grounded boat and retreated downstream.

The number of dead also differs. One report states 16 men in the boats died, and another that ten regular soldiers, a woman and a child were killed. In any case, after it was over, Black Hawk returned to his village and hoisted the British flag, as did the British in what became known later as Spencer Square, downtown Rock Island. The British and their Indian allies had won this battle. (War of 1812)

7 This quotation was taken from a special Fidlar & Chambers lithograph printing of Quad-City bridges and the accompanying short subjective and historical statements.

8 Since 1971, the Coast Guard is responsible for Mississippi River bridges.

9 Judge McLean presided in all three litigations against the railroads by riverboat interests. The first was in 1854 for the right of the Rock Island Railroad to go on government property. The second was after the "Effie Afton" hit the Rock Island Bridge (1856) two weeks after it opened. The case was tried in Chicago, September 1857, with Abraham Lincoln as lawyer for the railroad (ending in a hung jury) but was later decided by McLean. The third was "Hurd vs. the Burlington Railroad," an attempt to have the Clinton Railroad Bridge removed as an obstruction to river traffic in 1867. McLean ruled in the railroad's favor in all three cases and ended all further contests to stop Mississippi River bridge building.

10 Little Rock Island in 1866 was a 583-foot-long causeway, says General G. K. Warren. The railroad bridge going east from Little Rock Island crossed water and shoal with sandbars and willow trees before crossing the main Illinois channel. Today this shoal area has changed in shape and size for two reasons—wing dams have been added further north, and the 1930's Lock and Dam system has raised the channel-water, submerging parts. By 1943 the separate shoal area had grown into what the Corps of Engineers called Willow Island. Today it is all incorporated under the title "Little Rock Island." Today's "Willow Island" is about a mile further north, next to Joyce Island.

11 The "Lincoln Highway," one of the most important national routes before interstate highways appeared, passed through the city of Clinton from New York and Chicago enroute to Omaha and the West. To cross the Mississippi at Clinton, either the Lyons-Fulton or Clinton-Illinois Bridge could be used—both were considered part of the famous road. The "Lincoln Highway" was marked with red, white and blue stripes on utility poles and often on bridge posts or piers.

12 The Work Projects Administration (WPA) and Civilian Conservation Corps (CCC) built the long causeway in 1931, using horses and wagons to haul rock.

13 The S. N. Pearman Bridge in Charleston, South Carolina, has the longest continuous truss main span in the United States (1,350 feet), with Astoria, Oregon, second (1,232 feet), and Commodore Point, Jacksonville, Florida, third (1,088 feet), all built in 1966 or 1967. The Julien Dubuque Bridge

is fourth longest with an 845-foot main span.

14 Taconite is a fine-grained sedimentary rock of magnetite, hematite and quartz, mined as a low-grade iron ore. Found in the Taconic Mountains in New England, it is the raw material used in making iron and steel. A similar low grade iron ore is found in the Mesabi Range in Minnesota. What I found between the railroad tracks were 1/4 to 3/8 inch uneven metal balls, which had bounced out of or fallen through the freight cars' floor. The usual white rock between the ties was covered in places with these pellets.

15 I wish I could say that the side-frame was a "Bettendorf Truck," but I wasn't reading well from my precarious position. Many train wheel-trucks were built in the Bettendorf Company Car shops, Bettendorf, Iowa, the largest car shop west of the Mississippi from 1902 until 1927. The Bettendorf side-frame saved 1,000 pounds of dead weight and adjusted to the inequality of the track. One casting combined the arch bars, columns, spring seat, and journal boxes.

16 The Pontoon Bridge was the first bridge built from Prairie du Chien to McGregor, Iowa, 14 April 1874. Before that the railroad used boats to take passengers and freight across the Mississippi (traveling 4 miles around the end of the island). Next in the bridge evolution, tracks were placed on the island and boats were used on either side to get to them. Finally, the "Floating Draw-Bridge" was built, with wooden piles supporting the fixed portions, leaving a drawspan opening in each of the two channels for passing vessels and rafts. Three ordinary transfer scows were fastened together for a 393-foot total draw. It took one minute to open the bridge and 3 to 5 minutes to close it by means of a chain around a drum. (Warren 1878, 88) Before the first bridge, in the winter of 1868/69, "piles were driven across both channels, and the trains ran through without delay until the ice broke up in the spring." (Ibid 87) (Also see Burlington Bridge #49, 1855-56.)

17 Mount Hosmer was named after a well-known Eastern artist. In June 1851, Miss Hosmer was taking a trip up the river on Captain Orrin Smith's steamboat, the Senator. The crew was taking on wood and Miss Hosmer was discussing the beautiful scenery with the captain. She asked if she would have time to climb the bluff. "We'll give you time," was the captain's answer. A clerk who accompanied her on the ascent had gone only halfway when she reached the top and waved her handkerchief to the stewardess ringing the breakfast bell on the boat. Coming down, Miss Hosmer passed the clerk and returned victor in the race. The clerk asked her to wait while he went to a local proprietor to ask if the bluff had a name. He was told "not as yet." Then the clerk requested that the bluff be named Mount Hosmer after the lady who had just made a record ascent. (Tousley 1931, 21)

# BIBLIOGRAPHY

### Books

Allen, Lucius P., comp. 1879. History of Clinton County. Chicago: Western Historical Company.

American Waterways Operators. 1982. Big Load Afloat. Washington, D.C.: American Waterways Operators Incorporated.

[Aubry, Grace.] 1975. History of St. Mary's Parish, Moline, 1875-1975. Chicago: C.P.D. Corporation.

Billings, Henry. 1961. Bridges. New York: The Viking Press.

Bissell, Richard. 1973. My Life on the Mississippi or Why I Am Not Mark Twain. Boston: Little, Brown & Company.

Butterfield, C. W., and George A. Ogle, comp. 1884. "Railroads and Boat Landing." In The History of Crawford and Richland Counties, Wisconsin. 645-46. Springfield, Illinois: Union Publishing Co.

Flagler, D. W. Brevet Lieutenant Colonel. 1877. The History of the Rock Island Arsenal. Washington, D.C.: Government Printing Office.

Historic American Engineering Record (HAER). 1986. Behemoths: The Great River Bridges of George S. Morison. Loveland, Colorado: Fraser Design.

Pierce, Bess. 1981. Moline, A Pictorial History. Virginia: Donning Co., Publishers.

Plowden, David. 1974. Bridges, The Spans of North America. New York: W. W. Norton and Co.

Price, Willard. 1963. The Amazing Mississippi. New York: The John Day Co.

St. Louis Division Engineer, Upper Mississippi River Valley, comp. 1940. The Middle & Upper Mississippi River, Ohio River to Minneapolis. 2nd ed. Washington, D.C.: Government Printing Office.

Steinman, D. B. 1953. Famous Bridges of the World. New York: Random House.

Tousley, Albert S., ed. and comp. 1931. The Book of the Black Hawk Bridge. Lansing, Iowa: The Tepee Press.

Twain, Mark, 1917 edition. Life on the Mississippi. New York: Random House.

U.S.Coast Guard. 1984. Bridges Over the Navigable Waters of the U.S.: Gulf Coast and Mississippi River System. Commandant Publication P16590. 2, 75-80.

Warren, G. K. Brevet Major General. 1878. Report on Bridging the Mississippi River Between St. Paul, Minnesota and St. Louis, Missouri. 2nd ed. Washington D.C.: Government Printing Office.

### Reference Books

Book of Knowledge, 1963 ed., s.v. "explorers of North America," and "the flight of Black Hawk."

Clinton City Directory, 1869 ed., s.v. "Clinton history."

Clinton and Lyons City Directory, 1870-71. 1871 ed., s.v. "first train bridge." 17-19.

Collier's Encyclopedia, 1993 ed., s.v. "bridge."

Compton's Encyclopedia, 1982 ed., s.v. "bridge."

Encyclopedia Britannica, 15th ed., s.v. "bridge," and "Natchez."

History of Clinton County, 1879 ed., s.v. "first railroad bridge."

World Book, 1993 ed., s.v. "bridge," and "Davenport."

### Journal Articles

Ashton, Ned. "The Design of a 1540-Foot Three-Span Continuous Tied Arch Truss." The Iowa Transit, College Engineering Magazine (April 1944): 5-22.

Baier, Gustave J. "Santa Fe Dedicates New Bridge Over Mississippi River at Fort Madison." Santa Fe Magazine (September 1927): 28-36.

"Dubuque to Complete Span." Engineering News Record (10 December 1987): 15.

Fraser, Clayton B. "Behemoths—The Great Bridges of George S. Morison." Historic American Engineering Record (October 1986): 267-357.

Morison, Elting E. "The Master Builder." Invention and Technology Magazine (Fall 1986): 34-40.

Nothstein, Ira O. "The First Railroad Bridge to Cross the Mississippi." Museum Quarterly, Davenport Public Museum 1, no.2 (April 1956.): 1-10.

Orth, William A., Jr. "The Quincy Bridge, A Portrait of Pinpoint Design and Construction." Construction Digest, Illinois DOT Publication (4 August 1986): 1-5.

"Reaching to the Crescent City." Engineering News Record (26 April 1984): 30-32.

Riebe, William. "The Government Bridge." Rock Island Digest (1982) 2: 68-79.

Rolfe, William E., and Lucius H. Cannon. "The Municipal Bridge of Saint Louis." St. Louis Public Library Monthly Bulletin (August 1922): 167-198.

Trowbridge, Arthur C. "The Mississippi in Glacial Times." The Palimpsest 40 (July 1959): 257-288.

### Newspaper Articles

Allbee, E.A. "Tells of Building the First Bridge Across the Mississippi." Rock Island Argus, Centennial edition, 29 April 1941, 23.

Arpy, Jim. "Arpy Takes a Look at the Bridge (I-80)." The Times Democrat, Davenport, Iowa. 23 October 1966.

—. "Arsenal Stems From 'Oddball' Roots, Presidents Plotted, Settlers Squatted During Early Years." Quad-City Times, 26 July 1987, 4D.

—. "Ghosts Along the Mississippi." Quad-City Times, 15 September 1978, Tempo Section 1 & 2.

—. "Hungry Bridge Is Waiting." Quad-City Times, 22 October 1979, 7 Tempo Section.

—. "Take a Trip Down the Mighty Mississippi." Quad-City Times, 15 December 1985, 9D.

Ashcraft, Michael. "Since '47, He's Had the Loneliest Job in Town." The

Leader, Davenport, Iowa, 6 February 1988, 1A & 4A.

"A Bridge At Last; Commemorating the Opening of the Greater New Orleans Bridge No. 2." The Times-Picayune, Special Section, 30 September 1988, F1-F12.

Barr, Linda. "Centennial Bridge Marks It Golden Anniversary." The Quad-City Times, 12 July 1990, 1A & 2A.

Bergendoff, R.N. "Centennial Structure Ranked Among World's Notable Spans." The Daily Times, 10 July 1940, 15.

"Bet-You-A-Million's Bridge." The Times-Democrat, 23 October 1966, 3D.

"Bridge Closed for a Decade." Allamakee Journal, Lansing, Iowa, 24 October 1990, 1 & 13.

"Bridge Completed in October." Allamakee Journal, 28 May 1957, 1B.

"Bridge (Prairie du Chien) Won 1976 Aesthetics Prize." Des Moines Sunday Register, 8 February 1981, 10A.

"Bridging the Mississippi." The Palimpsest, May 1922, 133-141.

Brown, Dee. "The Day the Iron Horse Crossed the Mississippi." The Chicago Tribune, 22 May 1977, Perspective Section, 1 & 2.

"Centennial: Unique On the River." The Times-Democrat, 23 October 1966, 3D.

Clayton, Teresa. 1976. "The Impossible Dream's Come True." The Democrat Argus, Caruthersville, Mo., 1 December 1976, 1.

"Covered Bridge Across River Last of Kind." Daily Gate City Newspaper, Keokuk Library's Bickel Collection, 22 April 1932.

Finch, Hortense. "Tale of Two Bridges." The Times-Democrat, 30 November 1969, 11-12.

"Future of Black Hawk Bridge." Allamakee Journal, 26 September 1990, 1 & 16.

Hente, David. "Floods, Fires and Collision Don't Sway 82-Year-Old Thebes Bridge." Southeast Missourian, 19 April 1987, 1A & 6A.

Hagen, Barbara. "Crossing the Father of Waters, A Giant Leap Connecting Iowa and Wisconsin." Allamakee Journal, 17 October 1990, 1,2 & 20.

Kulp, Jim. "The Clark Bridge: a 50-year span." Alton Telegraph, 29 July 1978.

McPartland, Phil. "The Goose Has Been Laying Golden Eggs for Fifty Years." The Hawk-Eye, Burlington, Iowa, 29 March 1967, 14.

Parker, Ron. "Building the New Bridge: How It Went." Daily Gate City, Keokuk, Iowa. 22 November 1985, 1-6B.

Peters, Frank. "Twin Arches Over the Mississippi." St. Louis Post Dispatch, 23 August 1987, 4D.

Raffensperger, Gene. "Davenport's Biggest Asset, It's Not Just Any Old Bridge." Des Moines Sunday Register, 18 October 1970, 4-8.

Rockhold, Carolyn. "The Old Swing-span Bridge: Its History." The Daily Gate City, 22 November 1985, 6B.

"Sabula/Savanna Bridge Officially Opened Saturday Night." Sabula Gazette, 31 December 1932.

Schmidt, William. "Engineer Tells Technical Side of Big Project." The Daily Times, 10 July 1940, 22.

Theobald, Bill. "I-74 Bridge Is a Real Marvel." Quad-City Times, September 1985, 1-8.

Weiss, Richard H. "Old Chain of Rocks Bridge For Sale." St. Louis Post-Dispatch, 5 March 1986, 7.

## Unpublished Material

Ashton, Ned. 1944. "Comments on Design and Construction of Various Mississippi River Bridges." Lecture for Tri-Cities Civil Engineers, 6 April, 1-42. Historical Society file, Iowa City, Iowa.

Bouilly, Robert H. 1981. "The Moline Bridge and Its Predecessors." Four-page presentation at the dedication of new Moline-Arsenal Bridge, 16 February. Historians' Office, Rock Island Arsenal, Rock Island, Illinois.

City of Clinton Bridge Commission. 1956. "The Gateway Bridge at Clinton, Iowa." Seventeen-page grand-opening booklet, 30 June.

Comp, T. Allan, and Donald Jackson. 1977. "Bridge Truss Types: a Guide to Dating and Identifying." Twelve-page Technical Leaflet #95, May. For the American Association for State and Local History, Nashville, Tennessee.

Engineers, Modjeski and Masters. 1957 "Gateway Bridge, Clinton, Iowa, Over the Mississippi River." Twenty-six-page Engineers' Report.

Fowle, Frank F. 1940. "The Original Rock Island Bridge Across the Mississippi River." Fifteen-page paper presented at Rock Island Rotary Club, 30 July. Public Library, Rock Island, Illinois.

Freitag, Joan. 1991. "Designing Clark Bridge: a Hanson Team Effort." In-house newsletter entitled "Hanson Engineers' Insights," Summer. Springfield, Illinois.

Glaser, W. R. 1988. Telephone interview with author on 6 September from City Hall, St. Louis, Missouri.

Hallberg, Carl. 1980. "The Sylvan Island Wagon Bridge: Sylvan Island's Handicap." Research paper, 12 May, for Dr. Norm Moline's Geography class, Augustana College, Rock Island, Illinois.

[Hayes, W. E.]. 1970. "The Iron Road to a New Empire." 23 July, photocopied six-page paper, Rock Island County Historical Society, Moline, Illinois.

"History of the Mississippi River Bridge, Fort Madison, Iowa." Six-page presentation given about 1975, Regional Freight Office Two, Fort Madison, Iowa.

Julio, Mary Antoine de. 1988. Historian's letter to author, 18 September.

Langworthy, Jerry L. 1968. "Conference to Determine Legal Problems Concerning Sylvan Island." Conference minutes, 10 December, Riverside Park Office, Moline, Illinois.

Pelo, Gregory V. 1989. "The Mystery Remains Over 100 Years After the

Event." n.d. Two pages written by local historian, photocopied.

Tweet, Roald. 1980. "A History of Navigation Improvements on the Rock Island Rapids." April, fifteen-page government publication #1979-652-796.

### Interesting Reading

Arpy, Jim. 1983. The Magnificent Mississippi. Grinnell: Iowa Heritage Gallery/Publications.

Curry, Jane. 1983. The River's in My Blood: Riverboat Pilots Tell Their Story. Lincoln: University of Nebraska Press.

Dorsey, Florence. 1947. Road to the Sea: The Story of James B. Eads and the Mississippi River. New York: Reinhart & Co., Inc.

Glazier, Willard. 1887. Down the Great River. Philadelphia: Hubbard Brothers, Publishers.

Jackson, Donald C. 1988. Great American Bridges and Dams. Washington, D.C.: Preservation Press.

Peterson, William J. 1967. Mississippi River Panorama, by Henry Lewis. Iowa City: Clio Press.

—. 1968. Steamboating on the Upper Mississippi. Iowa City: State Historical Society of Iowa.

Roba, William, ed. 1987. William F. Cody 1846-1917: Buffalo Bill, The King of the Border Men. Davenport, Iowa: Service Press, Inc.

Russell, Charles E. 1928. A-Rafting on the Mississip'. New York: Century House Americana.

# GLOSSARY

**Abutments** — heavy supports at the extreme ends of a bridge; receive thrust from an arch or strut; retain earth under roadway approach.

**Anchor arm** — part of a cantilever span that reaches between the shore abutment and the pier.

**Arch bridge** — one of the oldest types of bridges; each span forms a curved top or arch. The early ones were stone blocks wedged together to form the arch. Today short spans are concrete or wood but long span arches are concrete or steel. They can be either above or below the deck. The arch pushes downward and outward against its massive abutments, which must be heavy to resist the thrust. (Types: deck arch, half-through arch and through arch).

**Archimedes' screw** — a device attributed to Archimedes, a Greek physicist and mathematician, consisting of a coarse screw incased in an open cylinder, used to withdraw water when building early bridges. (Used on the original Rock Island Railroad Bridge, #53).

**Art Deco** — a style of architectural decoration developed in 1925 at the Paris "Arts Décoratifs" Exhibition from which the term came. Art Deco decoration is not applied but achieved by dividing surfaces into shapes by line or carved motifs.

**Askew** — Set or turned to one side. Used to describe bridges with piers and abutments not perpendicular to the span of the bridge. (Sylvan Island Railroad Bridge, Moline, #57).

**Baluster** — upright support in a railing.

**Balustrade** — row of balusters topped by a railing.

**Bascule bridge** — earliest of all movable bridges; a counterpoised or balanced drawbridge; swings upward on a horizontal axis, like a trapdoor or an ancient drawbridge over a moat. It may have one leaf or two.

Bascule Bridge

**Beam bridge** — simple log/s or board/s across supports.

**Bent** — framework on land supporting loads as does a pier.

**Bollman trusses** — diagonals run from end posts to every panel point; one of the first notable truss designs in America; designed by Wendel Bollman across the Mississippi at Clinton, Iowa, in 1865. (Clinton Railroad Bridge, #64).

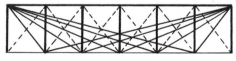

Bollman Truss

**Bow arch** — or Bowstring arch — as opposed to a round arch; a structural member of a bridge; an arch that is shallow like an archer's bow. (Jefferson Barracks Bridge, #23).

**Box girder** — a strong box-shaped horizontal member of a bridge; a part on which the weight of the deck is carried.

**Bridge-tender** — a person responsible for opening and closing movable bridges.

**Bullnose** — name given the protection pier near a bridge turnspan.

**Burr arch** — a wooden arch added to a truss to keep the span from twisting; used on the first Mississippi River railroad bridge at Rock Island, 1856; arch addition to a wooden bridge is attributed to Theodore Burr of Pennsylvania, in this case added to a Howe truss.

**Cables** — thick, strong wire ropes used on suspension bridges. John Roebling, Trenton, N.J., invented wire cable in his back yard and manufactured it in the 1830's. (Later he designed and built the Niagara Falls Railroad Suspension Bridge, 1855, and the Cincinnati Suspension Bridge, 1865; Roebling's son Washington built the Brooklyn Bridge, 1883, after his father's death.)

**Cable-stayed bridge** — combines features of cantilever and suspension bridges. One or two towers support a balanced section of the deck with cables that reach out at increasing angles from the perpendicular. If there are two towers, the bridge is built out from each and meets in the middle. The cables form a radiating pattern, a fan or a harp, depending upon points on the roadway and the tower at which they are connected. It is a variation of an old bridge style first perfected for use in a long span in Dusseldorf, Germany in 1955. (Luling Bridge, #3; Alton, #34; Quincy Bayview Bridge, #40; Burlington, #48)

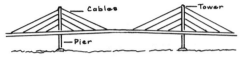

Cable-stayed Bridge

**Caisson** — a watertight box or chamber used for construction work under water. Caissons can be either pneumatic or open-dredged.

**Caisson disease** — a disease that is sometimes fatal, marked by neuralgic pains and paralysis, induced by too rapid decrease in air pressure after a stay in compressed atmosphere such as a pneumatic caisson.

**Camelback span** — section of a bridge with a polygonal top chord having exactly five slopes.

Camelback

**Cantilever bridges** — consist of two independent beams called cantilevers that extend from opposite banks of a waterway. The two cantilevers are joined together above the middle of the waterway. Each finished cantilever is self-supporting, balanced on its pier and braced by triangular trussing. The most famous cantilever is the Firth of Forth Bridge, Edinborough, Scotland, 1889. (Crescent City Connection Bridges, #1).

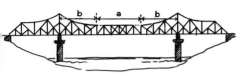

Cantilever Bridge
a. suspended span
b. cantilever arm

**Cantilever arm** — part of a cantilever bridge; one end of the cantilever arm is supported by the pier and the other end extends freely over the waterway.

**Cast iron** — a hard but brittle commercial metal; melted and poured into molds to solidify into desired shape.

**CCC** — Civilian Conservation Corps, organized by President Roosevelt during the Great Depression, to put people to work doing civil projects, such as building the causeway between Sabula, Iowa, and Savanna, Illinois.(#69 and #70)

**Channel span** — section of a bridge that crosses the deepest part of the river; navigation channel. Bridge engineers compare lengths of bridges by the main-span distance, center to center. However, the Corps of Engineers measures this distance without interference to navigation (deducting any part of pier, rock or other obstacle) so that their total "clear" channel span can be as much as 50 feet less than that of the engineers. I have included both distances, "clear" and "total" for all navigable parts of the river.

**Cherry picker** — a small mobile crane; will "pick and carry" loads; has a telescopic boom with a hook or detachable basket from which a man can work. Originally used in

an orchard to telescope a man up to pick cherries. Generic term to cover many styles and uses. (Baton Rouge's Huey P. Long Bridge, #7).

**Chord** — one of the principal members of a truss bridge, usually horizontal; at the top and/or bottom.

**Clearance** — as used in this book's statistics, means vertical clearance, distance between the underside of the bridge and normal water level.

**Cofferdam** — a steel box without top or bottom; a watertight enclosure from which the water is pumped to expose a rocky river bed for excavation work to be done there. (If river bottom is sand, work can be done and concrete poured without removing the water.)

**Combination bridge** — more than one type construction used on main part of the bridge, such as a suspension and a girder. (I-74 Bridge, Bettendorf, Iowa, #59).

**Composite plate-girder** — concrete deck works with stiffened girders and connectors, all used to strengthen the bridge. Usually the girders alone support the bridge. (Iowa/Wisconsin Approach Bridge, Dubuque, #74).

**Compression** — a force which pushes or squeezes from the outside; one of the stresses put on a bridge.

**Continuous truss** — a style bridge that spans continuously over three or more supports, with depths over intermediate piers greater than anywhere else. First came onto the American scene in 1917. The continuous truss can include a tied arch. (Julian Dubuque Bridge, #71).

Continuous Truss

**Corten steel** — a tradename by Bethlehem Steel for weathering steel; composed of copper and steel which rusts to a degree and stops, forming a brown color; never requires paint unless there is pocketing of water on or within the members. (Jefferson Barracks Bridge, #23).

**Creosote** — a preservative made from coal tar for timbers such as railroad ties; makes them last ten times longer than usual.

**Crossings** — in the South, water between pools. See pool.

**Deck truss** — a truss under roadway. Usually on small bridges or for strengthening suspension bridges— since the Tacoma Narrows Bridge failure in 1940. (Winneshiek Slough Bridge, #86).

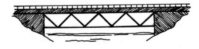

Deck Truss

**DNR** — Department of Natural Resources.

**Doric column** — the oldest and simplest of the Greek orders. It has  a capital with a square and round pillow and a fluted column. (Tourist center near Vicksburg Bridge, #10).

Doric Capital

**DOT** — Department of Transportation.

**DOTD** — Department of Transportation and Development.

**Drawspan** — technically a movable bridge that can be drawn up, down or aside to admit or hinder passage. Although today we seem to differentiate between drawbridges as lifting, and swingspans as turning, in the 1860's and 70's, G.K.Warren referred to those that swing as drawspans. Therefore, I will be using "swing," "turn," and "draw" interchangeably. A drawspan is balanced on a pivot pier and turns to allow boats to pass. Its span is measured by including the length of both arms. All drawspans on the Mississippi are railroad bridges. (Rock Island Arsenal Bridge, #53).

**Embayment** — formation of a bay; in early times the end of the Mississippi River; later filled by sand, gravel and clay from the north as land and river pushed south.

**Eyebar** — a flat piece of steel with a circular head at each end having a hole in the circles. Pins connect the eyebars. (Harahan Bridge, #15).

**Falsework** — a temporary scaffolding built of timber or steel to hold a bridge up until it is self-supporting.

**Flair and bury** — a corrugated steel guardrail on which the end is flush with the ground, with no end post.

Flair and Bury

191

**Flange** — a rib or rim for attachment to another object and for strength.

**Ford** — a place in a river crossed by walking or on horseback. (Near Norfolk Southern Railroad Bridge, Hannibal, Missouri, #38).

**Gallows frame** — a tall wooden arched framework added for a short time to the first railroad bridge's swingspan. Although this construction was not there in the very beginning, it was built a short time later, for what reason we do not know — possibly to help riverboat pilots locate the span that opened. (#53).

Gallows Frame

**Gandy Dancer** — a section hand who lays rail and repairs or maintains railroad track. The name derives from Gandy Manufacturing Company of Chicago, which made many of the tools used by section hands.

**Girder** — a strong horizontal member used on edge to bear the weight of a floor or partition. Girders are made of wood, steel or concrete. Girders in iron or steel can be in many different shapes: I or H section, T section, or Z section to name a few.

**Girder bridge** — a bridge with two or more parallel girders connected by steel beams bearing the weight of the roadway or railroad track.

(Iowa/Wisconsin Approach Bridge, #74)

**Guard rail** — inner track which prevents derailed train wheels from going further astray if train goes off the main track. (Dubuque Railroad Bridge, #72).

**Gusset** — a rectangular or triangular insert to give strength or width.

**Gusset plate** — a metal plate over each meeting place of truss members. The gusset plates, two per kingpost in bridge #1, weigh 51.4 tons each. (Crescent City Connection Bridges, #1)

**Hangers** — cables or steel shapes that hang from an arch or suspension bridge cable to support the roadway; they help distribute the weight of moving loads more evenly.

**HNTB** — Howard Needles Tammen and Bergendoff; bridge designers.

**Horizontal strut** — overhead bar or piece designed to resist pressure or compressive stress; heavy overhead connection on truss.

**Howe truss** — a truss which utilized both wood and wrought iron; metal verticals functioned as tension members and wooden diagonals functioned as compression members; an improvement over all wooden bridges; used by early railroads; designed by William Howe of Massachusetts in the

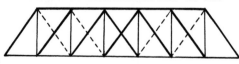

Howe Truss
(wood with metal verticals)

1840's. (First Rock Island Railroad Bridge, 1856, #53).

**Humpback truss** — a term used by bridge workers; synonymous with camelback; truss with convex top chord.

**I-beams** — beams in the shape of the letter "I" with flanges top and bottom; a standard shape used in bridge construction both in steel and precast concrete . (Two 36-inch-deep I-beams 50 feet long will carry a train.)

**Jetties** — structures jutting into the river to influence the current; designed by Eads near the mouth of the Mississippi to keep the channel open by scouring itself and depositing the load of silt at sea; also called spur dikes or wing dams. (Eads Bridge, #26).

**Kingpost** — a vertical bridge member connecting the apex of a triangular truss with the base; also a small triangular-shaped wooden bridge type with origins in the Middle Ages. (Baton Rouge I-10, #6).

**Kudzu Vine** — a member of the pea family of plants brought to the South to hold the soil. Since it is hard to kill, it has taken over some areas with uncontrolled growth; it totally covers and often smothers young trees. (Vicksburg Bridge US 80, #10).

**K truss** — a truss design with the appearance of the letter "K"; has a curved top chord. (New Cairo Bridge, #19).

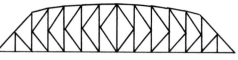

K-Truss

**Laced beam or Truss beam** — short bars that zigzag between two long vertical metal bars forming a beam; prefabricated, standard shapes used in older bridges as supporting members; the lacing prevents local buckling. (Crescent Railroad Bridge, #51).

**Lateral struts** — heavy diagonal bracing on bridge top or bottom.

**Length** — in this book, the total bridge length including approaches, unless otherwise stated.

**Lift bridge** — a movable span which rides up and down on towers like an elevator. During building of the present Rock Island Arsenal Bridge in 1896, an ice jam took away the falsework. A lift span was erected for use the following summer only. (Norfolk Southern Railroad Bridge, #38).

**MLW** — Mean Low Water, or normal water level, used in statistics for vertical clearance.

**Mullions** — slender bars between window panes.

**Milo** — a plant grown in the South which looks like Indian corn, but is shorter; rust-colored tops used for bird seed. (Seen beside Old Cairo Bridge, #18).

**Orthotropic Deck** — deck construction which consists of an assembly of steel plates welded together; has a strength-to-weight ratio higher than any previously used deck.

Orthotropic decks are not concrete but steel and the steel deck plate is the top flange of the deck girder; developed in post-war Germany, but the first major examples in the U.S. came in 1967, across San Francisco Bay and in St. Louis. (Poplar Bridge, St. Louis, #25).

**Parapet** — low wall or railing.

**Parish** — a civil division of land in Louisiana corresponding to a county in other states.

**Parker truss** — a common type truss; essentially a Pratt truss with an arched upper chord or camelback having five slopes. C.H. Parker designed it; popular in the mid-to-late 19th, and 20th centuries. (C&NW Railroad Bridge, Clinton, second span, #62).

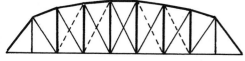

Parker Truss

**Petit truss or Pennsylvania truss** — arched top chord with a standard Pratt truss and added sub-struts and sub-ties for added strength. Called Pennsylvania because the Pennsylvania Railroad used this truss extensively from 1875 to the early 20th Century. (McKinley Bridge, St. Louis, #28).

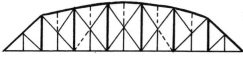

Petit Truss
(Pennsylvania with sub-ties)

**Phoenix columns** — unique iron columns made in four or five segments with flanges bolted together into one. Made in Phoenixville, Pennsylvania. In use after the Civil War. (Sylvan Island Railroad Bridge, Moline, #57).

Phoenix Column

**Pier** — an intermediate support under a bridge; heavy column or columns used to hold up a bridge.

**Pile** — a long slender stake driven into the ground to carry a vertical load; used as a base (footing) under piers.

**Pile and trestle bridge** — a braced framework of piles for carrying a road over a depression or water; dates back to the time of Julius Ceasar; a kind of beam bridge popular especially in military engineering, erected quickly and easily; for shallow quiet water with clay or fine-grained soil bed.

**Pivot pier** — a wide central pier supporting a horizontal ring girder on which the turnspan rolls as it is rotated parallel to the channel. There are two types: rim-bearing span, which is supported entirely on the ring girder; and a center-bearing span, which pivots on a large bronze center bearing and is merely stabilized by the ring.

**Plate girder** — a built-up beam strengthened by riveting and welding together a combination of steel plates and angles; for long spans requiring deep strong

sections. (Harahan Railroad Bridge, Memphis, #15).

**Pneumatic caisson** — a huge timber box with a heavy roof and sides but no bottom; bottom edges are sharp to cut into the earth. Water is pumped out of caisson when it is in place, and compressed air is pumped in. Men work inside, removing dirt, rock or sand until the desired depth is reached. The pier is constructed on top to sink the caisson until it reaches rock or hardpan at the river bottom, after which the working chamber is filled with concrete.

**Pony truss** — a half-through truss with short side trusses; too shallow to have overhead bracing.

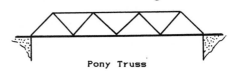

Pony Truss

**Pontoon bridge** — a floating bridge. Read's Landing, Minnesota, and Marquette, Iowa, each had one until after the 1950's. The boat pilot would blow for the bridge to open and the bridge-tender would release the pontoon span and let the current carry it parallel to the shore. The bridge-tender would pull the floating span back into place when the vessel had passed, with the help of a steam-powered engine. (Marquette/Prairie du Chien Bridge, #78 is located on the pontoon site).

**Pool** — two distinct meanings: in the South, the water area where the river hits the bank and erodes to the

bottom; in the North, the water area between dams on the river.

**Portal** — entrance to a through-truss bridge.

**Pratt truss** — a strong, simple straight-forward truss with vertical compression members and diagonal tension members; patented by Caleb and Thomas Pratt in 1844. Virtually the standard American bridge form from 1890 to 1925.

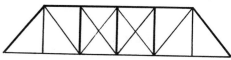

Pratt Truss

**Prestressed concrete** — created by imbedding a series of parallel high-grade steel wires, tightened for a powerful compressive stress through the full length of a concrete beam. More economical than reinforced-concrete, pre-stressed concrete can use up to 50 percent less steel and 25 percent less concrete to make slender and graceful modern bridges; widely used after 1950.

**Protection pier** — a barrier that juts out from a pivot pier; wooden pilings filled with riprap to guide boats and protect the pivot pier.

**Relief** — the projection of sculptured figures or ornament from the background. The kinds of relief are named according to the amount of projection. "High relief" is half or more than half the natural thickness of the figure. "Low or bas relief" is slight, as on a coin.

**Reinforced-concrete** — steel rods placed in the part of the beam which is under tension. Extensively used for buildings in Chicago. Used previously for shorter span bridges, like road crossings. Current drawback is the need for extensive field labor to build forms.

**Riprap** — irregularly shaped chunks of limestone which line riverbank to minimize current and wave erosion that would otherwise wear away the wall and destroy its effectiveness.

**Rocker link assembly** — complicated parts that hold the sections of a suspension bridge together and allow it to move, as well as lengthen and shorten with the change in temperature. (I-74 Bridge, Bettendorf, #59).

**Sandhogs** — workmen who dig out the earth inside caissons.

**Scour** — result of river current hitting the bank or pier; whirlpools circle downward and dig deep holes in underwater sand or ground. To minimize this, piers are set with the current. On a river without dams, the normal river bottom scours. In the life of a bridge the normal bottom may lower significantly and the pier footings must be placed deeper to account for this. (Sabula Back Channel Bridge, #69).

**Sheer Boom** — if there are two protection piers by a bridge, the second would be called a "sheer boom"; also describes a floating structure that guides the river traffic into the proper channel to pass through the drawspan.

**Shoe** — intermediary unit which connects pier with tied arch; line bearing hinges between the tied arch and the pier where it rests. (Centennial Bridge, #52).

**Sleepers** — railroad ties lying by tracks.

**Slough** — an inlet from a river.

**Span** — part of a bridge between two piers; another term for bridge.

**Spandrel** — area between the exterior curve of an arch and the horizontal deck above.

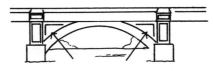

Spandrels

**Split bridge** — really two bridges connected and topped with concrete (Iowa/Wisconsin Approach Bridge, #74).

**SR** — state road.

**Steel** — material used in building bridges; made by refining molten pig iron. More ductile than iron, wood or stone; withstands the effects of impact and vibration. Strongest bridge material — 20% stronger than wrought iron. Flexibility makes steel ideal for suspension towers.

**Stringer** — a longitudinal member extending the length of the bridge panel to support the deck.

**Suspended span** — in a cantilever bridge the last span inserted between the two cantilever arms, completing the connection.

**Suspenders** — see hangers.

**Suspension bridge** — bridge with roadway that hangs from steel cables supported by two high towers. Primitive man accidentally and then purposely built suspension bridges. Best bridge style for long distances. (I-74 Twin Bridges, Bettendorf, #59).

Suspension Bridge

**Substructure** — part of bridge below the deck; pier and footings.

**Superstructure** — the portion of a bridge above the pier.

**Swingspan** — another term for turnspan or drawspan; movable span that turns on a pivot pier; requires considerable space in which to turn.

**Taconite** — a fine-grained sedimentary rock of magnetite, hematite and quartz, mined as a low-grade iron ore; raw material for making iron and steel; shipped in railroad cars as 3/8 to 1/2-inch irregularly-shaped balls. Found in the Taconite Mountains in New England. (CC&P Railroad Bridge, Dubuque, #72).

**Tailrace** — the channel into which the water from a water wheel or turbine is discharged. (Sylvan Island Railroad Bridge, Moline, #57).

**Tension** — a force which pulls the ends of an object apart.

**Through-truss** — a truss bridge on which the roadway goes under the superstructure; carries its traffic

load level with the bottom chord.

**Tied-arch** — a steel arch in which the bottoms of the ribs are tied together by a strong girder. The tied-arch is a self-contained unit. (Iowa/Wisconsin Bridge, Dubuque, #73; also Centennial Bridge #52).

Tied Arch Bridge

**Trestle** — a braced framework of timber, piles, or steelwork for carrying a road over a depression. A series of wooden beams crossbraced together with planks laid on the supports.

**Trompe l'oeil** — (Fr.) art that "fools the eye."

**Truck** — a group of four railroad wheels in a rectangular frame; found at the beginning and end of a railroad freight car.

**Truss** — a frame made in the shape of a triangle; the most rigid form of framework.

**Truss Bridge** — one in which a series of triangles is used in simple or complicated superstructures. The main members of a truss are either stiff, heavy struts or posts or thin flexible rods or bars. Common truss designs are Pratt, Warren or Parker.

**Turbine** — a rotary engine actuated by the reaction, impulse or both of a current of fluid subject to pressure; usually a series of curved vanes on a central spindle which spins or whirls around. (Sylvan Island Railroad Bridge, #57).

**Turnspan** — see swingspan

**Truss beam** — see laced beam.

**Unloaded backstays** — aft-slanting stays or cables that run from a bridge tower to the reinforced concrete anchorage of a suspension bridge without suspenders. (Clinton Gateway Bridge, #65).

Unloaded Backstays

**Vertical lift** — see lift bridge

**Viaduct** — a steel structure made up of short spans carried on high steel towers; a bridge that goes straight over land with no ups or downs; the metal railway viaduct which evolved about 1850 from the timber trestle is uniquely an American form. A metal or wooden bridge in which the different spans are supported directly upon legs or towers composed of two or more bents braced together in all directions. (Huey P. Long Bridge, Baton Rouge, #7).

**Warren truss** — a simple straight-forward design whose diagonals are alternately placed in tension or compression. Designed by Captain James Warren, a British engineer, in 1848, and quickly adopted by American bridge designers; still used by present-day bridge engineers.

**Weathering steel** — a mixture of copper and steel which stops rusting after a certain point; like Corten steel but without the tradename given by Bethlehem Steel Company.

**Web** — consists of entire area between the top and bottom chords of a truss bridge.

**Whipple truss** — a double-intersection Pratt truss; used the basic form of Pratt but lengthened the diagonals to extend across two panels, thus allowing longer spans; designed by Squire Whipple in 1847. (Burlington Railroad Bridge, #47).

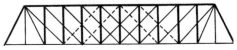
Whipple Truss

**Wind tongue assembly** — device below each tower of a suspension bridge; keeps roadway in line and prevents it from swaying. (I74 Bridge, #59)

**Wing dam** — a navigation structure built out from and often perpendicular to the river bank, to increase the flow of the river.

**WPA** — Work Projects Administration; started under President Franklin Delano Roosevelt to put men to work during the Great Depression. A part of the National Recovery Act, NRA.

**Wrought iron** — a tough, malleable and relatively soft commercial form of iron used for railway bridges between 1850 and 1890.

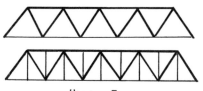
Warren Truss
(with or without verticals)

# *Railroad Changes*

Since 1995 and Volume I's first edition, there have been many changes in railroad ownership used in the bridge stories. Rather than change the copy on each story, I have listed here the railroad changes and the year they took place. The asterisk in front of the listed railroad bridges on the next page indicates that there is a change in that bridge's railroad. The reader can find the new railroad name or owner below:

The Santa Fe (SF) and Burlington Northern (BN) Railroads merged in 1995. The new name is the Burlington Northern Santa Fe (BNSF).

The Union Pacific (UP) took over the Chicago Northwestern (CNW) in April 1995.

The Southern Pacific (SP) was taken over by the Union Pacific (UP) in 1997 .

The Canadian Pacific  (CP) absorbed at least part of the Soo Line in 1992.

The I&M Rail Link (served four states—Illinois, Iowa, Minnesota and Missouri—two I's and two M's) was created in 1997 from the Soo Line and in July 2002 became the IC&E Railroad (Iowa, Chicago and Eastern Railroad).

The Burlington Northern Santa Fe Railroad (BNSF) took ownership of the Crescent Bridge beween Rock Island and Davenport in 1995.

The Canadian National Illinois Central Railroad (CNIC) took over the Chicago, Central and Pacific Railroad (CC&P) and bridge in Dubuque in 2000.

The Kansas City Southern Railroad (KCS) has taken over the Gateway Western Railroad (GW) Bridge in Louisiana, Missouri, beginning 1997 and the Mid-South Railroad (MSR) which used the Vicksburg Highway/ Railway Bridge in Mississippi, in 1993.

# MISSISSIPPI RIVER RAILROAD BRIDGES
## From Louisiana to Minnesota

[+]Original bridge, 1856, the first railroad bridge on the Mississippi River

*Bridges with changes in ownership or railroad users since 1995

## NEW BRIDGES and BRIDGE CHANGES

There has been a great deal of activity since 1995 with bridges along the lower and middle Mississippi River. Below is a table of spans that are started, being built, or have officially been planned in this part of 'Old Man River'.

| | Bridge | Location | Style | Dates | Comments |
|---|---|---|---|---|---|
| 1 | Greenville | .5 mile downstream from existing bridge | Cable stayed (2 towers) with 77 approach spans | Started December 2001; Completion expected by August 2005 | |
| 2 | Burlington Railroad Drawbridge | Same | Vertical-lift will replace swingspan | Expected start 2003 (Depends on funding) | New 300' clearance instead of 153' |
| 3 | Cape Girardeau | Directly below the existing bridge | Cable-stayed with 2 towers and girder approaches | Started 1996 Completion May 2004 | New 815' clearance instead of 460' |
| 4 | Eads Bridge | Same | No change | Redecked in 2002; Expected completion September 2002 | |
| 5 | Old Chain of Rocks | Same | Renovated deck for bike and pedestrian safety | Opened: 1 June 2002 to 31 May 2003 daily | Open from 1/2 hour before sunrise to 1/2 hour after sunset including holidays |
| 6 | I-70 St. Louis | Relocated north of existing I-70, presently on the Poplar Bridge | Cable-stayed with no piers in water; 8 lanes | No permit yet; hoped to complete by 2010 | Approximately 2,000' river span |
| 7 | Proposed Julian Dubuque Companion Bridge | Adjacent to downstream side of existing bridge | Style unknown; will be 2 lanes | Unknown, start or completion; no permit or plans yet | |
| 8 | The McKinley | Same | No change | Repaired In 2002 | |